The
Adjunct
Faculty
Handbook

The
Adjunct
Faculty
Handbook

edited by
Virginia Bianco-Mathis
Neal Chalofsky

SAGE Publications
International Educational and Professional Publisher
Thousand Oaks   London   New Delhi

For information address:

SAGE Publications, Inc.
2455 Teller Road
Thousand Oaks, California 91320
E-mail: order@sagepub.com

SAGE Publications Ltd.
6 Bonhill Street
London EC2A 4PU
United Kingdom

SAGE Publications India Pvt. Ltd.
M-32 Market
Greater Kailash I
New Delhi 110 048 India

Printed in the United States of America

Library of Congress Cataloging-in-Publication Data

The adjunct faculty handbook/editors, Virginia Bianco-Mathis and
  Neal Chalofsky.
    p. cm.
  Includes bibliographical references and index.
  ISBN 0-7619-0277-5 (cloth: acid-free paper).—ISBN 0-7619-0278-3
(pbk.: acid-free paper)
   1. College teaching—Handbooks, manuals, etc. 2. College teachers,
Part-time—Handbooks, manuals, etc. I. Bianco-Mathis, Virginia.
II. Chalofsky, Neal, 1945-   .
LB2331.A37   1996   96-4516
378.1'2—dc20

This book is printed on acid-free paper.

96 97 98 99 10 9 8 7 6 5 4 3 2 1

Sage Production Editor: Vicki Baker
Sage Typesetter: Marion S. Warren
Sage Cover Designer: Candice Harman

Contents

Preface   vii

Introduction   ix

1. Program Policies and Administration   1
   Virginia Bianco-Mathis
   Lorri Cooper

2. Adult Learning: Philosophy and Approach   13
   Kathy M. Naylor

3. Developing Instructional Objectives, Lesson Plans,
   and Syllabi   28
   Theodore E. Stone

4. Teaching Methods and Strategies   55
   John Fry
   Karen Medsker
   Dede Bonner

5. Connecting With Cooperative Learning   115
   Barbara J. Millis

6. Active Learning Designs: Simple Techniques
   to Make Your Teaching Dazzle   132
   Rebecca Birch
   Cynthia Denton-Ade

7. Facilitating Classroom Learning   142
   Margaret Sears
   Penny Ittner

8. Evaluation of Students   158
   Linda M. Raudenbush

9. Evaluation of the Course and the Adjunct   186
   Edward J. Marits

10. Professional Development of Adjunct Faculty   220
    Edward J. Marits

11. Putting It All Together   227
    Cynthia Roman

   Index   249

   About the Editors   259

   About the Contributors   261

Preface

Both of us have been adjuncts and are now full-time faculty working with adjuncts, and one of us is a program administrator hiring and evaluating adjuncts. We have experienced most of what has been written in this book.

Dr. Virginia Bianco-Mathis conceived the idea of this handbook. She suggested that we apply for a grant from the Consortium of Universities of the Washington Metropolitan Area to research the issue and develop a resource, and it was approved. Our plan was to collect already existing material from area universities and to conduct seven focus groups to collect information: two for full-time professors and administrators, four for adjuncts, and one for graduate students. We formulated an outline based on the results of our information-gathering effort and then solicited potential authors for chapters from among the focus group participants.

AUTHORS' NOTE: The development of this Handbook was made possible through a grant from the *Consortium of Universities of the Washington Metropolitan Area*, One Dupont Circle, N.W., Suite 200, Washington, DC 20036-1166.

We would like to thank the consortium for giving us the chance to get involved in this project. We had worked together as dissertation chair and doctoral student, and it was a pleasure to be able to work together as colleagues. We are indebted to all the participants in our focus groups and especially those who became our chapter authors.

Special thanks go to Helen Roberts—Vice President, Consortium of Universities of the Washington Metropolitan Area—for her continued support. Finally, we were constantly amazed at the work of Allison Pinckney, who was able to take any document, handwritten scribble, or software package and somehow make it all work.

Introduction

This book is for the "unsung heroes" of academia: the adjunct and part-time faculty who come out, mostly at night, to teach in our colleges and universities and then disappear, only to reappear the following week at the same day and time and in the same room. These are the people who bring current real-world expertise to the classroom. These are the people who are living their disciplines daily by virtue of their full-time jobs and who teach to share their experience and expertise with students. They are much valued by their students and fellow full-time program faculty, yet are often not given the support they require to fulfill their responsibilities. In 1995, Eugene Arden, provost and vice-chancellor emeritus of the University of Michigan at Dearborn, wrote in an editorial in the *Chronicle of Higher Education:*

> During the first semester or two of employment, adjuncts may be advised by an assistant department head or an unlucky senior faculty member whose turn it is to perform "service." The oversight, however, may consist of no more than a single meeting, which ends with the professor saying, "Let me know if you need any more help." Barring a crisis . . . the adjunct thereafter is pretty much on their own. Often an adjunct is told only what textbooks to use and what the minimum requirements are . . . and everything else is left up to the individual adjunct.

[Adjuncts] typically live hectic lives, on killer schedules. Many of them hold a full-time job elsewhere or are managing a household, in addition to moonlighting as adjuncts. . . . The situation would ordinarily be hopeless, except that the current criticism of higher education is so vitriolic that even the most stubborn faculty members and administrators concede that changes must be made. (p. A44)

This book has been designed to help

- Adjuncts and part-time faculty members (hereafter also referred to as adjuncts) who need to know how to "work the system" at their university so they can obtain the resources, including instructional support, that they need to be as effective as possible
- Program, department, and school administrators, who need to be mindful of their obligation to their adjuncts and to their students
- Full-time faculty who work with adjuncts, and *all* faculty who are interested in improving their teaching and facilitating skills

The chapters on instructional strategies and techniques (Chapters 4 through 7) are also applicable to teaching assistants. This book cuts across all disciplines and all levels of academia, from certificate programs to doctoral programs and from main campuses to satellite campuses.

The philosophical foundation of this handbook is adult learning and instructional design theory. All instruction should have a sound theoretical basis no matter what the discipline. Although this handbook heavily emphasizes teaching strategies and methods for adult learners, we believe these techniques are equally applicable to college undergraduates. (In fact, much of adult learning methodology is also applicable to primary and secondary school students.)

The sequence of the handbook is from administration to teaching to evaluation to professional development and professional conduct. Most of the chapters have checklists, job aids, and other practical resources that we encourage all readers to use to their full advantage.

The chapters do sometimes overlap because they were written by different authors and were designed to stand alone for reference purposes. The structure of each chapter and the style of writing also differ, due to the purpose of the chapter and the background of the author(s).

Chapter 1, "Program Policies and Administration," covers the items the adjunct and the administrator should consider in ensuring a successful teaching-learning experience. Everything from the contractual agreement between the adjunct and the program administrator to parking arrangements is discussed in both narrative and checklist form.

Chapter 2, "Adult Learning: Philosophy and Approach," discusses the need for student-centered learning facilitation with both young adult undergraduates and older returning students. The role of both content and process and the setting of a learning climate are emphasized.

Chapter 3, "Developing Instructional Objectives, Lesson Plans, and Syllabi," goes into the instructional planning and preparation for a course. A taxonomy of educational objectives and process for goal analysis, as well as a guide to lesson planning, is discussed. Samples of syllabi and course schedules are provided.

Chapter 4, "Teaching Methods and Strategies," reviews various traditional and nontraditional teaching strategies, including interactive lectures. Checklists and job aids are provided, as well as guidelines for selecting the appropriate methods for different kinds of learning experiences.

Chapter 5, "Connecting With Cooperative Learning," presents an innovative teaching strategy that is predicated on active learning, cooperation, and respect for individual learning styles. It promotes student participation and interaction, yet is highly structured. It also supports skill development in group process, problem solving, and critical thinking.

Chapter 6, "Active Learning Designs: Simple Techniques to Make Your Teaching Dazzle," shares six different learning approaches that generate high motivation by getting students interested in learning while having fun. Specific activities are described that can add variety to a lesson plan.

Chapter 7, "Facilitating Classroom Learning," discusses the role of adjunct as a learning facilitator rather than expert authority. This chapter extends the concepts presented in Chapter 2 into practical techniques and job aids and wraps up the series of chapters on instruction.

Chapter 8, "Evaluation of Students," covers criterion-referenced approaches to evaluation, developing an evaluation plan, and the feedback process. University and program policies and adult-learning-based evaluation methods are discussed. Specific evaluation tools for the adult learner are emphasized.

Chapter 9, "Evaluation of the Course and the Adjunct," deals with the evaluation of the course and the adjunct by the university to provide feedback to the adjunct for the improvement of the learning experience and for the adjunct's professional growth. How to create self-evaluation methods is emphasized.

Chapter 10, "Professional Development of Adjunct Faculty," addresses the strategies for continuous formal and informal professional development in terms of the adjunct's discipline base and teaching style. Criterion-referenced development and mentoring are addressed.

Chapter 11, "Putting It All Together," presents four scenarios that dramatize the mistakes any adjunct can make and the lessons that can be drawn from the material in this book.

Well, it is time for class to start. We hope everyone at your institution has done everything possible to help your adjuncts provide a meaningful learning experience to your ultimate customers—your students. And we hope you adjuncts feel confident and prepared. Good luck!

Reference

Arden, E. (1995, July 21). Ending the loneliness and isolation of adjunct professors. *Chronicle of Higher Education*, p. A44.

1

Program Policies
and Administration

VIRGINIA BIANCO-MATHIS
LORRI COOPER

Bianco-Mathis and Cooper kick off this book by orienting the adjunct instructor to his or her first challenge: coping with university administration. In this chapter, they provide pragmatic advice, ranging from the specific to the general—from "Where do I park?" to "How do I grade?" Adjunct instructors tend to be practicing experts in their chosen field who teach because they find the experience personally rewarding. Nonetheless, the authors warn us that universities vary in how much help they provide to adjunct faculty. The authors encourage adjuncts to become involved in their academic community and stress the necessity of forming supporting networks.

This chapter provides checklists and guidelines for signing a teaching contract, coordinating classroom details, and managing student administrative procedures. The chapter ends on an interesting and caution-

ary note with a matter-of-fact discussion of ethics that addresses freedom, diversity of perspectives, and professional limits to teacher-student interaction.

Any adjunct professor will appreciate the tips provided by Bianco-Mathis and Cooper. They present an outline for how to simplify the process of orientation by identifying issues in a straightforward manner.

Program Approaches

The relationship between adjuncts and universities varies and is anything but predictable. Some setups are very organized, and you, the adjunct, will be supported and recognized. Others are "sink or swim" situations in which you will be left to fend for yourself.

"Continuous education" schools within universities, such as the School of Inservice Education at George Mason University, the University of Maryland University College, and the George Washington University Continuing Education Program, depend almost totally on adjunct instructors. Given this dependence, resources such as administrative help, coaching, orientation programs, development seminars, joint meetings, and regular communications are provided to support adjunct faculty.

Unfortunately, this is not usually true for the main schools and departments within a university. Usually, main campuses and programs that rely on full-time faculty are not given additional resources (time, money, extra staff) to support adjunct faculty. Consequently, adjuncts in these settings tend to have to "fend for themselves," and the experience can be frustrating. This situation is further exacerbated when adjuncts are asked to teach at satellite locations.

Luckily, adjuncts are dedicated individuals who find the adjunct experience personally rewarding. They tend to succeed despite the system because of the enjoyment they gain from imparting knowledge, watching people grow, promoting intellectual interchange, and undergoing the continuous learning that teaching involves.

Adjunct positions are filled not only by formal calls for applications but by contacting those who have sent in resumes for full-time positions and by informal networking with other professors or related departments, professional organizations, and industry contacts. Possible candidates include successful executives who wish to "give back" to the field, former graduates (following a waiting period), and retired military personnel.

Most adjuncts can tell interesting stories of how they were hired and their first few classroom experiences. You and the university coordinator will need to discuss the following points:

- What is the interviewing process? Will you be required to give a presentation or prepare a sample lesson?
- How are decisions made concerning salary, title, and schedule? By whom?
- Will there be a formal acceptance letter and/or contract? When will this be received?
- What criteria are used for hiring and determining pay, title, and increases?
- What is the title structure for adjuncts (instructor, assistant adjunct, associate adjunct, etc.)?
- How is salary paid?
- When and how will communication be made concerning selection, schedule, class size, class location, class roster, and books?

Depending on whether the adjunct population is specifically supported, you may or may not receive ongoing communication from your department or program. Some universities make a special effort to include adjuncts as part of the academic community. Efforts along these lines might include

- Invitations to faculty meetings
- Receipt of faculty minutes
- Special meetings between adjuncts and full-time faculty
- Developmental workshops
- Mentorship programs
- Mailboxes on site
- Awards
- Luncheons/dinners

Such activities create a sense of belonging to the academic environment and reinforce commitment and quality.

If you find yourself in a less supportive environment, you are encouraged to take a more proactive, resourceful, and creative approach. Seek out relationships with library and bookstore personnel, key professors, and secretaries. "Give back" when you can: Redesign a course, develop special lessons or case studies that full-time faculty have not had time to do, or research and discover a better text.

Preparing for the Teaching Term

Every adjunct hopes to arrive at the first class confident in his or her knowledge of the subject matter and prepared to dazzle a room full of willing and talented students with an impressive teaching style. Before this occurs, however, the adjunct must spend advance time attending to certain details that will ensure a successful beginning to every class. The remainder of this chapter takes you through a series of questions to resolve before you actually start teaching. The list is not intended to be all-inclusive. We hope that as you read through the guidelines and the questions, you will consider what is particular to your situation and record additional items for discovery on your own.

Coordination of the Class

To begin with, you must have a contract between the university or college and yourself. The terms of the contract should spell out the dates of your teaching assignment, the course(s) you will be teaching, the form and timing of payment, and any other pertinent information. You will need a copy of the contract showing your signature agreeing to the terms and the signature of the provost or academic dean for your records.

Next comes the scheduling of class meetings. The university may already have a set schedule of dates, times, and places that you must adhere to. Or you may have some input in the scheduling process. Everyone experiences scheduling conflicts. It will be helpful for you to prearrange any makeup classes or schedule changes due to your un-availability early in the process. Students lose their flexibility and patience after the first class!

Finally, your university "contact" is an extremely valuable resource. Whatever position he or she holds (maybe dean of the program, department chair, or senior professor), this is the person to contact with your questions and requests for assistance. It will also be helpful to know your contact's support person. This gives you the ability to relay information, and often the support person will be able to answer your questions.

Physical Location of the Class

For planning purposes and to help relieve any "first-night jitters," arrange to visit the classroom (or similar setting) in which you will be teaching. This gives you advance information on whether the room will need rearranging to accommodate your teaching style or special students, as well as familiarity with parking, restrooms, snack availability, and so forth. It also gives you the opportunity to visualize which instructional media forms are possible.

To begin, is the building in which you will conduct class sessions located on or off campus? Are parking facilities available? Are you required to have a sticker? (If so, where do you obtain one?) If parking is some distance from the classroom location, is there a shuttle available? What are the hours of operation? Are there any personal safety concerns about returning to your car after class? Are the classroom and the building accessible for all students? On the basis of your list of enrollees, will there be any requirements for special accommodations in the classroom? Now that the Americans With Disabilities Act is law, instructors may need to find interpreters, "signers" for the deaf, tape recorders, or other accommodations. Where are the restrooms and water fountains located? What are the locations and hours of operation of sources of snacks, drinks, or meals? If any problems should arise, how can security be contacted, and where are they located? Finding the answers to these questions may seem administrative and outside your concerns for teaching. But this is part of your planning process, and you can be sure that students will ask these same questions and more because you are accessible!

As for the classroom itself, will it accommodate the proposed number of students? If for group exercises students need to spread out, what other meeting spaces are located and available nearby? If the room needs to be rearranged either to meet your teaching needs or to accommodate special students, is any permission required to rearrange the classroom? Are there any requirements to return the room to a preset configuration? For your teaching methods, is the room furnished with adequate chairs or tables, chalkboards and chalk, marker boards and markers? Is there a policy that prohibits food and drink in the classroom?

Some classes require students' work to be done in a lab setting. It will be beneficial to know beforehand the availability of the facilities, where they are located, and the hours of operation. If you plan to conduct a class session in the lab, what prior arrangement needs to be made, and with whom? This same information is also pertinent for the library. Where is it located, and what are the hours of operation? If a computer lab will be used, what is the process for passwords, e-mail, and scheduling?

Student Administration

For your planning purposes and information (students will ask you!), familiarize yourself with the university's registration procedure and dates. A general knowledge will be most helpful. As for your particular class, find out the dates for drop/add and whether a signature or approval is required of you. Before the class begins, you will receive an enrollment roster. Knowing when to look for a final registration roster is helpful. Sometimes students may ask you how late registration is conducted. Be prepared.

Next come the all-important grades. What is the grading system used by the university? Are you required to file a midterm grade? When, where, and how must your final grades be turned in? This knowledge will have an effect on the timing of any final assignments completed by students and your availability to grade them. What are the provisions and deadlines for Incompletes? And have students fulfilled the requirements for class attendance as set by the university? Becoming familiar with the university attendance and absentee policy is important because it is an area that can be subject to much argument and can vary from state to state.

Teacher evaluations are useful tools for the advancement and development of your teaching style. Does the university use them? If so, how?

When and how are they accessible to you? What arrangements are made for the completion of the evaluations? Most schools require that the evaluations not be handled by the adjunct and that the adjunct not be physically present in the room when the forms are being completed. Again, for planning purposes, you may need to schedule time for this exercise in one of the final classes.

Adjunct Support

As we become more skilled and as students' attention span grows shorter, the use of instructional media is encouraged in the classroom. Overheads, projectors, VCRs, and computers are a reflection of the changes. Gone are the days when the teaching standard was strictly lecture. Therefore, as you plan your class sessions, you will need to know what instructional media the university can make available to you and how to arrange for the use of the materials.

Depending on the department with which you are affiliated, some administrative support may be offered. It will be worthwhile to discover the types of support available and what arrangements are necessary. The same applies for photocopying. It will be helpful to know how long it takes and whether you may be reimbursed for any expense you incur by completing this task yourself.

Then there is the subject of class text(s). Are you responsible for choosing the text yourself, or does the department have a recommended text? Is there a textbook committee to which you may have input? And how are the selected textbooks ordered? Must you make arrangements at the bookstore? Who is responsible for checking to see that texts arrive in time for students to purchase? What are the hours of operation of the bookstore? Must you make special arrangements for your students to purchase texts? Will the university provide you with your own personal copy?

Knowledge of the library will be key in your planning process. As you decide the scope of assignments for students, consider the resources available to them. What materials does the library have on the particular subject matter? What assistance does the library offer students in their research process? How available is the library to you and your students? If necessary, what is the procedure for placing materials on reserve?

Finally, are there any perks for an adjunct? How do you get (and are you required to have) a faculty ID card? What will this card do for you? Will you be admitted to the faculty dining hall? If so, at what charge? Can you gain admittance to any recreational facility with your ID card? Can you attend any entertainment events sponsored on campus? The greatest rewards of teaching are intrinsic, but anything else is nice!

See Appendix 1.1 for a checklist summarizing the administrative details on which you may need to prepare.

A Word About Ethics

Every profession has ethical standards, and the professorate is no exception. As an adjunct faculty member, you represent the same model to students and the outside world as any full-time professor. The difference may be that you have no responsibilities for faculty governance or service to the community. But as for any matter concerning students and the institution, the same ethical standards apply.

The institution's standards of academic freedom imply that along with your freedom to teach and pursue scholarly work goes the responsibility to represent yourself and your views accurately, both in and outside the classroom. This responsibility demands that when you are stating your beliefs and ideas, you make it clear that these are yours and not the institution's. Likewise, you have the responsibility of accurately portraying your relationship with the university—that of adjunct faculty, not professor.

Within the realm of your classroom and your relationship with students is a whole other set of ethical standards. In the classroom, you have the responsibility of ensuring students' freedom to learn. First, you must protect students' freedom of speech: As part of the learning process, all students should be encouraged to express themselves and their ideas. Students must realize, however, that along with the freedom comes responsibility, and you may find yourself as arbiter in the classroom when the speech becomes harmful toward others. You should be aware of your institution's policy concerning free speech.

Second, you must protect students' right to privacy. Private conversations between a student and you are confidential; so are any of your comments on any written work and any grades given. Third, you must protect students' right to due process, within both your classroom and the institution. And fourth, you must foster honest academic conduct. This involves not only representing yourself and your views appropriately but exhibiting professional standards that protect the integrity of your course and protect honest students. You may want to consult the university's policy for dealing with academic misconduct.

Another area in which ethical standards apply is the selection of course content and course materials. Whatever you choose must be valid and credible, with a clearly defined purpose. Be careful not to present materials that exclusively support your ideas and views, and do not present as final truth an idea that may still be undergoing scholarly debate. You have a responsibility to inform students that other views exist in a manner that does not distort or misrepresent those modified or opposing ideas. You have an obligation to guide students through their own scholarly pursuit, wherever it may lead you and them.

Another area in which you must be aware of the power and responsibility of your position is that of testing and comments on student work, both on papers and in recommendation letters. Testing is used to determine and support student achievement. As a faculty member, you have the responsibility to design instruments and testing procedures that do not allow any one student or groups of students an unfair advantage. And you are the person responsible for protecting student honesty and avoiding any violation of the integrity of the test. Students put time, effort and a part of themselves into each paper they prepare. Remember this when writing your comments in the margin. Criticisms and comments should be constructive and encouraging. Writing recommendations for students requires a certain finesse. An accurate portrayal of the student's performance and abilities is the goal, yet inflation of these is sometimes the result. Consult with your department head or dean for guidance. Also, it is not uncommon for students to ask a faculty member to write a letter of reference. Check to find out if there is a policy and how you are to represent yourself in the letter.

Finally, there is the issue of friendship. As a teacher in the classroom, you have the responsibility of not only treating each student fairly but maintaining the appearance of impartiality. Favoring a particular student or group of students, however tempting or natural it may seem, compromises every student's learning process by raising questions of performance based on ability. Students observing such inappropriate friendships may begin to doubt your credibility, thereby weakening your ability to model scholarly behavior and serve effectively in an advisory role. Almost all schools have policies prohibiting sexual harassment. This helps ensure that student, faculty, and staff may work and learn in an environment conducive to intellectual, professional, and social development. Be aware of the operative policy at your respective college or university, as well as the formal grievance procedure for resolving such complaints.

You are human, and the profession of teaching is full of passion. Effective teaching demands the use of your emotions and knowledge plus your ability to deliberate and judge each student with impartiality. Do not compromise yourself or your standards.

Suggested Readings

Cahn, S. (1986). *Saints and scams: Ethics in academia.* Totowa, NJ: Rowman & Littlefield.
Cahn, S. (Ed.). (1990). *Morality, responsibility, and the university.* Philadelphia: University Press.
Rich, J. M. (1984). *Professional ethics in education.* Springfield, IL: Charles C Thomas.

Appendix 1.1
Administrative Details to Check Before the Term Begins

▧ Coordination of the Class

_____ Do you have a copy of your contract signed by the provost or academic dean indicating responsibilities and payment?

_____ What are the date, time, and place of your class meetings? Have you prearranged any scheduling conflicts or makeup classes?

_____ Have you spoken with your university contact? Do you know how to obtain whatever support you will need?

▧ Physical Location of the Class

_____ Where is the classroom located, and what parking is available? Have you obtained any necessary permits?

_____ Have you visited your classroom? Will you need to rearrange anything to accommodate your teaching methods?

_____ Have you addressed personal safety concerns for yourself and the students both coming to and going from class?

_____ Have accommodations been made both in the building and in the classroom for all students?

_____ Have you located restrooms, water fountains, telephones, concessions, etc.?

_____ Do you know how to contact safety and security personnel in the event of an emergency?

_____ Where is the library (or laboratory facility) located, and what are the hours of operation?

Student Administration

_____ Do you have a general knowledge of registration procedures? Drop/add procedures?

_____ Have you been given an enrollment or registration roster? Have you confirmed actual enrollment information?

_____ Have you been given information regarding the university's grading system and procedures, especially the deadline when final grades are due?

_____ Are you aware of the procedures and expectations for teacher evaluations?

Adjunct Support

_____ Have you made arrangements for any instructional media materials you will need?

_____ Are there any provisions for administrative support—typing, photocopying, etc.? Do you know how to arrange for anything you may need?

_____ Have you made arrangements for the students to obtain the required textbooks?

_____ Are you familiar with the university's library and the resources available pertaining to your subject? Will the library offer you or your students assistance with research? Do you know the procedure for placing materials on reserve?

_____ Finally, are there any perks? Will your faculty ID card serve any other purpose besides campus identification?

Adult Learning
Philosophy and Approach

KATHY M. NAYLOR

So the adjunct has signed a teaching contract. Now what? At this point, it is wise to step back and analyze the client population: namely, under- graduate and graduate college students. By fully understanding this group, the adjunct is in a better position to develop materials, design classroom activities, and create syllabi that are appropriate for adult learners. This entire book has been built on a framework of adult learning theory as it applies to both undergraduate and graduate college students. Grasping adult learning concepts is essential before moving on to chapters dealing with goals, objectives, teaching methods, and evaluation.

As field practitioners, adjunct instructors are mostly familiar with traditional classroom approaches: namely, lecture, lecture, and more lec- ture. In this second chapter, Kathy Naylor provides a primer on the psychology of adult learning that emphasizes student-centered teaching practices. Naylor reminds adjunct instructors that they are learning facilitators—individuals who guide the student through the transforma-tional process of learning. To do this, adjuncts must manage two distinct dimensions in the classroom: content and group process. Naylor points out that the learning facilitator must demonstrate not only subject matter competency but also skill in managing motivation, feelings, tone, atmo-sphere, influence, participation, leadership issues and struggles, conflict, communication, and competition.

By citing her own experiences and the works of learning theorists such as Carl Rogers and Malcolm Knowles, Naylor presents a series of adult learning principles, including such researched propositions as "Adult learners want guidance, not grades," "Adult learners must be challenged through critical reflection," and "Adults are problem centered rather than subject centered."

Naylor offers tips and checklists on adult interaction skills, such as listening, communication, and feedback skills. There is also a useful discussion of the necessity of matching teaching style to learning styles: For example, a "global" ("right-brained") learner will learn best by participating in a group exercise or case study before getting into specific facts.

This chapter offers the adjunct an appropriate backdrop for the entire university teaching experience. Naylor presents theory with substantive lessons that adjunct instructors can put to use immediately.

The Learning Process

Learning involves change in the learner, and very little change occurs in individuals or groups unless there is a commitment to change. To commit to learn, individuals need to shed old attitudes and behaviors; negotiate expectations and goals; and assume new attitudes, thoughts, and behaviors. This is often very threatening and challenging. A key factor in this transformation process is the "champion of change" who promotes and supports the new way of being and helps individuals and groups discover the value of transformation. This champion—the ad-junct instructor—can be referred to as a *learning facilitator.* With the facilitator's help, the learner challenges existing paradigms and ex-plores new mental models (Brookfield, 1988; Merriam & Caffarella, 1991).

Basic Competencies of the Learning Facilitator

To fulfill his or her role successfully, the learning facilitator needs to become adept at

- Understanding adult learning styles
- Relationship building
- Motivation enhancement
- Communication and feedback

Understanding Adult Learning Styles

Instructors need to be familiar with what Malcolm Knowles (1973) called *andragogy*—"the art and science of helping adults to learn." Adults learn by five different methods: reading, hearing, seeing, saying, and doing. Research indicates that they absorb 10% of what is read, 20% of what is heard, 30% of what is read and heard, 50% of what is heard and seen, 70% of what is said by themselves, and 90% of what is done by themselves with others.

Said more simply, adults learn best by *doing*. This means they learn best by practicing skills and by using the skills to work on realistic problems. Also, they learn best when they are "ready" to learn, which means they see the importance and usefulness of the learning if the environment is adequate and comfortable. In addition, they learn best when material is presented in small amounts arranged in an organized way, when they have time to absorb it, and when they have a sense that they are making progress. Table 2.1 lists these and other characteristics of the adult learner. It is wise to keep these in mind whether you are a new or seasoned adjunct instructor.

Because of the pragmatic and problem-centered focus of adult learners, the learning facilitator should develop and carry out any presentation or classroom exercise with careful attention to its goals, applications, and efficacy. W. Edwards Deming's "Plan, Do, Check, Act" cycle (see Walton, 1986) provides a useful framework (see Table 2.2).

Many factors contribute to the learning experience, including psychological factors, such as anxiety level and self-esteem, and physical factors, including current health. Combined with these factors are style

Table 2.1   Characteristics of Adult Learners

Adults must want to learn.

Adults will learn only what they feel a need to learn.

Adults look to learning what can immediately be applied.

Adults want to know if what they are asked to learn is relevant to their needs.

Adults seek to learn what they have identified as important rather than what others deem important.

Adults learn by doing.

Adults are problem centered rather than subject centered.

Adults have a broad base of experience on which to draw and share with others.

Adults learn best in an informal environment.

A variety of methods should be used in instructing adults.

Adult learners tend to be less interested in survey courses.

Adults want guidance, not grades.

Adults' concepts about themselves directly affect their behavior and desire to learn.

Adults have expectations, and it is critical to take time up front to clarify and articulate all expectations before getting into content.

Programs need to be designed to accept viewpoints from people in different life stages and with different value "sets."

SOURCE: Wilson (1986).

differences. Some people are "detail learners" who prefer to focus on specifics and not the big picture. Others are "main idea" learners who pay more attention to the overview and skip instructions and details. Some are active learners who prefer to seek out data, usually by asking a lot of questions; however, they tend to jump to conclusions. Others are passive learners who need to be encouraged to learn.

In addition, individuals can be either "right-brain-dominant" ("global" learners) or "left-brain-dominant" ("analytic" learners). Right-brain-dominant people tend to be more intuitive, imaginative, concrete, impulsive, tacit, and free. They like open-ended learning experiences, and their preferred learning approach is to start with a broad idea and then gather supporting information. They learn best by seeing and doing in an environment that is informal, busy, and relatively unstructured. They work best with others and are concerned about people and processes. Left-brain-dominant people, on the other hand, tend to intellectualize more and to be deductive, rational, abstract, directed, ana-

Table 2.2   Guidelines for Continuous Quality Improvement in Classroom Presentations and Exercises

Stage	Guidelines
Plan	What are my goals?
	Am I thoroughly familiar with the material?
	What is the experience level of class members?
	Have prerequisites been clearly identified?
	Do I have a lesson plan?
	What handouts will I use?
	What exercises will I use?
	What flip charts and/or transparencies will I use?
	Are classroom and breakout rooms reserved?
	Have the class members been notified of goals, any preparation required, time, and place?
	Is the equipment I need available?
Do	Know/introduce the concept or tool.
	Why is it important or useful?
	When would you use it?
	How would you use it?
	Show/give an example, the "classroom" one or one directly related to the work of your class members.
	Practice.
Check	Get feedback:
	How did the exercise go?
	Did everyone achieve the objectives?
	What behavior indicates that the class members learned your material?
	Ask how members would use this concept or tool in their jobs.
Act	When appropriate:
	Slow down if team members are struggling.
	Speed up if they're way ahead.
	Repeat.
	Clarify.
	Use other examples.
	Do other exercises.

lytical, and objective. They enjoy step-by-step, structured experiences and well-organized lectures and activities. Their preferred learning approach is to learn many facts and then put them together to arrive at a general understanding. They learn best by hearing and reading in an environment that is organized and quiet. They work best alone in a job that produces something concrete. One can ascertain students' learning styles by (a) using inventories or psychological tests, (b) observing students and paying attention to their questions, and (c) discussing learning styles with students and asking them to share their preferences.

To facilitate the learning process, it is essential to understand the different styles of individual learners and then to tailor the course design and methods to accommodate the group. The following are approaches to transferring knowledge or skill that work particularly well with left-brain-dominant learners:

- *Lecture:* In this common training method, the learning facilitator "stands and delivers" the information. For adult learning, it is best to use lectures sparingly. Short lectures are useful to introduce a major topic.
- *Readings:* Assigned readings can contribute to the learner's store of information.
- *Programmed instruction:* Printed, video, audio, or computer programs allow the learner to follow a sequence of planned instruction at his or her own pace.
- *Demonstration:* The facilitator shows the learner how to perform a given task.

The following are approaches that work particularly well with right-brain-dominant learners:

- *Group discussion:* The facilitator or leader guides the sharing of the learned information and experience.
- *Simulation and role play:* Learners are assigned a role to act out in a given situation. This technique shows how to solve problems and encourages understanding.
- *Games:* These competitive activities use preset rules to govern players' activities and determine outcomes.
- *Panels:* Three to five "experts" read prepared statements and then discuss the statements among themselves. The experts also respond to audience questions.
- *Case study:* The facilitator explains a problem or "case" that the group discusses to find a solution.

Relationship Building

All human interactions have two aspects: content and process. Content is the subject matter or the task. Process is what is happening between and to the people who are interacting. Learning facilitators should become very sensitive to group process, including issues of motivation, feelings, tone, atmosphere, influence, participation, leadership, competition, conflict, communication, and cooperation/collaboration or the lack of it. Such awareness is important because it can provide valuable information not only about the individuals in the class but about the group as a collective and can help the facilitator to rethink and adjust his or her approach to maximize the learning experience.

In addition, to accomplish adult transformation, it is critical to view students as "clients" with whom you will interact to provide a "service." A way to begin this relationship is immediately to establish "ground rules," or group behavioral norms that respect students' adultness by mutually creating and agreeing on expectations. Ask students how they feel concerning their learning needs, class goals, assignments, grades, methods of evaluation, self- and group assessments, deadlines, communication methods, learning activities, schedule of progress, and so forth. Determining the needs and values of individuals up front and gaining consensus allows for program and process buy-in. By taking the mystery out of the process, it creates a comfort level that minimizes fear and threat.

Looking at risk, trust, expression, creativity, participation, confrontation, collaboration, and communication processes is primary when engaging a new class in the learning journey. The behaviors that the facilitator models can make all the difference in whether individuals are receptive to the learning process. For success, facilitators need to

- Understand quickly the context within which they are functioning, the class culture
- Envision the environment they want to create
- Engage the group in creating the learning environment
- Provide experiential opportunities within that environment
- Foster personal ownership and integrity
- Negotiate mutual expectations and methods of evaluation and communication

Central to relationship building in the classroom is what Carl R. Rogers, the therapist, author, and teacher (Knowles, 1973), called "student-centered teaching." This approach is based on five assumptions:

1. No one can teach another directly; one can only facilitate another's learning.
2. A person learns the most those things he or she perceives as being involved in the maintenance or enhancement of self.
3. A person is naturally threatened and resistant when confronted with the reorganization of him- or herself.
4. New experiences inconsistent with the organization of self can be assimilated only if the current organization of self is relaxed and expanded to include it, so it is important to provide a nonthreatening environment with a great deal of focus on student responsibility.
5. The learning environment that promotes reduced threat to the learner and enhances a differentiated learner perception tends to be the most effective. Differentiated perception is defined as the tendency to see things in less than absolute terms; to become more aware of variations in phenomena, values, and ideas across space and time; to anchor facts, not concepts; to evaluate in multiple ways; to become more aware of different levels of abstractions; and to be more willing to test inferences and abstractions against reality.

Creating a nonthreatening environment basically means displaying acceptance of people and their ideas. Traditionally, instructors tended to lecture and serve as subject matter authorities who focused on one-way communication: telling and evaluating. Effective learning facilitators need to assume a participatory approach that fosters two-way communication and collaboration. Behaviors a learning facilitator can model to cultivate a nonthreatening environment are outlined in Table 2.3. By taking a more accepting stance, the facilitator removes the impression that performance will be judged and then creates balance in the relationship with the group so that the task becomes a collaborative effort.

Motivation Enhancement

Motivation is the need to learn and the readiness to learn. More often than not, individuals need to choose for themselves whether and when

Table 2.3 Creating a Nonthreatening Environment: Accepting Versus Nonaccepting Behaviors

Behaviors	Results
Accepting	
Listening	Cooperation
Accepting another's ideas	Feelings of closeness
Sharing information	Willingness to work interdependently
Showing interest in the other person	Positive anticipation of the instructor's
Expressing appreciation	return
Nonaccepting	
Criticizing	Antagonistic feeling
Making unfair comparisons	Noncooperation
Ignoring	Avoidance
Giving advice	Noncompliance with suggestions or advice
Rejecting the other's ideas	Feelings of relief when the relationship is
Laughing at, not with	terminated
Pretending (to listen, to be interested, to be concerned, etc.)	

they will learn something. Usually they become motivated either when they are dissatisfied with some aspect of their lives and feel the need to act or when they become aware of greater payoffs for acquiring certain skills. Some of the blocks associated with learner motivation are

- Fear of the unknown
- Complacency
- Fear of failure
- Lack of skill
- Lack of time
- Fear of additional expectations, responsibility
- Fear of rejection
- Fear of relinquishing comfortable habits
- Fear of change and the effort it will require

Some of the payoffs are

- Increased skill and effectiveness
- Increased productivity

- Increased opportunities and recognition
- Increased responsibility
- Increased sense of achievement
- Increased self-worth

During the first class with a new group, the learning facilitator might want to take a survey by asking individuals to review the above lists of blocks and payoffs and allow time for students to answer the following questions:

- Which three blocks affect you the most?
- How can the facilitator and the group work together to reduce the impact of the blocks or cope with the blocks so to maximize our learning opportunities?
- What are the payoffs to gaining the skills associated with this class?
- How can I personally benefit by acquiring new behaviors?

What motivates one individual may not motivate another, so it is important to get a handle on what motivates particular individuals as well as the group as a collective to enhance one's teaching effectiveness and students' desire to learn.

Competency is a natural motivator because, as Schermerhorn (1986) pointed out, "Most individuals gain great satisfaction" from having mastery over their environment (p. 38). Learning facilitators can tap into this natural motivator by

- Acknowledging the learner's existing skills and abilities
- Building on existing skills and aptitudes to complete tasks
- Empowering learners with the vision that they can achieve and the rewards that achievement garners

Communication and Feedback

Rogers sees learning as an internal process controlled by the learner. The facilitator, then, can only attempt to engage the learner to interact with his or her environment as he or she perceives it and to stimulate the learner to differentiate his or her way of relating and behaving for growth and maximum learning experiences. It is imperative, therefore, that facilitators be, above all, good communicators, skilled in both listening to (receiving) and relaying (sending) information.

Listening is the most important (though often the most overlooked) component in any communication exchange. Active listening is critical to the facilitator for two reasons: It establishes a climate of trust between the other person and facilitator, and it enables the facilitator to gather needed information from the other person. The facilitator must draw out information to clarify and expand on the issues involved, and active listening encourages the other to respond more openly than does poor listening.

The following are listening responses that inhibit communication:

- Ordering/directing: "you must," "you should," "you have to"
- Advice giving: "my advice is," "why don't you," "it would be best to"
- Lecturing: "the fact is," "you must understand," "nevertheless"
- Diagnosing/evaluating: "your problem is," "what you need is," "your duty is"
- Devaluating: "it's not so bad," "don't worry," "look at the bright side"

The following are some listening responses that increase communication:

- Listen attentively to the other person's words and feelings.
- Do not judge, evaluate, censor, or try to control the conversation. Keep an open mind; do not allow your feelings, attitudes, or opinions to interfere.
- Reinforce what the other person is saying. Examples of reinforcement include *nonverbal signals,* such as smiles, head nodding, eye contact, squarely facing the other, and leaning slightly toward the other, and *verbal signals* (which do not include those already mentioned), such as short questions for clarification only and statements such as "I see," "yes," and "I understand."
- Listen for the other person's feelings by observing his or her nonverbal behavior carefully. Make a conscious effort to "read" these signals—a process that we generally do without conscious thought. Be aware of eye contact, posture, tone of voice, facial expression, and gesture. These nonverbal behaviors can signal a speaker's emotions, such as fear, anxiety, hostility, tension, distress, and defensiveness. A facilitator must be aware of these emotions to communicate effectively.

- Give the other person feedback, summarize the words, and reflect any strong emotion which you have observed. Without feedback, you cannot be sure you have correctly interpreted the other person's meaning. Also, feedback reassures the other person that you have listened carefully, understood, and valued both the feelings and the statements expressed. Some examples of feedback statements are "As I understand it, what happened was . . . ," "I can see you are concerned about . . . ," and "I get the impression that . . . worries you."
- If you are not certain of the other person's words or feelings, phrase your feedback in the form of questions: for example, "Do you mean . . . ?" "Is this what happened?" "Were you disappointed about . . . ?"

The following are overall tips for effective communication:

- Try to understand the other's needs and mind-set (where he or she is "coming from"). Rather than challenging or disputing his or her feelings and attitudes, try to change the other's mind-set through persuasion by means of objective reasoning. Be well prepared with facts on the interpretation, use, and significance of the issue involved; present these facts calmly and logically.
- Be realistic rather than idealistic. You are not going to achieve total conviction and change with every person. Adapt your goals to the individual situation, remembering that you are not a problem solver or solution giver, but a helper. Often you will do well if you can simply help the person accept that a problem exists and that it may have some solution.
- Be goal directed. Try to find areas in which the other person has goals that are congruent with the goals of the learning. Emphasize the positive consequences of attaining these goals rather than the negative consequences of not attaining them. End the conversation on a positive note, agreeing on goals and possible steps for attaining them.

Often adults are still rookies when it comes to listening and communicating effectively with others, not to mention giving and receiving feedback, which is an essential element of the communications and learning process. Included in Appendix 2.1 at the end of this chapter is a suggested role play to build skill in this area.

References

Brookfield, S. (1988). *Developing critical thinkers*. San Francisco: Jossey-Bass.

Knowles, M. S. (1973). *The adult learner: A neglected species* (2nd ed.). Houston: Gulf.

Merriam, S., & Caffarella, R. (1991). *Learning in adulthood*. San Francisco: Jossey-Bass.

Schermerhorn, J. R., Jr. (1986, November). Team development for high performance. *Training and Development Journal*, 38-41.

Walton, M. (1986). *Deming management at work*. New York: Perigee.

Wilson, D. (1986). National Society of Performance and Instruction, Utah Chapter Newsletter, 1.

Additional Suggested Readings

American Society for Training and Development. (1989, September). *Coming to agreement* (Info-Line Publication Rep. No.). Alexandria, VA: Author.

American Society for Training and Development. (1990, March). *How to train managers to train* (Info-Line Publication Rep. No.). Alexandria, VA: Author.

Knowles, M. S. (1980). *The modern practice of adult education: From pedagogy to andragogy*. Chicago: Follett.

Knowles, M. S. (1988). *The making of an adult educator*. San Francisco: Jossey-Bass.

Knox, A. B. (1986). *Helping adults learn*. San Francisco: Jossey-Bass.

Kolb, D. A. (1984). *Experiential learning: Experience as the source of learning and development*. Englewood Cliffs, NJ: Prentice Hall.

NTL Institute. (1982). *Reading book for human relations training*. Arlington, VA: Author.

Appendix 2.1
Giving and Receiving Feedback

▩ Tips

If you are the giver of feedback:
— Speak to the listener, the behavior, or the situation without assuming intent.
— Explain how it affects you (why you are concerned).
— Use specific examples.
— Suggest one or more alternatives.
— Be positive, not just negative.
— Be helpful.

If you are the receiver of feedback:
— Do not explain or defend.
— Ask clarifying questions.
— Ask for additional specific feedback if you wish.
— Show appreciation.

After receiving the feedback, it is optional to explore jointly a resolution of the concern or conflict.

If you are an observer, you should
— Review the basics for giving and receiving feedback.

— Observe the feedback session, taking notes on what goes well or not well, including specific examples.
— After the feedback session, use the feedback principles yourself as you share your observations with the giver and receiver.

▓ Role Play

The following is an example of a feedback scenario that could be role-played:

Giver of Feedback: Your team meeting is nearly over, and it is time for a self-assessment. It has been bothering you that someone (the feedback receiver) has been arriving at least 30 minutes late to the meeting and did so again today. This always disrupts the meeting when the person shows confusion on issues that were decided during his or her absence. After getting oriented, the late member participates well, often suggesting creative approaches to the problem under study. Today, you express your concern about the lateness.

Receiver of Feedback: You have been arriving late for team meetings and did so today. After arriving, you are apologetic and try hard to make a contribution. Your regular work involves preparing reports on short notice, and it seems that you always have one to finish up before you can go to the team meeting. You have been assuming the team would understand. This time, a team member raises the issue.

Developing Instructional Objectives, Lesson Plans, and Syllabi

THEODORE E. STONE

Armed with the basics of adult learning theory, the adjunct is ready to design the course and develop lesson plans. Even if the adjunct is provided with a ready-made syllabus and chosen text, he or she must create appropriate lesson plans and learning activities. In this third chapter, Theodore Stone provides a guide for developing instructional objectives, lesson plans, and syllabi.

Opening with an anecdote about the perils of launching into teaching without setting forth a plan, Stone argues that it is absolutely critical to have, use, and communicate clear instructional goals and objectives. He breaks this down into three major activities: setting goals and objectives, planning lessons, and designing syllabi.

Stone uses Bloom's taxonomy of educational objectives to demonstrate the varying levels of learning that should take place in the classroom: knowledge, comprehension, application, analysis, synthesis, and evaluation. A five-step process for goal analysis—breaking down goals into enabling and terminal objectives—is provided. Through this explanation, Stone demonstrates how objectives can be used to organize each class lesson and determine appropriate activities and assignments. Building on the adult learning concepts from Chapter 2, Stone explains that lesson planning requires careful thought on the most effective way to deliver the instruction. Instructors must think through what their students expect and how they will best learn.

Finally, Stone discusses the elements of a good syllabus. He argues that a syllabus can be viewed as an informal contract between the instructor and the students. Consequently, the syllabus should be a road map to help students navigate the course, including information on texts, objectives, schedules, grading and evaluation, classroom policies, and student involvement.

This is a user-friendly chapter that provides examples from many disciplines. Adjunct instructors can easily use the checklists to construct solid lesson plans and syllabi.

It was the big night for the new adjunct lecturer. Teaching this course at the university was good for his career; it emphasized his credentials as an expert. Besides, he wasn't like the professors he had had when he was in college—they had no idea what the real world was like. His students would appreciate his hands-on experience.

He walked into the classroom and gulped. Gosh, they had a lot of material to cover in just one semester. But he was prepared; they weren't going to waste one minute of valuable class time. At the start of the hour, he handed out the course description and syllabus to the students and launched into his first lecture.

The next day, his coworkers at the office noticed that he seemed depressed. At the water cooler, they asked how his first night as an adjunct lecturer had gone. "Not so well," he moaned. "Instead of appreciating my background and knowledge of the subject, all they did was fidget the entire time. Instead of asking me about the lecture subject, they wanted to know how many tests there were going to be, or how long I wanted the research papers. Some of them didn't even know what I meant by a research paper. And these are college students!"

The next week, the adjunct lecturer felt his spirits sag as he walked into class to find only half as many students as there were the first week. Taking a deep breath, he launched into his topic for the evening. . . .

In designing a course, it is absolutely critical to have clear instructional goals and objectives. These goals and objectives should be stated in a course syllabus, along with a clear explanation of what is expected from the students, when it is expected, and why. Students should know, ideally before the beginning of the first class, what to expect, what will be required of them, what prerequisites are needed, and how their work will be graded.

Many college students today have families and careers, and their expectations of your class will probably be extremely high. They need to know when they walk into class on the first day why your class is important and what they can expect to know or do better as a result of their participation. Consequently, it is critical that you take the time to develop your course goals, objectives, lessons, and syllabus carefully to communicate this.

This chapter focuses on

■ How to write instructional objectives
■ How to develop lesson plans
■ How to write a course syllabus

In support of these goals, this chapter also examines

■ The differences between goals and objectives
■ Using Bloom's taxonomy of learner objectives
■ Writing terminal and enabling objectives
■ Organizing and developing each lesson on the basis of objectives
■ Components of a good syllabus

See the Additional Suggested Readings at the end of the chapter for a list of materials that you may want to examine as you develop your course and look for ways to improve the quality of your materials and planning process.

Setting Goals and Objectives

Goals are broad statements on what you want to accomplish in your course and how your course will meet the learner's needs (Kemp, 1985, p. 29). For example, if you are teaching a course in introductory statistics, the goal may be stated as follows: In this course, students will gain an understanding of the basic components of quantitative statistics. Emphasis is placed on understanding nominal statistical measures and how they apply to understanding research published in scholarly journals.

Goals have been described as the "warm fuzzies" in the course-designing process because although they sound desirable, how to achieve them is unclear (Mager, 1972). The goal addresses the general *outcome,* not the *process:* It does not refer to a specific activity in which the student will engage. For example, an art history course may have the goal of "broadening the student's appreciation for the Impressionist period," but the goal does not specify how this will be accomplished.

Objectives, on the other hand, support the goals of the course by indicating, in specific language, what the learner will actually do to achieve the goal(s) of the course. A good objective is a clear statement of what the student is expected to learn and what specifically will be measured to determine success. If we go back to the example of the course in introductory statistics, the goal statement describes the aim of the course, but it would be difficult to know, just from reading the goal statement, what a student would need to do to achieve success in the course.

Thus, at some point before the course, the instructor needs to translate the goals into specific learner objectives. For example, in the introductory statistics course, one objective that supports the course goal could be "Given a sample of data, the student will calculate the mean, mode, and standard deviation." In this case, the objective supports the goal of understanding nominal statistical measures and specifies a task that can be tested.

The process of writing objectives that are derived from goals is called *goal analysis.* Frequently this involves thinking about how people behave after they achieve the goal. For example, in the art history course, people who appreciate the Impressionist period know and understand the history that led to that period and understand some of the techniques of applying a paintbrush to canvas. Thus learning about these areas could become *performance* or *learning* objectives toward supporting the goal. It is from the course objectives that more specific lesson plans and activities can be developed.

One way of performing a goal analysis is to follow a five-step process (Rothwell & Kazanas, 1992):

1. Identify, as clearly as possible, the goal that the instruction will achieve.
2. Write down examples of what people know, or do, when they have achieved the goal—identify behaviors associated with the goal.
3. Review the list. Eliminate duplications and objectives not clearly related to achieving the goal.
4. Describe in precise and measurable terms what learners need to do when they have achieved the goal.
5. Test the objectives. Can they be measured? Can they be tested through tests, class activities, or special assignments? Will the test/activity discriminate whether the student has successfully achieved the objective?

Using Bloom's Taxonomy of Educational Objectives

Mager, cited in Isaac and Michael (1987), named three elements for a good behavioral (or measurable) objective:

1. A statement of an observable behavior that will be expected of the student in demonstrating mastery (what the student must do)
2. A description of the conditions and constraints of the learning task under which the student will show competence (e.g., "Given a sample of data, student will calculate the mean")
3. A specification of the level of performance

The first two elements have already been discussed as part of the goal analysis process. Benjamin Bloom's *Taxonomy of Educational Objectives*, Handbooks I and II (Bloom, Engelhart, Furst, Hill, & Krathwohl, 1956; Krathwohl, Bloom, & Masia, 1956) can be useful in determining the third element, performance level.

Bloom and his colleagues grouped learning into three major categories: cognitive, affective and psychomotor. The *psychomotor* domain of learning involves eye-hand coordination instruction. For example, a driver's education course requires more than just learning the rules of the road. It is necessary to get the student behind the wheel of a car, on the road, and driving. For most adjunct instructors, the psychomotor domain of learning is rarely, if ever, dealt with. *Cognitive* learning is centered on knowledge such as facts, terminology, and analysis of elements. *Affective* learning centers on values and value systems: openness to or awareness of selected ideas, valuing of ideas, integrating values into a total world philosophy. These last two types of learning can be broken down into levels. The *Taxonomy of Educational Objectives* (Bloom et al., 1956) identifies six levels (or depths) of cognitive learning and five levels of affective learning:

1. Cognitive

    Knowledge: remembering something encountered

    Comprehension: understanding material, without necessarily relating it to other material

    Application: using abstractions in particular and concrete situations

    Analysis: breaking down communication into parts so that organization of ideas becomes clear

    Synthesis: putting elements into a whole

    Evaluation: judging the value of material and methods for a given purpose

2. Affective

    Receiving: being willing to attend to or receive certain stimuli

    Responding: being actively involved, participating

    Valuing: determining the worth of a thing, phenomenon, or behavior

    Organization: determining the organization, interrelationship, and ordering of values

    Characterization by a value or value complex: integrating values into a total worldview or philosophy

When writing an objective, it is important to keep in mind whether it falls within the cognitive or affective domain. In addition, the level of the learning objective should be reflected in the objective. For example, consider these three cognitive objectives, all of which concern the calculation of the statistical mean:

> The student will recognize the formula for calculating the statistical mean.
> Given a sample of data, the student will calculate the statistical mean.
> Given a sample of data, the student will analyze whether the statistical mean is the most appropriate measure of central tendency.

What distinguishes these three examples from each other is the level of learning performance required of the student. In the first example, the student merely has to recognize the formula. This corresponds to the first level of cognitive knowledge of Bloom's taxonomy: knowledge. The second example requires the student to use the formula for calculating a statistical mean. This corresponds to the third level of Bloom's taxonomy: application. The third example requires the learner to determine whether the statistical mean formula is the most appropriate one to use. This corresponds to a higher level still—the sixth level of Bloom's taxonomy, evaluation.

All three of these objectives can be tested. And because they can be easily tested, they can clarify the accountability of both the student and the instructor. The instructor can give a fair and honest grade to the student and the student can know what must be mastered to pass the course.[1]

Writing Enabling Objectives

Consider again the objectives of the introductory statistics course. We have discussed three, and we will assume that there are actually four altogether:

> The student will recognize the formula for calculating the statistical mean.
> Given a sample of data, the student will calculate the statistical mean.
> Given a sample of data, the student will analyze whether the statistical mean is the most appropriate measure of central tendency.
> Given a research article from a journal, the student will evaluate the use of the mean as a statistical measure in the context of the data reported.

Obviously, some of these objectives are more complex than others. Some require more background knowledge and skills than others. In fact, some require other learning objectives to support them.

For example, consider Objective 3: "Given a sample of data, the student will analyze whether the statistical mean is the most appropriate measure of central tendency." That is the *terminal objective:* what we want the student to be able to achieve as result of attending the course. But we might need to teach several things first:

- How to calculate the mean and what it is used for
- How to calculate other measures of central tendency (e.g., median, mode) and what they are used for
- Types of research and how statistics are used generally

There might be more, of course, depending on how the course is ultimately designed. However, these are the *enabling objectives* that must be achieved before the terminal objective can be met.

Writing enabling objectives serves several purposes:

- It facilitates the development of lesson plans and the generation of quizzes, tests, and assignments.
- It allows you to sequence properly the information in the course. It encourages you to plan the course from the simple to the more complex, from the concrete level of information to the higher level of critical thinking. For example, if you were teaching a course on the Constitution of the United States, you might first have students identify the amendments of the Bill of Rights and then have them analyze a specific law passed and critique whether it violated the Bill of Rights and, if so, in what ways.
- It enables students to get a better understanding of the direction of the course and its short and long-term goals and objectives.
- It enables both instructor and students to focus more precisely on problem areas in which students are struggling with the material.

Developing Lesson Plans

After the goals and objectives are determined for the course, you will need to develop individual lesson plans for each class meeting. Of course, you will not cover each goal and objective at every class meeting, so you will have to identify which objectives will be met during the class period. You will also have to decide on the most effective way to deliver the instruction. This means you need to think through what your students will expect and how they will best learn. You will want to survey the course material and look at naturally occurring relationships, which material students can best learn independently (e.g., by reading) and which material requires a collaborative approach in which students work together in groups to achieve an objective. You will need to decide which lessons can be passive (lectures, slides, videos) and which active (hands-on experimentation). For example, if you were teaching a course on architecture, a collaborative approach might involve giving small groups a case study in which they must identify and agree on the style and placement of a new structure in a particular neighborhood. A hands-on approach might require students to redesign the facade of a building in a case study, constructing a model as part of the assignment.

Of course, techniques can frequently be combined to make for a dynamic lesson filled with a variety of activities. However, in planning your lesson, the objectives should be driving which activities and assignments you select. For example, if you decide to show a videotape as part of the lesson plan, it should be because it supports a learning objective, not because it merely breaks up a boring lecture.

Remember, students learn both passively and actively. Passive learning takes place when students play the role of "receptacle of knowledge," and though "passive" sounds negative, much learning can take place this way (Ryan & Martens, 1989). If you need your students to think critically about a subject or to construct knowledge, then an active approach should be considered.

Designing Syllabi

A *syllabus* is more than a handout to students or an information sheet. It is also an informal contract between the instructor and the students (Millis, 1990) and a road map for the students, an aid to help them navigate through the course.

A complete course syllabus generally contains the following (Millis, 1990):

- Course name, number, section, and location
- Date or semester
- Your name and home and office telephone numbers and the best times to call
- Titles, authors, and editions of text(s)—required and recommended
- Course description, goals and objectives
- Tentative schedule of assignments and activities
- Testing, grading, and evaluation policies and procedures
- Attendance and participation policies
- Academic integrity policies

George Mason University recommends that a syllabus describe the balance among lectures, class discussion, and small group activities and that it spell out the instructor's expectation for student involvement. The course description ought to describe the extent of field work and experiential learning and the balance of theory and practice. Ultimately, a good syllabus is as much a statement of your educational philosophy as it is a navigational chart for your course.

Keep in mind that the language you use to describe the learning objectives to the students should perhaps be less formal than the language you would use to formulate the objectives for yourself. It is a good idea to walk students through the syllabus on the first night. Students can then study the syllabus more closely and ask further questions at the next class.

The University of Maryland University College provides its adjuncts with a syllabus checklist. A version of it appears in Appendix 3.1. It is followed by a good example of a complete syllabus (Appendix 3.2).

Using the Calendar

The syllabus calendar is a good vehicle for telling the students—up front—what the major learning objectives will be for each class session. Many instructors will also put the day's objectives on the blackboard at the beginning of class and leave them unerased on the board for the entire class period. This is useful for the students and the instructor. The daily objectives provide a visual aid for the introduction of the day's subject matter as well as a summary at the end of class. If all objectives are not achieved, the instructor has a visual reminder of what needs to be covered at the next class.

The class calendar's precise scheduling of reading assignments, quizzes, and tests helps the student prepare for each class and organize his or her time better. As an adjunct instructor, you are likely to be teaching in the evening and/or on weekends. Most of your students will be adult learners who have jobs or other full-time day activities. The class schedule you provide can help them break up large tasks into smaller, more manageable ones. For instance, the University of Maryland University College's *Syllabus Construction Handbook* suggests that for a research paper counting significantly toward the final grade, you might want to assign due dates for a working bibliography, an outline, and a rough draft (Millis, 1990).

In addition, by constructing a class calendar before the semester begins, you can be certain of not scheduling tests or major assignments on national or religious holidays.

Testing and Grading

If there are two areas in which instructors really take the heat, they are the areas of testing and grading. The syllabus is an excellent vehicle for telling your students, up front, how they will be graded and on what. There is nothing quite so awful as having an instructor change his or her grading policy in midcourse. Therefore thinking it through beforehand and explaining it in detail to the students through the syllabus can prevent some problems (see Chapter 8 on evaluating students).

Note

1. If you would like some more sources to help you with writing objectives using the levels of Bloom's taxonomy, you might want to read Kemp's *The Instructional Design Process* (1985), which devotes an entire chapter to this topic and includes examples.

References

Bloom, B. S., Engelhart, M. D., Furst, E. J., Hill, W. H., & Krathwohl, D. R. (1956). *Taxonomy of educational objectives: Handbook I. Cognitive domain.* New York: David McKay.

Isaac, S., & Michael, W. B. (1987). *Handbook in research and evaluation.* San Diego: EdiTS.

Kemp, J. E. (1985). *The instructional design process.* New York: Harper & Row.

Krathwohl, D. R., Bloom, B. S., & Masia, B. B. (1956). *Taxonomy of educational objectives: Handbook II. Affective domain.* New York: David McKay.

Mager, R. (1972). *Goal analysis.* Belmont, CA: Fearon-Pitman.

Millis, B. J. (1990). *Syllabus construction handbook.* College Park: University of Maryland University College.

Rothwell, W. J., & Kazanas, H. C. (1992). *Mastering the instructional design process.* San Francisco: Jossey-Bass.

Ryan, M. P., & Martens, G. G. (1989). *Planning a college course: A guidebook for the graduate teaching assistant.* Ann Arbor, MI: National Center for Research to Improve Postsecondary Teaching and Learning.

Additional Suggested Readings

If you would like to read other material related to the development of instructional objectives, syllabi, and lesson plans, the National Center for Research to Improve Postsecondary Teaching and Learning (NCRIPTAL) has several publications in this area. Write to NCRIPTAL, School of Education Building, Suite 2400, University of Michigan, Ann Arbor, Michigan 48109-1259. Among the publications you may wish to request from them are the following:

Lowther, M. A., Stark, J. S., & Martens, G. G. (1989). *Preparing course syllabi for improved communication.*

Stark, J. S., & Lowther, M. A. (1986). *Designing the learning plan: A review of research and theory related to college curricula.*

Stark, J. S., Lowther, M. A., Bentley, R. J., Ryan, M. P., Genthon, M., Martens, G. G., & Wren, P. A. (1989). *Planning introductory college courses: Influences on faculty.*

Stark, J. S., Lowther, M. A., Ryan, M. P., Bomotti, S. S., Genthon, M., Martens, G. G., & Haven, C. L. (1988). *Reflections on course planning: Faculty and students consider influences and goals.*

Appendix 3.1
Faculty Syllabus Checklist

▧ Information About Instructor

_____ Name
_____ Phone numbers
_____ Times when students may contact you

▧ Course Information

_____ Name and address of university
_____ Course number, section, title, location
_____ Required text(s)—titles, authors, editions
_____ Recommended books (not required)
_____ Course description; goals and objectives; prerequisites

▧ Schedule Information

_____ For the date of each class meeting, specify the subject matter/topics to be covered (e.g., lectures, field trips, guest lecturers), the preclass readings and other nongraded assignments due, and learning objectives for the meeting

_____ Graded assignment due dates, preferably highlighted in bold or capitalized (e.g., homework, quizzes, papers, projects)

_____ Exam dates, preferably highlighted

Grading Information

_____ Course requirements (exams, quizzes, projects, papers) and the proportion each counts toward the final grade. Discuss the content and format of each requirement. If class participation is factored in, please explain how you will evaluate it.

_____ Grading scale and standards

Additional Components

_____ Policies regarding late work and makeup exams

_____ A statement regarding academic integrity

_____ A statement about any university-specific policies regarding exams

_____ Attendance policy

_____ Unique class procedures/structures, such as cooperative learning exercises, panel presentations, case study methods, class journals or learning logs

_____ Procedures for special accommodations

Appendix 3.2
Sample Syllabus

AdSc 216: THEORIES AND MANAGEMENT
OF PLANNED CHANGE

Syllabus: Fall 1995

Professors:

Cindy Roman, Ed.D., Principal, Roman and Associates 703-569-4605
(phone and fax); e-mail: chroman@ix.netcom.com

Eric Dent, Ph.D. (ABD) Assistant Professor, George Washington
University, 202-676-8090 (phone), 202-676-5232 (fax); e-mail:
edent@gwis2.circ.gwu.edu

▪ I. Introduction

This course provides an introduction to theories of planned change, which can be described through the young academic discipline of organization development. OD helps organizations achieve objectives by increasing responsiveness to internal and external stakeholders and helping individuals improve performance within organizations. The objective of OD is to assist organizations in operating effectively both by adapting to changes in their unique environment and by effecting positive changes internally. This course introduces an OD process of contracting, assessment, intervention, institutionalization, evaluation, and termination. Specific foci are change and interventions, such as team building, process consultation, strategic planning, and Total Quality Management.

■ II. Course Outline

Week 1. Introduction to Organization Development
Week 2. The Evolution of Organization Development
Week 3. The Organization Development Practitioner
Week 4. The Nature of Change
Week 5. The Masters of Change
Week 6. Leadership of Change
Week 7. Workplace Design/Reengineering
Week 8. Midterm Examination
Week 9. Assessment Models, Data Collection, and Feedback
Week 10. Human Process Interventions
Week 11. Technostructural Interventions
Week 12. Human Resource Management and Strategic Interventions
Week 13. Evaluation, Institutionalization, and Termination
Week 14. Summary and Future of Organization Development
Week 15. Final Examination

■ III. Required Materials

Cummings, Thomas G., & Worley, Christopher, G. (1993). *Organization development and change* (5th ed.). St. Paul, MN: West. Listed below as ODC.

Weisbord, Marvin R. (1987). *Productive workplaces*. San Francisco: Jossey-Bass. Listed below as PW.

Other handouts to be read before the week listed.

■ IV. Schedule of Assignments

After each class, beginning with Week 2, you are required to send an e-mail message to your professor by midnight on Thursday. This message will include

1. Your understanding of the key points from the week's class.
2. Your "muddiest" point: something that you need clarification on, whether because it wasn't explained well or for some other reason.
3. Your own level of preparedness for class on a scale of 1 (unprepared) to 5 (fully prepared).

The purpose of the feedback is *not* to evaluate you. You will receive all 5 points for sending the messages, regardless of their content. The purpose of the feedback is to help *us* know how the class is being received, whether concepts are coming across clearly, and whether we need to make any adjustments. These messages are intended to be composed in 3 minutes or less.

Week 1 (August 29): Introduction to Organization Development
ODC: Ch. 1
PW: Ch. 1 and prologue

Activity: "Win as Much as You Can"—Prisoner's Dilemma
Cindy and Eric jointly deliver both classes.

Week 2 (September 5): The Evolution of Organization Development
PW: Chs. 2, 3, 4, 5, 6, and 7

Handout:
   Senge, Peter. (1995). The leader's new work: Building learning organizations. In D. Kolb, S. Osland, & I. M. Rubin (Eds.), *The organizational behavior reader.* Englewood Cliffs, NJ: Prentice Hall.

Week 3 (September 12): The Organization Development Practitioner
ODC: Chs. 2, 4
PW: Ch. 8

Week 4 (September 19): The Nature of Change
ODC: Ch. 3

Handouts:
   Bianco-Mathis, Virginia, & Roman, Cynthia H. (1995). *Change in organizations: Best practices* (abridged ed.). Washington, DC: U.S. Department of Agriculture.
   Bridges, William. (1986, Summer). Managing organizational transitions. *Organizational Dynamics,* 24-33.

Vaill, Peter. (1993). *Permanent whitewater action principles.*

Vaill, Peter. (1992, June). Notes on "running an organization." *Journal of Management Inquiry*, 130-138.

Vaill, Peter. (in press). Permanent whitewater II. In P. Vaill, *Learning as a way of being* (Ch. 1). San Francisco: Jossey-Bass.

Week 5 (September 26):   Masters of Change
ODC: Ch. 8
PW: Ch. 9

Handout: Bridges Case
Clark, Jim, & Koonce, Richard. (1995, August). Engaging organizational survivors. *Training and Development*, 23-30.

Week 6 (October 3):   Leadership of Change
PW: Chs. 15, 17

Handout:
Oakley, Ed, & Krug, Doug. (1991). The ultimate empowerment tool. In E. Oakley & D. Krug, *Enlightened leadership: Getting to the heart of change* (Ch. 8). New York: Simon & Schuster.

Week 7 (October 10):   Workplace Design/Reengineering
Assignment 1 due.
Double session: Both sections meet from 1:00 to 5:00.
ODC: Ch. 5
PW: Chs. 10, 11

Week 8 (October 17):   Midterm Examination for half the class time
Good luck!

Week 9 (October 24):   Assessment Models, Data Collection and Feedback
ODC: Ch. 6, 7, 9
PW: Ch. 12

Week 10 (October 31):   Human Process Interventions
ODC: Chs. 10, 11, 20 (pp. 597-606), 21
Argyris, Chris. (1994, July-August). Good communication that blocks learning. *Harvard Business Review*, 77-85.

Week 11 (November 7): Technostructural Interventions
ODC: Chs. 12-14

Handout:

Suarez, J. Gerald. (1992, July). *Three experts on quality management: Philip B. Crosby, W. Edwards Deming, and Joseph M. Juran* (TQLO Publication No. 92-02). Washington, DC: Dept. of the Navy, Office of the Under Secretary of the Navy, Total Quality Leadership Office.

Week 12 (November 14):   Human Resource Management and Strategic Interventions

ODC: Chs. 15-18

Handout:

Foster, Daniel R. (1991, January-February). The case of team-spirit tailspin. *Harvard Business Review*, 14-18.

Week 13 (November 21):   Evaluation, Institutionalization, and Termination

ODC: Ch. 19
PW: Ch. 16

Handouts:

Dent, Eric. (1993). Evaluation, institutionalization, and termination. In E. Dent, *Organization development* (Ch. 12). College Park: University of Maryland Press.

Reardon, Kathleen. (1993, March-April). The memo every woman keeps in her desk. *Harvard Business Review*, 16-22.

Week 14 (November 28):   Summary and Future of Organization Development

Assignment 2 due
ODC: Ch. 22
PW: Chs. 13 and 14 and Epilogue

Handouts:

Dent, Eric. (1995). Emerging management. In E. Dent, *Management: Perspectives, process, and productivity* (Ch. 13). College Park: University of Maryland Press.

Rothstein, Lawrence R. (1995, January-February). The empowerment effort that came undone. *Harvard Business Review*, 20-26.

Week 15 (December 5):   Final Examination
Good luck!

▆ V. Grading and Other Policies

5%:   E-mail submissions (all or nothing)
5%:   Class contribution (all or nothing, see section VII)
25%:   Assignment 1
20%:   Midterm examination
20%:   Assignment 2
25%:   Final examination
100%: Total

Due Date Extensions

We will model the work of a change professional in this course. A change professional who misses a client deadline faces dire consequences, usually losing the client. We expect papers to be handed in by the date due. Extensions without penalty will only be considered if an outline or two pages of the paper are handed in 1 week prior to the due date. Lateness penalties: up to 1 week—1-10% points; 1 to 2 weeks—11-16% points; over 2 weeks—17-25% points.

▆ VI. Assignments

Assignment 1

Find an organization that will allow you, at no fee, to conduct an organizational assessment (preferably the organization with which you will be interning). Try to get the client's permission, before the interviews, to distribute the report to each person interviewed.

Conduct individual interviews with at least five employees of the organization, using the interview protocol below. It will be easier for you if you select five people who all report to the same manager. If this is not possible, ensure that you ask about a common leader in the last section, perhaps a division head to whom everyone reports. You will probably have to ask dozens of additional questions to get the information you need. You must submit one additional question for each question below except those under the heading of "Introductory Information." Include your questions in your report. Be prepared to add new questions spontaneously during the interview if they will help you gather the information you need. Before you interview the employees, you may find it useful to practice with friends or family by having them pretend to be employees.

Write a report (at least 10-12 pages) of your results, including an overview of the organization selected, your additional questions, and the written feedback you would offer your "client." Your job is to write a narrative that presents a complete picture of the six areas listed below. Do not include your raw data, which consist of each respondent's answer to each question. You add value by content-analyzing the raw data for common themes, consistent responses, and unusual observations (e.g., all five people gave you different responses about goals). You should write one-and-a-half to two pages for each of the six headings. The best papers will read as narrative discussion so well synthesized that it won't be apparent which questions were asked. It helps to include some specific examples of responses as long as they don't compromise an interviewee's confidentiality. The assignment should be written to your client. The only exception is the introductory information section, which is necessary to provide a context for the professor.

Do not give the paper to your client until *after* you receive comments from your professor. Some changes may be necessary before the report is suitable to give to your client. You will need to use the techniques you have learned in the course, but it is not necessary to quote the textbooks. I suggest you start each interview with the questions listed in Cummings and Worley (1993, pp. 112-113).

Organize your feedback using the headings below. Be careful not to develop your own recommendations. As an OD practitioner, your role is to feed back the data and let the client system develop its own recommendations.

Interview Protocol: If the organization isn't your own, or if you aren't familiar with it, start with questions that provide you with that information.

— What does your organization do?
— Who are its competitors?
— What products or services does your work group provide?
— What specifically do you do?

Leadership

— Describe your manager's leadership style.
— What things should your manager do more or less of?

Motivation

— Do people in your work group enjoy their jobs?

— Are employees encouraged to show initiative?

Communication

— What are the primary forms of communication of information that you need to do your job?

— Is there adequate communication among separate work groups?

Decisions

— How are decisions made in this organization?

— Do you have the authority to make the decisions you need to accomplish your job?

Goals

— What goals has your organization established?

— What performance criteria are established for you and your work group?

Controls

— What is the one thing that you don't currently have the authority to do that if you did would most help you do your job?

— What is the process (who has to sign off) for purchasing a new computer (or other relevant acquisition) in your work group?

Assignment 2

Your first task in this assignment is to locate an OD practitioner who would be willing to be interviewed by you on the phone for at least 30 minutes (in person is even better if your interviewee is willing). Some of you will find a person easily; for others, some legwork will be required. Your selection of an appropriate OD practitioner is part of what will determine your grade on the paper. The more the individual has change agent responsibilities without "line" responsibilities, the better the learning experience for you. In determining whether someone is an OD practitioner, refer to the definitions of OD in the first week's reading.

You may want to begin with the Air Force to find an appropriate interviewee. The Air Force makes use of a tremendous number of external consultants, so they would be appropriate interviewees as well. Professional associations are another source of OD professionals. The Washington area is the headquarters for the NTL Institute for Applied Behavioral Science, 703-548-1500, and the American Society for Training and Development (ASTD),

703-683-9583. The national OD Network is at 201-763-7337. Keep in mind that it is *your* responsibility to find an appropriate person; that is part of the assignment.

In the past, students have found it helpful to be in touch with the interviewee very briefly for a second time. You may want to ask your interviewee if you may call again to briefly clarify any points once you have had an opportunity to summarize your notes and begin writing your paper.

Have your interviewees

— Discuss the types of interventions they conduct.

— Describe four interventions they have conducted. It is your responsibility (not the interviewee's) to categorize them under the four headings: human process, technostructural, human resource management, and strategic. Most OD professionals will not conduct interventions under all four headings. If possible, select an OD specialist who can share interventions in more than one category.

Your objective is to get their specific, nitty-gritty details of how an intervention *really* happens. Ask them where their real-world experiences differ from academic theory. Find out which parts of the intervention didn't go as planned and what your interviewee did as a contingency. The purpose of this assignment is to get a different perspective from that of the textbooks, which make the intervention sound straightforward and methodical.

Describe how they include evaluation in their practice. Ask whether they have specific measures they often use. Many who may not claim to use specific measures will say they assess whether the client was satisfied or whether the OD practitioner had repeat business. The first response only begs the question. You then have to ask, "How do you determine whether the client was satisfied?" Help them to make explicit, criteria that they may have used only implicitly. In all cases, these measures do not have to be of a quantifiable, objective nature.

Write up the interview in a paper of at least 10 to 12 pages, and include their commentary on all of the above.

For each question, your job is to make linkages in your paper between their discussion and the course concepts. They may never have heard of our categorization of human process, technostructural, human resource management, and strategic interventions. No such categorization is yet standard in the young field of OD. You are to take their practical, real-life experiences and place them within the academic models and concepts of the course.

▉ VII. Course Philosophies

1. Class Participation Versus Contribution

We are not interested in classroom *participation*. We are, however, very interested in classroom *contribution*. We place a value on thinking rather than talking. *Participation* connotes involvement, sharing, and simply taking part, all desirable attributes especially for the social dimension of a class. *Contribution*, on the other hand, connotes not only social, but also intellectual involvement and sharing of knowledge and knowledge construction. In addition, it also implies the willful intent to assist others in the forging of understanding. Contribution not only includes, but also enlarges upon the values represented by participation, because it rivets attention on the goal of generating knowledge. The litmus-test question: Does a student comment contribute to class process and peer understanding of the concept under discussion?[1]

Some ways to contribute are (1) providing recapitulations and summaries; (2) making observations that integrate concepts and discussions; (3) citing relevant personal examples; (4) asking key questions that lead to revealing discussions; (5) engaging in devil's advocacy; and, (6) disagreeing with the instructor, so that the difference of opinion serves as both counterpoint and a basis for exploring all sides of a concept, issue or practice.[2]

2. Writing Quality

We read your written work carefully. In fact, we read it for grammar, punctuation, syntax, organization, transitions, clarity and precision of expression. We read it for content. If you write well from a technical standpoint, then, if possible, write with creativity and flair. Strunk and White's *Elements of Style* should assist you in doing so.[3]

3. Responsibility for Learning

We do not take responsibility for what you learn, for the quality of your work, or for the consequences of the decisions you make regarding our class. We do believe that part of *our* work is to help you do the best you can at whatever you set out to do. But we do not live by the credo "If a student hasn't learned, the teacher hasn't taught." We are professors, not teachers in the sense that we *profess* (claim) skill in, or knowledge of, our field, but we do not necessarily *teach* it, for learning is your responsibility. Whether or not you make use of the knowledge that we offer to share is up to you. We respect you too much to try to teach you things you choose not to know.[4]

Notes

1. Dennis A. Gioia, "Contribution! Not participation in the OB classroom." *Organizational Behavior Teaching Review*, 11, no. 4 (1987): 16.

2. Ibid., p. 17.

3. William Strunk Jr. and E. B. White (1979). *Elements of Style*. New York: Macmillan.

4. Parts of these notes have been adapted from syllabi of other GW professors, including Jerry Harvey, John Lobuts, Erik Winslow, and Hamilton Beasley.

Assessment Form

AdSc 216: THEORIES AND MANAGEMENT
OF PLANNED CHANGE

Assignment 1

Name _____

Graduate-level standards will be expected for all written assignments.

1 = poor, 2 = fair, 3 = average, 4 = good, 5 = very good

Categories	**Grading Scale**
Information obtained from interviews	1 2 3 4 5
Synthesis of interviews	1 2 3 4 5
Probe questions	1 2 3 4 5
Classification of interview information	1 2 3 4 5
Completeness of information	1 2 3 4 5
Goals	1 2 3 4 5
Motivation	1 2 3 4 5
Communications	1 2 3 4 5
Decisions	1 2 3 4 5
Controls	1 2 3 4 5
Leadership	1 2 3 4 5
Communication skills and clarity of expression	1 2 3 4 5
Grammar, mechanics, and appearance	1 2 3 4 5

Additional Comments:

Grade/points _____

Assessment Form

AdSc 216: THEORIES AND MANAGEMENT
OF PLANNED CHANGE

Assignment 2

Name _____

Graduate-level standards will be expected for all written assignments.

1 = poor, 2 = fair, 3 = average, 4 = good, 5 = very good

Categories	Grading Scale
Selection of interviewee	1 2 3 4 5
Intervention #1	
Completeness of information	1 2 3 4 5
Linkages to course concepts	1 2 3 4 5
Intervention #2	
Completeness of information	1 2 3 4 5
Linkages to course concepts	1 2 3 4 5
Intervention #3	
Completeness of information	1 2 3 4 5
Linkages to course concepts	1 2 3 4 5
Intervention #4	
Completeness of information	1 2 3 4 5
Linkages to course concepts	1 2 3 4 5
Categorization of interventions	1 2 3 4 5
Completeness of evaluation discussion	1 2 3 4 5
Listing of evaluation measures	1 2 3 4 5
Communication skills and clarity of expression	1 2 3 4 5
Grammar, mechanics, and appearance	1 2 3 4 5

Additional Comments:

Grade/points _____

4

Teaching Methods and Strategies

JOHN FRY
KAREN MEDSKER
DEDE BONNER

Chapters 4 through 7 provide a series of discussions concerning classroom strategies and teaching methods. Practical checklists and job aids outline specific dos and don'ts for a full range of teaching approaches, from lectures to cooperative learning and from traditional to innovative.

In Chapter 4, Fry, Medsker, and Bonner have written a primer on instructional methods. This chapter serves as a baseline for new instructors and as a refresher for those of us who have gotten "lazy" in classroom techniques. This chapter is long but provides easy reading and application through the use of charts, guidelines, and extensive examples that cross a variety of disciplines, such as French literature, computer science, and business.

The authors stress that instructional methods must be chosen to match specific content, objectives, audience, and personal preferences. All methods—lecture, discussion, demonstration, case study—are described from the perspective of adult learning theory, which emphasizes involvement, interaction, facilitation, and participation. The chapter is based on the philosophy that students need to practice what you want them to learn. Of particular interest is the section "Making Lectures Interactive: Seven Designs." Innovative ideas are shared for panel discussions, simulations, dramatizations, buzz sessions, and field experiences.

The authors go beyond discussing structural techniques and also offer tips on process: for example, how to handle sensitive discussions, conflict, silence, and emotion-laden situations. These are more sophisticated techniques that a novice instructor may forget to consider. They take careful planning and practice to master.

Last, practice guidelines are given for choosing and using presentation aids, such as flip charts, white boards, transparencies, and videotapes. We often forget that these seemingly "simple" aids require thought and skill. They are channels through which key information is transmitted.

This chapter synthesizes information from numerous teaching strategy texts. The authors provide a fast and easy reference that adjuncts should use on a regular basis.

Once you have a course syllabus, complete with goals and objectives, you are ready to select appropriate teaching methods and strategies. Various traditional and nontraditional approaches are available to increase effectiveness and motivate your students. Many are explained in detail in this chapter, along with guidelines for selection, based on your content, objectives, audience, and personal preferences.

This chapter covers a wide range of instructional methods. Consequently, it is divided into four major sections:

1. Choosing Instruction Methods
   - Examples of Instructional Method Selection
   - The Lecture Method
   - Making Lectures Interactive: Seven Designs
2. The Discussion Method
   - When to Use the Discussion Method
   - Conditions for Facilitating Student Discussion

- Initiation of a Discussion
- Classroom Discussion Leadership Skills
- Requirements for Initiating Effective Discussions
- Basic Group Process
- Inclusion Activity: To Initiate Positive Group Dynamics
- Basic Discussion Topics and Strategies
- Using the Discussion Method in Large Classes
3. Participative Teaching Techniques
   - Definition and Description of Participative Techniques
   - Benefits of Participative Techniques
   - General Tips for Participative Techniques
   - Specific Participative Techniques
4. Choosing and Using Presentation Aids
   - Why Use Presentation Aids?
   - General Guidelines for All Presentation Aids
   - Types of Presentation Aids

Choosing Instructional Methods

An instructional method is an overall approach for facilitating learning. Examples of instructional methods are lecture, discussion, demonstration, reading assignment, and field trip. Within each method, various media can be used. Media are channels through which information is transmitted: for example, videotapes, overhead transparencies, print handouts, and electronic "slides." (Using media-based presentation aids is the topic of a later section.)

When choosing appropriate instructional methods, consider the following points:

- A variety of methods within each course and each class session stimulates student interest and therefore enhances learning. Using only one or two methods can become boring and sleep inducing!
- Adult learners generally prefer methods that actively involve them, preferably in simulated or real-world applications.
- The type of desired learning outcome may dictate certain methods. Generally, students need to practice the behaviors you want them to learn. For example, if students are learning to conduct experiments in chemistry,

laboratory exercises are essential. If students are learning to analyze organizational problems, then case studies are indicated. If many facts and labels are to be memorized, as in an anatomy course, then games and quizzes are very effective.

■ The time available in your class sessions will affect your choice of methods. Many graduate courses are taught in 3-hour sessions—too long for straight lecture, regardless of content. Interactive methods such as small group exercises and role plays are appropriate. One-hour classes are too short for certain interactive games and simulations. However, some interactivity should be included to supplement lecture.

■ Many instructors think that with large groups (above 30), they are limited to the lecture method. Actually, group size has little to do with method selection. Almost any method will work if the class is divided into smaller groups or if innovative classroom management techniques are used.

■ Student preferences should be considered when one is selecting instructional methods, but they should not be the sole determinant. For example, students with technical backgrounds may be accustomed to (and therefore most comfortable with) passive learning: The instructor "performs" and the students "absorb." They may resist methods that require active participation, even though such methods clearly produce more effective learning. Gentle stretching of their comfort zone is healthy and often necessary to achieve course goals. Yet wildly innovative methods may backfire with this population because they depart too much from tradition.

Table 4.1 defines a variety of instructional methods that can be useful in adult learning situations and describes their strengths. Using this chart and the considerations above, you should be able to select interesting and effective methods for your course. Remember that a combination of methods, rather than a single method, is probably best to achieve your goals.

Examples of Instructional Method Selection

Situation 1

Shirley Stevenson teaches a graduate course in French literature. A major goal of her course is for students to read and analyze French short stories, poetry, and novels. Shirley knows that analysis skills are

Table 4.1   Strengths of Various Instructional Methods

Instructional Method	Definition	Strengths
Lecture	Presentation of content by instructor/guest	Can cover lots of information quickly; instructor controls pace and structure
Discussion	Interchange of ideas and opinions by large or small groups of students	Gets students involved; increases interest; effective for controversial or open-ended topics and creative problem solving
Application exercise	Individual students or small groups practice applying the course content to real or hypothetical situations	Essential to develop competence on key course objectives; involves students actively; helps transfer learning to the real world
Reading or workbook assignment	"Homework" done individually or in study groups; based on print materials designed for self-study	Can cover content as efficiently as lecture; saves class time for other activities that require interaction or discussion; self-paced and can be reviewed as needed
Test or quiz	Questions that determine how well students are learning course material; can be short or long, graded by teacher or self-assessed	Provides feedback to students and instructor regarding student progress; change of pace for use of class time; can motivate students to do assigned reading
Case study	Actual or hypothetical situation that illustrates course content; can be open-ended or include a conclusion	Demonstrates real-world application of course content; provides exciting basis for discussion, exercise, papers
Role play	Students assume roles of individuals or groups and act out planned or free-form scenarios; amount of structure varies depending on purpose	Effective in teaching attitudes and interpersonal skills; provides practice on course objectives; enhances transfer of learning to real world
Demonstration	Instructor or student shows how to do something. Can be live or on videotape; hands-on physical activity or mental process explicated	Provides students with a model of how to perform; adds interest; if student-led, preparation is excellent learning experience

Table 4.1   Continued

Instructional Method	Definition	Strengths
Laboratory exercise	Students perform hands-on activity using real equipment, as in computer lab, kitchen, archeological dig, or video studio	Essential for learning to use specialized equipment; can get immediate, firsthand results; highly motivating and rewarding
Project	Individual or group activity done primarily out of class that applies or extends course content; results in a paper or concrete product	Provides practice on key course objectives; allows students to choose areas of most interest and apply to work setting; provides basis for substantive class discussion
Game	Simple to complex structure with rules; can be board game, "quiz show," or simulated "real life"	Fun, creative way to introduce or review course content; effective for teaching attitudes; can involve competition and/or cooperation, which is motivating

difficult for students working in a second language, and she has not been happy with the quality of papers in previous semesters. Her class meets for 1½ hours twice a week.

Solution 1

Shirley decides to use the following methods. Students read an assignment, such as a short story. In the next class, Shirley uses lecture/demonstration to explain and illustrate the steps for analyzing a short story properly. As an expert, she can explain and model the behavior she wishes her students to emulate. Students take notes and ask questions based on her lecture/demonstration. At the next class, students will have read another short story and will work in small groups to analyze the story according to the guidelines previously demonstrated. They will share their analyses with the total group and get feedback from Shirley and the class. Next, individuals choose a short story of interest to them and write an analysis to be turned in and evaluated by Shirley. This is an effective mix of methods, because students have been shown how to perform the desired behavior (story analysis), they have practiced with coaching, and then they practice again on their own. By now they should be able to analyze any French short story! A variety of classroom and out-of-class activities have been used toward this end.

Situation 2

Larry Brown is a computer science professor who teaches a graduate course on expert system software. The students are strong technically and need to develop better interpersonal skills. Yet they are accustomed to traditional instructional methods, primarily lecture. The class meets one night per week for 3 hours. Larry knows that lecturing the whole time is boring and ineffective. He wants to keep people awake and give them practical skills. An early lesson in the course is how to choose an appropriate expert system project.

Solution 2

For this lesson, Larry develops an exercise that is relatively non-threatening. It is a list of possible expert system applications, some of which meet all of the criteria for a good project, some of which are clearly poor projects, and some of which are ambiguous (meet some of the criteria). The first 45 minutes of class, Larry lectures on the criteria for project selection and gives examples from his own work experience. Next, the students work individually on the exercise for 30 minutes. After a break, they share their individual responses in small groups and try to reach consensus (30 minutes). The resulting debate is quite lively because the students have their own work experiences to draw on. The last part of the class Larry uses to summarize key points for the whole group and give an introduction to next week's lesson.

Situation 3

Doug Green teaches a graduate course in how to design adult/corporate training programs. Some students actually do training design in their work; others are preparing for a career change into the training field; still others work in human resource areas tangential to training and want a basic understanding of training development. The class meets six Saturdays from 9:00 a.m. to 4:00 p.m. Variety is extremely important in this class because of the long days.

Solution 3

Doug decides that the core of the course will be an individual application project. Each student must choose an actual or hypothetical but realistic training problem and design a training program to solve the problem. Because training development is a structured and sequential process, each set of skills will be taught and then applied to the projects. Although most of the project work will be done outside of class, class time can be used to practice the skills, discuss project difficulties, and get peer feedback on interim products. A typical day, then, may be as follows:

- Peer feedback on projects, done in small groups
- Question-and-answer session to review last session and reading
- Quiz on reading assignment
- Lecture with overheads and video on new set of skills
- Lunch
- Small group application exercise to practice new skills
- Lecture on new set of skills
- Individual worksheet assignment to practice new skills
- Three case studies (done in small groups) to integrate new skills learned today; report to large group
- Instructor guidance on next phase of project work

The Lecture Method

A lecture is a teacher's oral presentation to a group, usually to transmit information, explain ideas and principles, give examples, and integrate ideas from other sources. Primarily a one-way communication device, the lecture can be made more exciting and effective through the use of questions, presentation aids, and demonstrations and can be made more interactive through the use of the techniques explained below.

A lecture is a good choice of instructional method when

- A large amount of information must be covered quickly
- The information is not available from a more efficient source, such as a textbook or handout
- The information is original or is integrated from many sources
- The teacher wants to demonstrate or model how he or she organizes information, analyzes situations, or solves problems

The following, then, are advantages of (a good) lecture:

- It permits the dissemination of recent or unpublished findings.
- It allows the instructor complete control over the goals, content, pacing, organization, and presentation of the material.
- If delivered well, it can motivate and inspire students; the speaker's enthusiasm for the subject can be conveyed in a way not possible with other teaching methods.
- It is comfortable for learners who need structure, who learn best by listening, or who perceive active participation as threatening.
- It permits a great amount of content to be presented to a large number of people in a short time.

However, a lecture also has the following disadvantages:

- It tends to place the student in a passive role; this can hinder attention (which falters in 15-20 minutes) and learning (especially for students who prefer active methods).
- The instructor is not aware of how well students are understanding the material presented; straight lecture lacks feedback.
- The learner has no control over the goals, content, pacing, organization, or presentation; individual differences are ignored.
- If the instructor has mediocre or poor presentation skills, the lecture is the least effective method to use.
- Very difficult material and/or higher levels of learning are not suited to lecture because individual differences are greater.

When you use lecture, try to emphasize its advantages and minimize its disadvantages. Here are some tips for preparing your lectures:

- Prepare well in advance, including presentation aids.
- Ensure that the lecture content fits in with course goals and objectives.
- Consider the characteristics and needs of your students.
- Gain attention at the beginning with a provocative question, joke, cartoon, story, picture, quotation, or current issue. Gain attention again every 10 minutes or less.
- Provide students with the goals/objectives of the lecture.
- Tell students how you expect them to use the lecture material.
- Provide an overview of how the lecture is organized, or a mental model or framework into which students can fit lecture content.
- Relate lecture to previous class material.
- Provide an outline to facilitate student note taking.
- Make sure key points are covered in logical order.
- Ensure that all relevant concepts and principles have been included: no gaps.
- Make sure students have all prerequisite terms and concepts. If not, explain them.
- Use analogies to explain difficult concepts and principles.
- Do not try to cover too much; limit to just a few major points, and limit to less than 1 hour.
- Break up the lecture with other activities that get students involved.
- Change media frequently.
- Include examples wherever possible. Invite students to provide examples from their own experience.
- Frequently check for student understanding by watching for nonverbals, asking questions, allowing for student questions, and/or providing quick exercises or quizzes.
- Summarize key points and relate them to future course activities.

When lecturing, *do not*

- Lecture more than 30 minutes without some form of student interaction
- Read the lecture
- Face the blackboard or screen while lecturing
- Display distracting mannerisms
- Speak in a monotone
- Simply repeat what is in the textbook
- Simply read what is on your overhead transparencies
- Include material that is interesting to you but irrelevant to your students

Making Lectures Interactive: Seven Designs

Participative Lecture

Facilitate orderly brainstorming on a topic or question, based on previous student experience and/or reading assignments. Record all ideas on slickboards, flip chart paper, or computer. Then have the class organize and synthesize the ideas into coherent categories or meaningful chunks. Someone takes notes and makes copies for the whole class (unless you are using a computer with large projection capabilities, in which case simply print). The process is as important as the finished product.

Problem Solving:
Stories, Case Studies, and Demonstrations

Pose an intriguing problem or unfinished story, one that will hook students' interest. The answer unfolds gradually through alternating instructor minilectures and student hypothesizing and reasoning step by step until the solution is "discovered." Example: "What will happen when a major multinational communications monopoly divests its operating companies and is forced to compete?"

Energy Shifts

Every 15 to 20 minutes, change to a new activity. Specifically, energy should shift between teacher and students. When energy shifts to students, they can work individually on problems or quizzes, share ideas with a few people sitting near them, or break up into groups of five or six to discuss an issue or application.

Modeling, Practice, and Feedback

The lecture portion is a demonstration of how to do something: interpret a poem, solve an office motivation problem, formulate a strategic plan, or write a computer program. Next, let student volunteers practice in front of the whole group, getting feedback from the teacher and class.

Debates

Divide the class in half, and let each group come prepared to debate an important issue. (If the issue has more than two sides, use more than two groups.) Structure the interaction to allow fair representation of views from each team.

Role Playing

Begin class with a minilecture that clearly establishes the context and setting for a role play. Divide class into small groups (e.g., loggers, environmentalists, EPA officials), and assign each group a clearly defined role and a concrete task—for instance, to formulate a position and propose a course of action. Once the group results have been presented, the instructor can lecture on actual events or predicted events in the situation or can carry on the role play longer by simulating a meeting of the different roles. Debriefing helps identify what was learned and bring closure.

Bells and Whistles

For emotional impact when introducing a new topic (e.g., work satisfaction, social change, economic competition, a technical innovation, a historical era), put together a collage of quotations and present them dramatically at the beginning of the lecture. Introduce or summarize a topic with a slide-tape composed of music on the theme and corresponding slide images. This can be a stimulus to discussion or a meaningful wrap-up. To summarize a topic, let small groups write and perform raps, songs, or poems that incorporate key course content. This is effective and fun and builds group cohesion.

The Discussion Method

The discussion method is used by faculty (a) to use the resources of members of the class, (b) to elicit prompt feedback on how well course objectives are being attained, and (c) to motivate students to prepare for class and beyond. Typically, students analyze topics, issues, or problems and exchange information, experiences, ideas, opinions, reactions, and conclusions.

When to Use the Discussion Method

Research shows that the discussion method is especially effective in enabling students to learn to think in terms of the subject matter, to analyze problems, and to modify opinions and attitudes. The major benefits of the discussion method are that it enables students (a) to test their knowledge of the subject matter, (b) to receive prompt feedback, and (c) to learn to evaluate the logic of and evidence for their own positions and the positions of others.

If you wish to use the discussion method, you should be able to answer "yes" to the following questions:

1. The discussion method takes time. Are you willing to allow students to participate fully and develop their ideas even if it means that you may not be able to cover all of the content that you have planned?
2. Is your class small enough to allow meaningful participation? If not, are you willing to break the class down into groups of five to seven students and train them how to run their own discussion groups?
3. Are you willing to tolerate a mode of instruction in which the group rewards and motivates participation and controls the pace of, and to some extent the content of, the discussion? In other words, are you willing to learn from your students (rather than subtly "steering" them toward your predetermined answers or conclusions)?

Conditions for Facilitating Student Discussion

This section describes instructor skills that are useful in facilitating classroom discussion. They work best when the following conditions are met:

1. *When the number of students is less than 20; the optimal discussion group size is 5 to 7 students.* In a large class, the instructor can (a) select a random sample of 8 to 10 students for discussion purposes while the remaining students observe (this is called the "fishbowl" technique); or (b) break the

class into small groups of 5 to 7 students each and train students to be discussion leaders.

2. *When participants can easily see and hear each other.* In practice, this means that students sit in a circle or in a horseshoe-shaped configuration, with a board or flip chart at the open end.

3. *When the goal or purpose of the discussion is clearly stated:* for example,

■ *To discuss a commonly shared experience*—to understand better an experiment, a field trip, or a guest lecture

■ *To enter into an issue-centered discussion*—to clarify an issue and the values of participants

■ *To analyze and solve problems* for which there is no straightforward known solution and on which each participant has information to contribute

4. *When an agenda is agreed on.* The agenda might include the range of topics to be covered, the questions to be answered, and the time allocated for each.

5. *When "ground rules" or procedures for conducting the discussion are agreed on and enforced.* The following are typical ground rules for a problem-solving discussion:

■ All points of view will be accepted and posted.

■ Evaluation will be deferred until later.

■ Silence is okay; thinking takes time.

■ Interruptions will be "policed."

■ Disagreement is okay, as long as it is over ideas and does not degenerate into personal attacks.

6. *When roles and responsibilities are clearly stated.* For example, students should know what they have to do to prepare for class and then be held accountable.

7. *When the instructor assumes a task-facilitative role rather than an expert or authoritative role.* To elicit participation and to avoid dominance, the instructor must behave, generally, in a *nonevaluative* way and *accept* whatever ideas or opinions group members suggest. Whenever a discussion leader evaluates or criticizes group members, openly disagrees with their ideas, or expresses strong skepticism about their opinions, he or she may unwittingly cause students to be cautious about what they say. Instead of expressing their own ideas, they will begin to defer more and more to the instructor's opinions, even when he or she wants them to do just the opposite. Adopting a task-facilitative role means that the instructor is

■ Willing to *accept* and *explore* students' ideas and feelings, even though he or she may not agree with them

■ Willing to allow students to participate fully and develop their ideas, even if it means that all of the planned content may not be covered

■ Willing to tolerate a mode of instruction in which the group rewards and motivates participation and controls the pace of and to some extent the content of the discussion

Imagine yourself as a newspaper reporter who is interviewing a person. In assuming such a role, you would naturally be less inclined to express your own views and more inclined to ask questions that elicit open expression. Your mental set would be to elicit and collect all the relevant information possible. You would be less inclined to evaluate, disagree, or enter into an argument. That sort of behavior would only close up your contact; he or she would feel threatened. Or consider the television role played by Peter Falk in *Colombo* (an American detective television program). His behavior as a "dumb" or "naive" detective rarely threatens his suspects; they begin to trust him and tell him everything he needs to know to crack the "perfect crime." In contrast, "nonacceptance" language turns people off and makes them feel resentful, defensive, or inferior:

■ *Threatening:* "You'd better have some good ideas." (Or else!)
■ *Preaching:* "You shouldn't think that way; think this way."
■ *Judging:* "Your ideas won't work."
■ *Labeling:* "You're lazy in your thinking."
■ *Interrogating:* "Don't you have any facts to support your opinion?"

Initiation of a Discussion

Once the goal or purpose of the discussion has been announced and the agenda and ground rules have been agreed on, the instructor should write the problem, issue, or topic on the board, state that ideas are wanted ("Does anyone have any suggestions?"), and use nonverbal means to elicit them. Note that because nonverbal techniques eventually elicit participation, there is no need to call on individuals; such a move will typically generate defensive behavior, in which students start thinking up answers rather than listening to the discussion and responding spontaneously. Some examples of nonverbal techniques are as follows:

■ Indicate (coach) with hand gestures that ideas or opinions are wanted.

■ Cue with the chalk/marker that you are ready to write on the board.

■ Attend to students by approaching them, leaning forward, and making eye contact to "nudge" them into sharing their opinions or observations.

Classroom Discussion Leadership Skills

A number of techniques can be used to stimulate and motivate students to participate in group discussions. In general, these techniques encourage students to express their ideas and opinions openly by minimizing their fear of embarrassment or unfair criticism.

The first six skills discussed below help instructors to handle the flow of ideas and opinions, involve all students in discussion, and avoid emotion-laden situations. The second set of six skills will help the instructor to manage emotion-laden situations—those in which there are strong feelings such as anger, hostility, and fear. Emotion-laden situations are often critical and difficult to handle but are relatively uncommon when other (nonemotional) discussion situations are handled well. For example, if a student continually introduces irrelevant points into a discussion, other students may become highly critical of him or her and launch an attack that will lead to an emotional exchange. When such emotion-laden situations arise, they must be dealt with immediately because they interfere with rational discussion.

Information-Laden Situations

The six skills for handling information-laden situations are outlined in Table 4.2. Because situations where the skills should be used may arise at any time, they are displayed in an "If . . . then" format. Think of them as principles that can be used as necessary.

Situation 1: Active Contribution. In this situation, a controversial topic enters the discussion, and everyone wants to express an opinion. Some of the input is relevant and some is "irrelevant." The technique for dealing with this situation is to *post and confirm* all ideas, opinions, feelings, reactions, and related issues and problems that emerge from

Table 4.2   Six Skills for Handling Information-Laden Situations

If Students . . .	*Then the Instructor Should . . .*
Contribute relevant or irrelevant ideas/feelings/problems	Post ideas/feelings/problems and confirm
"Cut in" on each other	Gatekeep
Make vague or incomplete statements	Request examples or illustrations; check with others
Hesitate to contribute	Encourage and recognize any contributions
Appear to have exhausted their contributions	Test consensus
Come to the end of a part of the discussion	Summarize

the discussion. Record them on the board in your own words, as quickly and succinctly as possible. Abbreviations help. Then paraphrase each contribution and have the contributor confirm it before proceeding. However, if ideas are flowing fast or if "brainstorming" (a freewheeling "anything goes" format) is desired, confirmation can be delayed.

When students have their ideas and opinions posted, they know that they are being listened to and that you are concerned about their feelings and problems. Paraphrasing what they have said and asking them to confirm it greatly clarifies communication. (With new groups it sometimes pays to make a mistake in posting on purpose and then to paraphrase and ask for confirmation just to establish the norm that it is okay to correct the instructor.)

Posting also facilitates group discussion in other ways:

1. It is reinforcing to most people; it serves to increase their rate of participation.
2. It enables you and the group to handle information overload when too many ideas (7 ± 2) are generated too quickly.
3. It makes a public record of what was said so that information is not lost or forgotten and can be used later.
4. Emotion-laden issues or concerns can sometimes be defused by problem posting. When such issues or concerns are verbalized and written publicly on a board and then are restated in nonemotional, objective, and clear terms, exaggerated feelings are focused and often disappear.

5. If students dominate or keep repeating their ideas over and over, posting can help them to realize that they have been heard, thereby politely shutting them off.

Posting also helps you, the instructor, to be a better discussion leader. It slows you down and keeps you from talking; you have to listen to be able to write. It also forces you to pay attention and prevents you from dominating the discussion.

Situation 2: Cutting in. A student is elaborating on an idea when another student "cuts in" and contributes a completely new idea. (Whenever an active discussion gets underway, the flow of information often exceeds the capabilities of participants. In such situations, students may cut each other off or fail to recognize each other's contributions.) The technique for dealing with this situation is to *gatekeep the flow of information* by "cutting in," as a traffic cop would, to postpone the new contribution until you have completely recorded what the first student has stated, have confirmed it, and have allowed time for others to add to it or comment on it. For example, suppose that Joe is explaining one of his ideas and Sam cuts in to offer another idea. Before Sam gets a few words out, you cut in to say, "Could you hold that for a few minutes? We're still working on Joe's suggestion. But I'll get right back to you. I don't want to lose your idea either."

Joe is pleased to have you act as "traffic cop." In the past it seemed that every time he presented an idea, someone would jump in with his or her own idea. This not only made Joe angry but meant that Joe would have to bring up the idea again later, if it was not forgotten and lost in the meantime. Hearing out ideas certainly saves time and keeps the group focused. You quickly post Joe's idea by abbreviating it. Then you check with Joe for its accuracy. After Joe has confirmed it, you say, "Okay, Sam, thanks for waiting; let's have your idea now."

The intent of "gatekeeping" is to handle all ideas, opinions, and reactions as quickly, expeditiously, and efficiently as possible without losing ideas or irritating students. You can postpone dealing with ideas or problems that are irrelevant to the central theme of the discussion by posting them in a corner of the board with the pledge that they will be dealt with later. For example, suppose that Sam says, "I just wanted to point out that parking is getting to be a real problem." You respond, "That problem appears to be tangential to our discussion, but it sounds like a problem that bears discussion later. Would you be satisfied if I jot down 'parking' under our list 'other problems' and proceed with our discussion?" Sam sees your point and says, "Okay for now, but we've got to solve that parking problem soon!"

Although you should decide quickly whether to put "irrelevant" ideas on a "hold" list, it is important that the originator's acceptance of such an act be obtained before doing so—his or her ideas may really be pertinent to the topic at hand.

Situation 3: Vague or Incomplete Statements. Suppose a student seems to have something to offer but you do not understand what it is; it is vague or incomplete to you. The technique for dealing with this situation is to *request examples or illustrations.* Make requests such as "I'm not sure I understand what you said. Could you give us an example?" "How do you mean that?" "Can you elaborate on that?" Your questions should encourage expression; questions that suggest cross-examination or evaluation can be threatening and cause answers to become brief and guarded. For example, avoid asking questions such as "Why do you say that?" "Where's your evidence?" "How do you know?"

If you think you understand, you might test whether your understanding is correct. For example, you might say, "Let me see if I understand what you're saying." You might also check with other students to see if they would like to try checking out their understanding or if they would like to elaborate on or clarify what has been said. You might say, "Can anyone state in their own words what they understand is being said?" (Use nonverbal coaxing to elicit contributions.) "Can someone elaborate or give us some examples so that we can be sure we understand?" Here, as elsewhere, do not call on those who are quiet. If you do, you threaten those who have nothing worthwhile to contribute. Rather than listening to the ongoing discussion, they will become overly concerned about coming up with "good" responses.

Situation 4: Reluctance to Contribute. Students may be reluctant to contribute to the discussion for a variety of reasons, such as a previous embarrassing experience in which other students laughed at their contributions. The technique for dealing with this situation is to *encourage and recognize any contributions* by finding something good in them, by restating them in your own words, by posting and adding to them, and by asking others to add to them. Instead of forcing contributions, wait until the student makes any first, small attempt at contributing, or use nonverbal means (e.g., a coaching gesture with your hands) to elicit contributions. Then recognize the contributions by saying something such as "I'm pleased to hear your ideas. Keep it up. I like everyone to contribute." Finally, post the contributions on the board and add to them and/or ask others to add to them.

Verbal recognition of students' initial contributions, if positively stated, usually causes students to participate more often. Verbal recognition can be used whenever the opportunity arises: (a) when nonverbal behavior (such as a half-raised hand) indicates a readiness to respond, (b) when a hesitant first attempt occurs, or (c) when a student adds an idea or example to someone else's contribution.

Note that in the example above it is suggested that you recognize the act of contributing. Unless you can remember to find something "good" in every idea contributed, it is best to focus on recognizing only acts of contribution, not the ideas themselves. Otherwise, students whose ideas are not given your attention will feel that their ideas are somehow not as worthwhile.

Recognition is useful not only in getting shy or reluctant members to contribute but also when students contribute "half-baked" ideas—ones that just spontaneously "pop into their heads." If you accept these contributions by posting them and recognize them further with some words of encouragement, you may cause others to build or "piggyback" on the contributions and turn them, by synthesis of ideas, into really innovative results. For example, suppose that Ted suddenly throws out a tentative, partially thought-out idea. Instead of saying "Can't you be more clear about what you're talking about?" or "Does anyone else have a better idea?" you say, "I'm glad you brought that idea up. Let's see, can anyone add to it?" or "Thank you for sharing your ideas with us. What does that mean in light of what we have been discussing?"

Situation 5: Discussion Runs Down. Eventually, contributions to a discussion dwindle or run out: Students seem to have voiced all of their opinions, ideas, or solutions. When this happens, you should test to see if the group is prepared to go on to the next step in the discussion or problem-solving sequence. Your technique is to *test consensus* repeatedly until all participants are willing to go ahead. For example, you might say, "Has everyone expressed his or her thoughts on this issue? Are we ready to summarize what's been said? Take your time—I want to make sure we have exhausted the objections to the change."

To make certain that all students are really ready, you should encourage them to express their opinions. Consensus testing does not mean asking members to vote; it means seeing that each and every member is sufficiently satisfied to proceed and has had enough time to be sure.

Situation 6: End of Discussion Reached. Students who participate in a discussion usually want evidence that their time and energy have been spent productively. If discussion begins to drift to other topics or closure is felt, it is time to *summarize* what has been said and ask for confirmation. For example, suppose that during discussion of a topic, several ideas or feelings not associated with the topic have been captured on the board: "Group is apathetic, "Our goals unclear," "Wasting time here," and "Where are we headed?" You realize that you ought to try to summarize these feelings and identify the underlying problem. So you say, "It seems to me that a problem underlies our discussion today. Let me take a stab at identifying it: 'How can we state our goals so that they are clear and will elicit commitment to our discussion?' Is that correct?"

Of course, in any discussion, breaks occur that offer natural occasions for summarizing what has been expressed. Otherwise, summarize at least every 30 minutes or so. Obviously, if ideas and problems have been posted, summarizing is easy; you merely have to review what was written and get confirmation that your summary does in fact describe accurately what has been said.

Several summary-oriented functions that should be performed, if appropriate, are

- Combining two or more ideas into one
- Identifying (deducing) a problem from a number of examples of incidents (see above)
- Separating a series of ideas into two or more problems or issues

The intent is to provide closure to what has been written on the board.

Emotion-Laden Situations

The six skills for handling emotion-laden situations are outlined in Table 4.3. Emotion-laden situations are defined here as classroom situations in which there are strong feelings of anger, hostility, fear, etc. When emotion-laden situations arise, they must be dealt with, because they interfere with a rational discussion.

Emotion-laden situations arise from a variety of sources, particularly those in which the student feels that he or she is being evaluated. Students also react to such situations in different ways. Their reactions may be hidden or overt and may show up in the form of defensiveness ("don't blame me"), withdrawal, or attacks on others.

Situation 1: Silence. In this situation, you ask a question or pose a problem to the group, but students remain silent, whereas they normally respond to such stimulation. Sometimes students react with silence because the instructor, or a student, has inadvertently posed a problem, asked a question, or introduced an opinion that generates feelings of anger, hostility, or threat. The students may be afraid to reveal their real feelings for fear of the consequences. The technique for dealing with this situation is to *become silent* and use nonverbal means to indicate you would like someone to speak. By being silent you "force" students to begin talking. Once one student starts, others will soon follow.

Suppose, for example, that you express your concern about students arriving late. You do not realize that students are arriving after the hour because you have waited and started classes late. Each student is reluctant to state this fact and therefore remains silent. Sensing that silence signifies a reluctance to speak, you walk to the board, post the issue, repeat it verbally, ask for suggestions, and indicate with the cue of chalk in your hand that you are ready to write. You look about the room, make eye contact with a number of your more verbal students, coax them in an eliciting manner with your hands, and wait. Because of your tolerance of silence, one student finally says, "We ought to start at 6:15 instead of 6:00. The traffic is lighter then." Eventually, one student, seeing that all ideas are accepted, points out that you have contributed to the problem by starting class late.

Table 4.3   Six Skills for Handling Emotion-Laden Situations

If Students . . .	Then the Instructor Should . . .
Are silent	Tolerate silence
Exhibit guarded expressions	Make inquiry/probe
Display much emotion	Hear out
Display less emotion	Invite expression of emotion
Express emotion, but at a rational level	Feed back expression of emotion and confirm
Dispute/oppose/attack the instructor or class members with "loaded" questions	Turn "loaded" questions into problems to solve

In general, whenever you ask questions, pause. Students need time to think, and they need more time if they fear embarrassment or criticism.

Situation 2: Guardedness. Students sometimes reveal their hidden feelings with quick, but guarded, verbal expressions or with nonverbal behavior. Allowing these "loaded" or "hidden" expressions to go by unrecognized leads to misinterpretation and false conclusions. To deal with this situation, *inquire (politely) into the feelings behind the guarded expression.*

For example, suppose that after a change in classroom procedures is announced, one student says, "Oh, no!" and looks at the ceiling. You respond by saying (politely), "Correct me if I'm wrong, but I sense that you are concerned about this change. Could you share this concern with us? I'd like to understand how you feel about this change." (Silence.)

If you know your students well, you may be able to recognize any behavior that deviates from normal as a guarded way of expressing a hidden emotion. For example, folded arms may indicate disagreement. Nonetheless, any out-of-the ordinary behavior, especially nonverbal behavior, should be checked out.

Inquiry or probing into guarded expressions often reveals potential problems or sources of dissatisfaction before they have accumulated to an explosive level. If you are sensitive to student behavior, you can often prevent problems and misconceptions.

Once group members begin to express their feelings, the discussion leader should be careful to display an appropriate amount of acceptance of students' ideas, opinions, and feelings. The next three techniques can often be used in sequence to reduce emotion from a higher level to a lower level.

Situation 3: Much Display of Emotion. Sometimes, because of differences in basic values, several members of the group will actively display their displeasure with your "contrary" views by talking rapidly, loudly, or emotionally. In this situation, *hear out their views* by saying nothing and using nonverbal behavior to indicate that you are listening. Saying nothing is one way of demonstrating "acceptance" because it indicates that you are listening in a nonevaluative, nonverbal way. Nonverbal behaviors include maintaining eye contact, cocking your head to the side, leaning forward, moving in closer, and saying "um hum" or nodding your head up and down to indicate that you are listening.

When group members are obviously very emotional and argumentative, you may be drawn into an argument that polarizes differences and may generate anger. At this point, any hint of evaluation on your part, especially in your role as discussion leader, can elicit defensive behavior or attacks on you. But if you maintain your nonevaluative stance, emotions will eventually subside.

Situation 4: Emotionality Lessens. After you have heard them out, the emotional students will begin to slow down, hesitate, or pause. Your technique now is to *invite further expression of emotion.* Say, for example, "I'm interested in your point of view. I'd like to know how you feel" or "I'm not sure I understand; could you tell me more?" or "I'm learning something. This is news to me." By inviting more expression of feeling, you encourage sharing of ideas and feelings and demonstrate a nonevaluative stance. You might even appear to be slightly bewildered (Colombo), thereby suggesting that you have misunderstood and want to set yourself straight. This technique should not be overplayed, but it is useful when you are dealing with what appear to be inconsistent statements.

In any event, you must not appear to be evaluative by contradicting or "cross-examining" with such questions as "Why are you so angry?" Also avoid the use of the phrase "I understand." You cannot really understand until you are able to restate someone's feelings in your own words and have asked for confirmation (see the next technique).

Situation 5: Emotions Still Expressed, but at a Rational Level. At some point, your acceptance and nonevaluation will reduce emotion even further. Because their views and emotions have been accepted and heard out, students will calm down to a point at which you can risk saying something to demonstrate that you are listening and accepting. Your technique now is to reflect or feed back, in your own words, what you think or feel the emotional students are saying and then to ask for confirmation of the accuracy of your statement.

We all recognize that strong feelings frequently lie behind surface messages and that the reasons for these feelings may also be hidden. But most of us rarely attempt to clarify either the feelings or the reasons. You should try to state (take a "stab" at) what you think the feelings and reasons are for emotion-laden messages and then ask for confirmation. In such cases, you will either elicit confirmation or get corrected; you cannot miss getting better understanding.

Here are two examples. In the first example, the instructor and the student remain at the same level; they do not clarify the feelings expressed or the reasons for them. But in the second example, the instructor, by making a specific probe and seeking confirmation, helps to bring out the feelings and the reasons behind the original message.

■ Example 1: Parroting
Joe: Sue should never have been made a group discussion leader.
Sam: You think that Sue shouldn't lead group discussions?
Joe: Exactly! Group leadership is not the right job for her.

■ Example 2: Probing
Joe: Sue should never have been made a group discussion leader.
Sam: You mean you feel she's too easygoing? Maybe even permissive?
Joe: Oh, no. I mean she posts our ideas too slowly. We all get bored.
Sam: Oh, I see. You think that until she can learn to post more quickly, someone else should lead group discussions?
Joe: Exactly! That's my analysis.

Notice that in the Example 2 the instructor was wrong in his first guess at the underlying reasons for the message, but that his guess nevertheless helped elicit the "true" reasons for the message. It does not really matter if you are wrong in your probe as long as you ask for confirmation.

When you are confronted by emotional students, it may be difficult for you to provide feedback about their feelings to them. Strong emotions usually generate defensive behavior on the part of both parties. Both of you will probably want to argue or attempt to defend and clarify your position before you try to understand the other person's point of view. Even if you discipline yourself to listen, you still may distort or deny parts of the message. In such cases, feeding back feelings and confirming them become crucial; it helps to ensure that the real message gets through.

Although ideas are generally easy to elicit, most people are not used to identifying and restating feelings. Yet for accurate communication of acceptance, recognition of feelings or emotions is essential. Also, remember that if students' feelings are not recognized for what they really are, they will probably just "simmer" and come out later and be directed at you or someone else in the class.

Here is a final example:

> **Tom:** I really don't appreciate the way you are running this discussion! It seems to me that you are only interested in Sue and Hal's input, not mine!
>
> **Ben:** What you seem to be telling me is that this discussion would be more meaningful for you if I asked you for more input; is that right?
>
> **Tom:** No, that's not right—now you misread my intent!
>
> **Ben:** You're angry because I'm showing favoritism; I seem to be recognizing their contributions more. Is that correct?
>
> **Tom:** Right! Now you understand me.

Situation 6: Attacks With Negatively Loaded Questions. Sometimes when students become defensive, they attack the instructor. Typically, their attack takes the form of a negatively loaded question directed toward the discussion leader. You can deal with this situation by turning the attack into a problem for the group to solve. For example, suppose that because one student likes structure in his life, he is "uptight" with what he considers to be a permissive attitude on your part toward enforcement of the ground rules for conducting group discussions. He says to you (in an obviously hostile way), "Suppose a group member deliberately violates a ground rule. Do you mean you're going to let him get away with it?" If you answer "yes," you may appear permissive and have to defend yourself, thereby slipping into an argument. On the other hand, if you answer "no," you may appear to be backing down and may again slip into an argument. Instead, you might say, "Let's do some problem solving; let's see how the rest of you feel about this question. Does anyone have a recent specific example of a class member who has violated a rule and gotten away with it?"

If the question is technical in nature, you might express your own ideas, but if you do so just to prove you are right, you will probably slip into an argument. Instead, you should accept any disagreement, encourage others to express their opinions or feelings, and summarize what is said. With intense emotions present, this will do far more to influence attitude change constructively than will authoritative facts and opinions. By turning attacks into problems for the group to solve, neither the questioner (attacker) nor the leader is placed in a defensive posture.

Requirements for Initiating Effective Discussions

Numerous analyses of effective and ineffective discussions have determined that there are five basic requirements (Daniels, 1986):

1. *Agreement on a common focus.* Humans have a natural tendency to jump too quickly from one problem or topic to another. To overcome this tendency you need to
   - Elicit agreement on agenda topics
   - Determine priorities
   - Record the group's ideas publicly
2. *Agreement on a common stage/process.* Humans also have a natural tendency to jump too quickly from one stage or process to another. To overcome this tendency, you need to
   - State what process (procedure) is to be used
   - Elicit agreement on the process
3. *An open and balanced flow of information.* Aggressive and dominant individuals can easily prevent others from presenting their ideas. You need to
   - Gatekeep the flow of information

- Recognize and accept all ideas
- Protect "minority" opinions

4. *An absence of personal attack.* Conflict and disagreement over ideas can be used to elicit better ideas—but only if each participant's self-esteem is maintained and enhanced. You need to

- Turn personal attacks into problems to be solved
- Redefine conflict in terms of needs rather than solutions

5. *Equal power and influence.* Related to the above two conditions is the need to balance power and influence. With the role of discussion leader comes power. If that person is also viewed as an "authority," the amount of influence attached to the role can be counterproductive. Discussion leaders can easily sway the group's thinking unless they

- Arrange the meeting place to equalize power
- Provide an inclusion activity
- Enforce ground rules
- Accept and record all ideas

Basic Group Process

Three stages of group process are basic to all task-oriented discussions and meetings. For an orderly discussion, you should complete each stage before attempting the next.

Stage 1: Build an information base.

- Elicit all the facts and opinions about the topic as possible
- Obtain common agreement, by encouraging clarification and elaboration. Note: Do not permit analysis at this stage.
- Test consensus ("Are we ready to analyze?").

Stage 2: Analyze the information base.

- Encourage disagreement and handle conflict constructively.
- Encourage a variety of opinions/alternatives.
- Test consensus ("Are we ready to come to a resolution?").

Stage 3: Resolution: Agree on what to do with the information.

- Elicit summaries of what the group members want to do with data.

■ Obtain a final agreement/resolution: For example, check to :
  "cause" that has been identified is the real one.
■ Begin to look at potential problems for the decision that has been
  agreed on.
■ Complete the action plan that has been agreed on.

Unskilled discussion meeting leaders allow all three stages of group
process to happen at once. When the three group processes are followed
in the above sequence, results are usually superior and are imple-
mented by group members with greater commitment and efficiency.

Inclusion Activity:
To Initiate Positive Group Dynamics

When individuals enter a group, for whatever purpose, they immediately begin trying to influence each other. Primarily this is to establish
a "pecking order" or "norm state."

Once a "norm state" has been established, it has great staying power
and is very difficult to modify. In "natural" groups, those that have
formed as a result of influence or power, individual members do not
have equal influence. For example, those at the bottom of the "pecking
order" will not be willing to be risk takers, and their contributions
(especially innovative and creative ideas) will never be heard.

To create a "norm state" of equality, you need to require all group
members to enact the *same behavior at the beginning of each meeting.* Once
a norm state of equality is in place, group members will fight to
maintain it, just as they do to maintain counterproductive norm states.
An inclusion exercise, such as having each group member, in turn, offer
his or her opinion on the first item on the agenda (60 seconds each), will
establish and maintain a norm state of equality in influence and promote free sharing of ideas/opinions.

Basic Discussion Topics and Strategies

There are three basic discussion topics: (a) a shared experience, (b) an
issue, or (c) problem solving.

Shared-Experience Discussions

Students frequently have a shared experience that can be understood better, and can perhaps take on new meaning, if it is discussed in a small group setting. Sometimes these experiences arise spontaneously, but more often they result from an outside assignment (e.g., an assigned reading) or a planned class activity (Davis, Fry, & Alexander, 1977).

As noted above under "Basic Group Process," the discussion leader follows a three-step strategy. First, the leader helps students to *build an information base* by asking them to *identify* or sort out the key points that emerge from the shared experience. Second, the leader asks students to *analyze the information base* by asking them to *analyze* cause-and-effect relationships until consensus conclusions are reached. Third, the leader asks students to *reach resolution or agree on what to do with the information* by asking them to *generalize* their conclusions to new settings. This strategy is based on an experiential learning process or model, which consists of five separate but interlocking questions. As implied by the name of the model, the emphasis is on the direct experiences of the students, rather than vicarious experiences. Because adult learners bring a great deal of experience to the classroom, this strategy for discussion is especially appealing to them.

To demonstrate how an experiential discussion strategy can be used, a topic that is familiar to you will be used: "Insufficient Wait-Time." This topic, in and of itself, should be of interest to you; it is a behavior exhibited by many instructors that is counterproductive to open discussions. Because all students (including you) have experienced it, by definition it becomes a common experience.

Let us assume that you ask your students the following series of questions:

> *Question 1: What is "insufficient wait-time"?* Students will come up with a number of definitions. When they are finally summarized, the definition of *wait-time* usually is "the amount of time after an initial question has been posed before the instructor answers it him- or herself; repeats, rephrases, or adds further information to the question; or accepts an answer from a student." The definition of *insufficient wait-time* is "a wait-time of less than 3 to 5 seconds."
>
> *Question 2: Why do instructors exhibit this nonfacilitating behavior?* Students again will come up with a number of reasons:

- Instructors are anxious; they cannot stand the silence primarily because of time pressure.
- Instructors really want students to learn from them, not from other students.
- Instructors want to show off their knowledge.

Question 3: What are the consequences for student learning? Here students can relate to all the times that they have experienced the negative results of this behavior. Their answers usually are:

- Students have little chance to think; they become dependent on the instructor for answers.
- Slow thinkers never have a chance to respond.
- It stifles interaction and discussion among students.

Question 4: What generalizations can we make from this analysis? By considering the answers to the above two questions, it is not difficult for students to develop principles or extract generalizations that they can take away from the discussion for use in the future. When students are asked to come up with a generalization that is in the form of a proverb, they give examples such as

- Insufficient wait-time causes brain downtime.
- Question and answer all in one breath surely results in a thinker's death.
- For applause, pause.

Question 5: How can one avoid exhibiting this behavior? Because this discussion is about a behavior that every instructor wants to avoid, the question has to be worded in a negative way. But when you are discussing positive topics and questions, this question should be worded positively to elicit ways in which your students can apply the principles that they have derived. For our "insufficient wait-time" discussion, typical answers would be the following:

- Announce that you will wait; enforce ground rule that "silence is okay."
- Count to self; have students help you count.
- Have students pair up and discuss their answers; then ask for answers. (Students will be more confident if their answers have been confirmed by a peer.)

In general, you can use five questions along these lines (what is it, why does it happen, what are the consequences, what generalizations can we make, how can we make it happen/keep it from happening) to discuss any common experience that your students have encountered. Because students have a tendency to begin to analyze as soon as you ask them for the definition of the topic you are about to discuss, it pays to list the questions (headings) across the top of a board. Then, as you begin by asking for answers to your "what?" question (the first heading), you can capture their analysis answers as they arise by posting them. Of course, you want to refocus the group back to the first heading/column until consensus is reached before proceeding to the next question/heading.

This process of "brainstorming" and posting all of the students' ideas under each question/heading and then reaching consensus not only ensures that all ideas are elicited but that the topic is thoroughly analyzed and a resolution is derived. Note that adults will be most interested in the last question/heading: how to apply what they have just analyzed.

Issue-Centered Discussions

Issue-centered discussions focus on a topic over which there are differences of opinion. Disagreement arises because there is no obvious right or wrong answer to an issue, and therefore the issue becomes a matter of controversy and debate. The purpose of an issue-centered discussion is to clarify the issue and the values of the individuals participating in the discussion.

There are four steps for conducting an issue-centered discussion. The first step is to *present an issue*. Issues may be presented for the group in a wide variety of ways. For example:

- Present a brief case study that describes a real-life issue. The case may be in print (a newspaper article for example), on audiotape, or on film.
- State all sides of an issue directly and objectively at the outset of a class meeting. Alternatively, identify issues when they arise and focus the attention of the group on the new issue by stating both sides.
- Collect data from the class members based on their past experience and use the data to delineate the issue: for example, "How many of you have noticed that instructors often answer their own questions?"
- Pose an unusual problem. Take a stand and challenge the class to debate the issue with you.

The second step is to *help students to clarify the boundaries of the issue*. Unless the issue is stated in a relatively unambiguous way, the discussion is apt to go off in several different directions. Post the issue on the board or a flip chart, and make certain that only one issue is being discussed and that students agree on the use of the terms. Try to ensure that the issue, as defined, can be covered in the time available. If not, encourage students to redefine it. It is generally better to phrase a topic as a question than as a general statement. A question defines and limits the scope of discussion more than a statement can. Also, when presenting a question to a group, be careful not to include a solution in its wording.

The third step is to *discuss the issue*. In the course of the discussion, help students to clarify why they feel as they do. Encourage them to express themselves, but try to get them to cite evidence, define their terms appropriately, and make points by reference to shared experiences. Focus the discussion on one point at a time until all points are made and understood. It may help to post key points on the board or flip charts for a common reference.

The fourth step is to *summarize the discussion*. After all points have been made and understood, draw out the implications of the discussion by citing generalizations that seem valid and applying them to specific related cases, settings, or problems. Crystallize points of agreements and disagreements so that lingering differences among participants stand out clearly.

Problem-Solving Discussions

Students are frequently taught how to solve specific problems with known solutions. For example, in mathematics, physics, chemistry, and other scientific disciplines, obtaining a solution to such problems involves following a relatively fixed sequence of steps. In contrast, the discussion method can be used to solve problems for which there is no straightforward, known solutions.

There are six steps for conducting a problem-centered discussion. The first step is to *assign a problem to one or more groups of students*. The same problem may be assigned to different groups to compare problem-solving techniques or the quality of solutions later.

The second step is to *define the problem*. Before students attempt to solve a problem, they should be encouraged to define it precisely and arrive at some consensus regarding what the problem is. In many cases, defining the problem means specifying precisely what the words used to describe the problem mean. For example, here is a problem: "If the city decides to rezone the area north of town and allow a new mall to be built, what will be the environmental impact?" Clearly, before students can begin to solve this problem, they need to specify precisely what the area under consideration for rezoning includes and the aspects of the environment that are to be included in the study.

Sometimes a stated problem is actually not one problem at all, but many problems: for example, "What are the obstacles to providing better health care in the inner city?" Different people, generally, have different perceptions of problems of this type. The residents of the inner city may say the "real" problem is a shortage of doctors or the high cost of drugs. Doctors may say the problem is the high cost of liability insurance or crime or vandalism. Public officials may say the problem is in the state capitol.

One good method for bringing to light different perceptions of a problem area is to define the problem area in a preliminary way and then ask students to state their perceptions of it. The students' contributions are posted on a flip chart in one or two words. Contributions are encouraged from all students, but they are not discussed at this time except to be certain that they are understood. The focus is on problem definition, not solutions. In a discussion of birth control, for example, the "cost of contraceptives" is a legitimate problem, but to suggest that the "government should furnish contraceptives" is a solution. Actually, there are numerous ways of dealing with the cost of contraceptives, only one of which is having them furnished by the government.

The problem-posting process generally results in numerous suggestions as to what the problem "really" is. After all problems are posted, these can be ranked and a decision made as to which problem will be discussed first.

The third step is to *provide students with appropriate sources of information for attacking the problem*. This involves readings, cases, and so forth.

The fourth step is, after study of the available information, to *have students post possible solutions to the problem as described*.

The fifth step is to *have students report the results to the instructor and/or the rest of the class.*

The sixth step is to *evaluate the process.* Here the instructor leads a class discussion directed primarily at identifying problems encountered with the method and clarifying the steps used with this type of problem solving: that is, specifying precisely what the problem is, searching appropriate literature, and generating and evaluating possible solutions.

Using the Discussion Method in Large Classes

As noted above, the upper limit for the discussion method is 20 students. To handle classes of 20 or more, it is suggested that you select, at random, a group of 10 to 20 students to sit at the front of the class to serve as members of a discussion group. The rest of the class observes the discussion. New students are selected to serve in the discussion group for each session of the class. In this way, discussion rotates throughout the class during the semester or term.

Another solution is to have your students form groups of five to seven and train them to facilitate their own group discussions. Each discussion group should elect a discussion leader and a process observer. These roles can be rotated through the group each time they meet. Appendix 4.1 at the end of this chapter provides the leader with a useful checklist for facilitation and the process observer with possible dimensions of feedback after each discussion so that the next discussion leader will learn from the current one. Appendix 4.2 gives further tips on group membership behavior.

Participative Teaching Techniques

Definition and Description
of Participative Techniques

Some challenges never change for instructors. How do you keep distracted, unmotivated, or demanding students interested in what you have to say and the importance of your topic? One simple solution is to adopt a "participative style" of teaching.

In the traditional lecture method, the focus is on the instructor. What is common to all lectures is the loss of the dynamic of interaction between the student and the speaker. No dialogue exists. Lectures are speeches or presentations in a format of one-way communication.

In a participative style of instruction, which is either discussions or exercises, the focus is on the learner. Typically, students work together in small groups or in pairs to arrive at answers to problems or questions posed by the instructor. In fact, in a highly participative learning environment, a great deal of the total learning experience becomes student controlled. It is not unusual for students to teach each other and themselves. The secret is in the application of key concepts to students' own experiences and interests. Dialogue is highly encouraged and rewarded by the instructor. Traditional lectures are often supplemented by discussions and group exercises; there is no reason an instructor must choose one method over the other because a participative style of instruction is often used to reinforce key lecture points.

Benefits of Participative Techniques

Creation of a Motivating Learning Environment

A participative style of instruction can be motivating and stimulating for the students. Adults learn best when they feel free to make contributions and can clearly see a direct application and relevance in their own lives. By making the learners' successes depend on their interaction and involvement with your topic, you have captured their interest, and the facts are more likely to stick. Participative learning is active learning; lectures are passive learning.

Creating an environment in which the students are motivated to learn may be even more important to you as an instructor if your class is a required (and dreaded) one, if you typically have low enrollment or a high dropout rate, and if your course content is especially complex or advanced. A balance between straight lecture and a learner-controlled experience may make the difference for many students in terms of having a positive attitude about succeeding in your course and sincerely wanting to learn about your topic.

Demonstration of Your Interest in Your Students

Another benefit is that a participative style of teaching demonstrates your concern for and interest in your students. If you express your commitment to their individual learning, they will reward your efforts by showing higher levels of enthusiasm and interest in your class.

A participative style of instruction also creates a supportive learning environment for slower or more anxiety-prone students. You will have time during in-class exercises to mingle with these students and provide one-on-one coaching or advice.

Fewer Demands on the Instructor as Compared to Lecturing

Participative learning can be less demanding on the instructor than lecturing. The ability to give top-notch presentations for long periods of time is truly a skill that most adjunct instructors have not had the time or inclination to master.

Because the lecture format simply involves telling or talking to the students, the instructor does not know whether his or her students have actually learned anything. By using a participative style, the instructor has a constant feedback system in place to gauge the effectiveness of his or her delivery and the depth of the students' mastery of the topic.

Practical Applications

Experts in adult learning agree that adult students learn best by doing. Using a participative style of teaching gets students beyond the rote factual recall level of comprehension and to a point at which they can internalize the concepts. This is especially valuable for skill-based training—that is, training in how to do something.

Class members bring together and share their individual skills, capabilities, knowledge for collective accomplishments in solving real-life problems. Topic-related, practical exercises simulate the students' current or future workplaces. This often can go a long way in solving the often-heard complaint in college classes "This doesn't apply to the 'real world.' "

Greater Flexibility in Teaching Methodology and Timing

Students generally enjoy the mental and physical flexibility that the participative style of instruction brings. They can get up and move around, change seats, and talk to other classmates. Group input, analysis, and choices in problem solving are more effective than individual contributions. Depending on the exercise or discussion, a participative style of instruction allows opportunities for students to work with other students interested in the same subtopics or from common backgrounds. Because students differ on preferred learning modes, the flexibility built into a participative style of instruction accommodates a wider variety of learners than lecture does.

The amount of time on the various exercises is generally more flexible than lecture time. It usually takes a fairly consistent amount of time to cover materials via lecture unless sections are deleted for the sake of time. On the other hand, an experienced participative instructor knows how to adjust the time for exercises according to the students' needs, interests, and attention span and the amount of available time. Thus a participative style can also be the instructor's secret strategy for time management in the classroom.

General Tips for Participative Techniques

Be Well Prepared

You must prepare for exercises and discussions just as much as, if not more than, for lectures. If you do not organize your learning objectives and activities, the discussion or exercise may become directionless and end up frustrating both you and your students.

For a *discussion*, think through carefully in advance what discussion questions to ask. Where is your emphasis? How can you get the students to go deeper, to analyze, and to apply your key points? Ask solvable but challenging questions. Get them engaged; arouse their curiosity. If the discussion lags, ask a thought-provoking question or take an unpopular opinion to further stimulate the students. Act as moderator, recorder, and catalyst by guiding the comments and the learners' energy. Conclude with a summary or closing remarks, and refer to any discussion items you posted on the board or flip chart.

For an *interactive exercise,* mentally walk through the exercise to note all the logistical considerations (e.g., where the students sit), to clarify your instructions, and to ensure that you will have all needed supplies and audiovisual aids (e.g., handouts). Handouts such as checklists, observer sheets, and questionnaires help to organize the students' thoughts and keep them focused on the task. During the exercise, ask each group if they understand their assignment and clarify with any needed instructions. Then keep them on task by walking around and watching the time. Call out frequently the amount of time left for the exercise. Afterward, as you process the exercise with the whole group, consider what questions you will ask and determine the preferred order and format for group reports.

Keep the Group Size Small if Possible

Although participative learning is not impossible with a class of up to 100 or even 200 students, it is much more difficult. The ideal size for interactive exercises or discussions is approximately 10 to 25 students. This size allows maximized "air time" for most students and is generally quite manageable when organizing students into small groups.

If you do have a very large class, here are some tips for making your lectures more participative:

■ When you ask questions to be discussed in small groups or pairs, have the students talk to the people sitting closest to them. This minimizes the confusion of many people moving around and saves time. If you anticipate a wide difference of opinions or viewpoints on your question or exercise, a "pair share" gives students someone to talk to but minimizes the likelihood of strongly differing opinions or a deadlock on making a decision.

■ Instead of getting in-depth reports from each small group or pair, ask for quick sample reports from various corners of the room. Even though fewer students actually make verbal contributions, most appreciate the fact that student representatives are being listened to.

■ Ask simpler questions or assign simpler tasks to the small groups or pairs. This again saves time that can be used for more reports from all groups.

Be Sensitive to Interpersonal and Group Dynamics

Look out for students who are highly vocal, dominating, or overly passive or for any existing cliques. Plan ways to minimize these distractions or draw out silent students by planning which students should work together in which discussion groups or exercises. Try to imagine any possible negative reactions from students.

Arrange seating so that all students can easily hear and see each other. U-shaped or roundtable configurations are optimal for discussion groups. If space allows, plan for small group "breakout sessions" by locating or creating separate areas where the small groups can go to talk or work together in private. Structure the discussions and exercises so that students can relax and feel comfortable in a nonthreatening but well-organized environment.

Specific Participative Techniques

This section will address seven specific techniques that can be used as participative replacements for the straight lecture format. The characteristics, advantages, and disadvantages for each technique will be addressed.

Demonstration

Characteristics. This technique illustrates functions, processes, ideas, relationships, and activities in a skillful performance of precisely how something should be done. Demonstrations typically present skills and techniques in action. They appeal to the five senses, especially vision, thus increasing the retention of knowledge beyond the oral qualities of a lecture.

Students can test new skills in a controlled environment. Demonstrations usually stimulate interest and engage attention. Learning is reinforced if the process is shown, repeated slowly, and followed by thought-provoking questions.

Advantages. Because this technique is flexible, it can easily be adjusted to accommodate many different student needs and topics. The transfer of learning to the application level is high. If you give your students an opportunity to demonstrate the skills, functions, or relationships themselves, they can correct errors in the classroom. Demonstrations do not need to be expensive or complicated to be effective.

Disadvantages. Facilities and seating arrangements must be carefully planned in advance to maximize student viewing. If the students do not actually directly participate in the demonstration, interest level may be low at times. Demonstrations work best with small classes (under 25 students) unless closed cable TV is available.

Dramatization (Also Called Role Play and Skill Practice)

Characteristics. A dramatization is a combination of a discussion and a demonstration. The demonstrators are the students who, without the benefit of a script, act out specific scenarios to illustrate key skills or learning points. Following the role play, the class discusses the implications of the performance to the situation or problem under consideration.

First, the instructor explains the background situation and outcomes to be expected, gives each actor instructions on his or her character, behaviors, actions, and reactions, and helps to clarify all goals and roles. Roles are assigned or volunteers requested by the instructor. Sometimes other students are employed as "coaches" for the key role players to help them clarify further their anticipated behaviors and dialogue. After a few minutes of strategizing and practice, the role players dramatize the scenario in front of the class.

During the dramatization, it is a good idea to have the other students take notes on observer sheets to reinforce key learning concepts. After the dramatization, ask the role players for their personal reactions to how it went. Follow this discussion with a structured discussion, either from the students' observer sheets or in a more general format.

Advantages. Dramatizations teach and entertain at the same time. They can explore possible solutions without the risks involved in a real trial-and-error approach. The students who play the roles often become thoroughly engaged in the scenario and consequently the topic. This helps to create enthusiasm and interest among the students in general and is especially useful for distracted or even "trouble-making" students. Some students enjoy the chance to assume another identity for a short time. The collective analysis by the students encourages the class to pool their experience and knowledge. Shyer students can still be actively involved as observers and/or as coaches. Costs for development and props are usually minimal.

Disadvantages. This technique can be time consuming during class time if the instructor does not stick to a tight schedule for rehearsal and delivery. If the dramatization does not go as the instructor planned, or if one of the role players perceives his or her performance as something of a "failure," skillful handling by the instructor may be necessary to boost self-esteem and encourage positive learning outcomes. Devising the scenarios and roles takes a certain amount of imagination and creativity. Roles must be carefully written to include enough details but not too many and to make the roles "come alive" for the participants but to leave enough room for personalization and ad libbing. Even with careful preplanning, the roles are somewhat dependent on the personalities of the volunteers to play them, and this may negatively affect the key learning points you hoped to make. The best application of this technique is limited to a small class.

Buzz Session (Also Known as Small Discussion Group)

Characteristics. A buzz session is a technique for involving every member of a large class in the discussion. Divide the class into small groups of about five to seven students for a limited time (about 5 to 7 minutes) for discussion. Assign limited and specific objectives. Each buzz group selects a leader and recorder. The leader's responsibility is to ensure that every member gets to voice his or her opinion, while the recorder writes down the group's comments, preferably as a public record on a flip chart or white board. Either the leader or the recorder reports orally to the rest of the class the group's key points. You will use many of the common principles for group discussion. Buzz groups sometimes evolve into brainstorming sessions.

Advantages. Buzz sessions give quieter students a chance to interact, ask questions, and share ideas; this can be especially useful in a large class. Depending on how you structure the task and your subject, buzz sessions can also be an effective means of reinforcing key concepts and getting the students to apply their new knowledge to practical situations. For example, after you have lectured on several key themes or points, divide the students into as many buzz sessions as you have key themes, and ask questions such as "How does this theme apply to . . . ?" or "Describe this theme in your own words and how it might affect. . . ." Many times students will have a fresh perspective and be more likely to identify with and internalize the learning.

Another technique is to take sections of the textbook and assign each buzz group a section on which they are responsible for reporting. Buzz session members work together on tasks such as defining key terms, providing relevant personal examples, or analyzing deeper implications for their assigned passages. This technique is a welcome break from the monotony of a straight lecture and can be used with even the most technical content.

Disadvantages. You will have to be a tight timekeeper to ensure the buzz sessions do not go beyond their expected time limits. Because of the time restrictions, all students may not get as much opportunity to speak as you would prefer. Another disadvantage is that when several buzz sessions are in progress simultaneously, you cannot monitor all of them at once. There is the slight possibility that erroneous information may be shared by the students that you will not overhear and correct. Sometimes the oral reports become too lengthy and must be abbreviated. You will have to referee on any conflicting results from different buzz groups. At other times students are reluctant to volunteer for the roles of leader and recorder, or you must make those assignments for them.

Panel

Characteristics. A panel is a group of experts who have a structured conversation on a certain topic in full view of the students. Typically a moderator introduces the panel members and asks prepared and/or spontaneous questions to stimulate discussions. Sometimes each panel member will begin with a short, prepared speech (usually about 5 minutes); at other times the format is a more informal exchange among the panel members and the moderator. Usually the panel discussion is followed by an open question-and-answer period with the students.

Advantages. Several different opinions can be presented in a compressed amount of time. Students frequently enjoy the chance to interact with experts in the field and to ask them questions. Informal panels often result in open and stimulating discussions.

Disadvantages. Sometimes complex subjects are oversimplified or misrepresented by panel members. In some extreme cases, panel members may have conflicting or even radical viewpoints of which you were unaware, or they may challenge some of the points on which you have previously instructed the class. You may have to intervene if students try to challenge seriously one or more of the panel members. Make sure you choose a strong moderator who can handle such interpersonal situations and is knowledgeable enough on the topic to ask intelligent and thought-provoking questions.

Field Experience

Characteristics. A field experience is a well-structured, preplanned event in which a group or an individual visits a place that has a related interest to the topic. The visit can be a one-time event or can last over a period of time. Field experiences give students a firsthand look at a real-life situation and put theoretical concepts into practical applications. Depending on circumstances, advance arrangements are made by the student(s), the trip coordinator, or the instructor. These advance arrangements may include preliminary meetings with key personnel on site, setting a schedule, agreeing on roles and responsibilities, obtaining supplementary materials or learning aids, and advising students what they will be seeing or doing. Students visit or work on site doing predesignated tasks. Following the field experience, the instructor reviews what has been seen or accomplished and its significance to the classroom topic.

Advantages. Student interest in the topic is typically stimulated because the topic now can be put into a more meaningful context than more passive learning formats. A direct relationship to the "real world" and the classroom is often made by students, thus overcoming a frequent student criticism with many subjects. Because students are usually entertained, they are more likely to retain key learning concepts. Classroom discussions and lectures can be tied directly back into the students' field experiences.

Disadvantages. Advance preparations often take considerable time and effort. Sometimes the results can be uneven. Factors such as the responsiveness of on-site personnel often have a major impact on the value of the experience. Learning objectives may not be clearly explained to the students in advance, or students may have difficulty relating classroom points or a theoretical model to a more complex or diffuse experience. A well-structured review or worksheet procedure is needed to reinforce the key learning objectives and the overall significance of the field experience.

Picture Making

Characteristics. Picture making is an activity that can be used at any time during more conventional classroom presentations to reinforce key learning points, give students an opportunity to interact, and provide a creative, "fun" break. Divide students into small groups (between three and nine students each) and give each group flip chart paper and a series of colored markers. The students work together to draw a composite picture that represents some aspect of your topic, such as a flowchart of a process or a representation of an issue. For example, if you are teaching a military history class, have the students draw a representative sample of weapons from a certain time period. If you are teaching a psychology class, ask your students to draw visual representations of various abnormal behaviors. After the groups have finished drawing, ask a group spokesperson to explain the picture to the whole class. At times you may want to lead short discussions immediately afterwards to emphasize key points or prod the students to analyze the topic more deeply. Hang the pictures up in full view, and keep the pictures up throughout the class. Sometimes you may let the groups keep their pictures or bring them to later classes.

Advantages. If you are teaching an unpopular subject or a required class that you suspect students resent having to take, this technique can be used as an initial warmup activity during the first class to let the students vent their frustrations. For example, ask the students to draw a "Chemistry Monster." You can use this technique as a useful "yardstick" to gauge your students' frustrations, issues, and problems. Some students are highly "visual learners," and this technique will appeal to them especially. Many students feel a sense of accomplishment and expression by having their artwork displayed.

Disadvantages. Students tend to take as much time as you allow on this type of project, so you will have to monitor and restrict the time closely. You may have to sacrifice precious time from more conventional learning practices. Be sure you use later discussions to tie key learning points to the students' pictures. Picture making requires the extra markers and flip chart paper.

Simulation

Characteristics. A simulation is a detailed account of an event or a scenario that is usually presented as a "case study." The instructor prepares a written description of the fictional or real-life background, key players, assumptions, and sometimes anticipated outcomes or results. Usually the written handout page includes directions to the students about what actions they are to take concerning this information (e.g., answer these questions in small groups) and key questions for them to answer. Divide the class into small buzz groups for them to compare their answers or analysis of the scenario. Ask for oral reports from the small groups, and follow with a general discussion to reinforce your key learning points. Some simulations can be done in several parts spread out over several class sessions, with each part building on the learning acquired from earlier classes and/or readings.

Advantages. Many students like the detailed focus on a practical, "real-world" aspect of a theoretical model. Students may be stimulated by the discussions to see different viewpoints and possible solutions to the problems being presented by the simulation. Another important advantage is that simulations encourage students' analytical and problem-solving skills.

Disadvantages. Some students may dismiss the scenarios as irrelevant to their situations. Others may think the simulations are either too simplistic or too complex. Instructor skill, time, and practice are requirements for writing effective and meaningful scenarios. Development time for perfecting the simulation can be deceivingly long, and often the instructor will not be able to gauge the simulation's true effectiveness until he or she has actually tried it out with a class. Again, simulations will require extensive classroom time and a closely monitored clock.

Choosing and Using Presentation Aids

Why Use Presentation Aids?

Why should you use presentation aids? Because you want to communicate. As much as 85% of the information received and stored by the brain comes through the eyes. Thus visual aids are crucial in a training or education setting. Both hearing and seeing something greatly increases the chance of retention by the learner.

The most common presentation aids used in the college classroom are handouts (print), flip charts (easel with large pads of paper and markers), slickboards (white boards used with dry-erase markers) and chalkboards, transparencies (for overhead projectors) and slides, and videotapes. These are the types of presentation aids discussed here.

General Guidelines for All Presentation Aids

Presentation aids are used to
- Keep participants' attention by providing visual stimulation and changing the pace of a lesson
- Demonstrate and illustrate your messages, adding credibility to your presentation
- Emphasize key points to help aid retention

Your presentation aids should
- Convey your intended message
- Supplement the presentation, not dominate or distract
- Be colorful—use two or three colors to add interest and clarity
- Concentrate on one or two key items at a time
- Be used at the right moment and put away when not needed
- Be visible *(large and legible)* to entire group
- Be prepared in advance whenever possible
- Be accurate

When using any presentation aid:
- Prepare yourself: Familiarize yourself with the aid, practice using it, and plan when you will use it.
- Prepare the environment: Arrange the furniture, equipment, lighting, and materials for maximum viewing and hearing; test equipment; ensure extra bulbs, pens, etc.
- Prepare the group: Explain the aid you will be using, its purpose, and what you expect students to gain from the experience. Allow those with poor vision/hearing to position themselves to best advantage.
- Use the aid properly.
- Solicit feedback to find out whether your purpose is achieved.

Types of Presentation Aids

There are five basic presentation aids: handout materials, flip charts, slickboards and chalkboards, overhead transparencies and slides, and videotapes.

Table 4.4   Handout Materials

Use of Handouts	Suggestions
Support lecture	Correlate handouts with your lecture; cover all points in sequence. Include a small to medium amount of detail, depending on the topic and audience. Leave plenty of space for note taking. Hand out before lecture.
Support in-class activities	Hand out schedules, charts, and materials that are too long or detailed to show in slides or transparencies. Hand out in-class exercises, self-assessments, role plays, and other materials needed for class interaction. Distribute prior to session or as needed during the session. Number pages and put in sequence to be used.
Summarize	Hand out copies of flip charts, slides, or transparencies used in class. If handouts are intended for note taking, hand them out at beginning of class. Brief summaries of key points can be handed out at end of class.
Supplement class content	Hand out articles and exercises that extend or enrich what was presented in class. (Get permission from copyright holder.) Limit the amount of material that is *most* relevant to the course. Explain the importance of the handout and give a brief summary. Hand out at end of session. Allow time now and later for questions/discussion of the material.

Handout Materials

Some uses of handout materials and suggestions for their use are included in Table 4.4.

Further suggestions are as follows:

- When designing handouts, use lots of white space, headings, indentation, bolding, fonts, point sizes, and so forth for emphasis of key points, and use flowcharts, boxes, and decision tables for easier "digestion" of information. Your handouts will look more professional and communicate better.

■ Check for content accuracy, spelling, and grammar. Make originals as "clean" as possible for better quality reproduction.

■ Present your handouts in systematic fashion: well organized and ready to go into a folder or notebook, punched if students prefer.

■ Use colored paper for emphasis or to separate sections of material.

■ Bind the materials for use in class separately from materials for later reference.

■ Seal selected handouts (such as case study or exercise solutions) with adhesive labels, and state that they should not be opened until the appropriate time.

■ Develop a format page with graphics or logo that can be used for printing each handout. This will give the material a packaged, uniform look. Keep it simple, though, to avoid a cluttered look.

Flip Charts

Flip charts can be used to gather ideas from the group or to structure, define, and explain your presentation. They can be created in advance or spontaneously during the session. They are easy to use, permanent, inexpensive, and always available. Avoid using flip charts with groups of over 40 people because the entire group will not be able to see them.

Here are some tips for preparing flip charts:

■ Keep them simple: one idea per page.

■ Use no more than eight lines per page, as few words as possible.

■ Use colored markers: dark for text, light for highlighting.

■ Use both words and pictures.

■ Use large print: 3 inches high for average room.

■ Paper-clip preprepared pages for easy finding at the right time.

■ Make changes by cutting out section with a razorblade and taping clean paper to the back. No one will notice.

■ For a look of spontaneity, prepare flip charts in advance with light pencil. Then copy over during the session.

■ With preprepared flip charts, write light pencil notes to yourself in the margins. Your audience cannot see them.

■ Use graph paper or colored paper as alternatives.

Here are some tips for using flip charts:

- Use two or more flip charts: one for spontaneous material and one with prepared visuals.
- Use flip charts to outline results of work groups for presentation and discussion with whole group.
- Talk to the participants, not to the flip chart.
- As pages are completed, tape them individually to the wall for future reference. Pretear the tape and stick to side of flip chart stand.

Slickboards and Chalkboards

Slickboards and chalkboards are best used for spontaneous presentations. They can illustrate diagrams, charts and graphs, key points and calculations and can record group thoughts. They are most useful for groups of 40 people or fewer because people in the back of a large room will not be able to see. A disadvantage is that the content cannot be saved without someone taking notes.

Here are some tips for effective use of slickboards and chalkboards:

- Begin with a clean board, several pieces of chalk or markers, and clean erasers.
- Use dark colors for text, light colors for highlights.
- Keep writing brief. Use key words or phrases.
- Keep letters 2 inches high for every 25 feet of viewing distance.
- Print clearly in upper- and lowercase letters for legibility.
- Talk to the students, not to the board.
- You can predraw your material and conceal it with flip chart paper until ready to use.
- Use one section for prepared material that will stay during the entire session, another section of board for spontaneous "creations."

Overhead Transparencies and Slides

Transparencies and slides can be used in large rooms and with large audiences. Slides require a dark room, whereas transparencies can be used with the lights on (promotes wakefulness of students and allows note taking). Slides must be preprepared and can provide excellent color, photographs, realistic illustrations, and special effects. Transparencies may be less expensive and can be preprepared or spontaneous.

Most university media centers will help you produce slides and transparencies using photography and/or computer-generated graphics. You can make your own transparencies using word processing and/or graphics packages. Print out onto acetate sheets on a laser printer, or print out on paper and then make the transparency on a copy machine.

Here are some tips for preparing transparencies and slides:

- Limit to one idea or concept per screen.
- Use no more than six words per line, no more than six lines.
- Use pictures. "A picture is worth a thousand words." Really!
- Use cartoons and illustrations from magazines. Get permission.
- Use Helvetica typeface at size 36 and 32. Use upper- and lowercase letters. Stay away from any type less than 24 point and ornate fonts.
- Check for readability at a distance.
- Limit use of borders, banners, and underlines.
- Arrange horizontally (landscape) if possible.
- Allow at least a ⅜-inch border.
- Proofread for errors, check sequence.
- Use colored acetate backgrounds for interest appeal.
- Use overlays on the basic transparency to build an idea. The same effect can be achieved with successive slides, or electronically if slides are on a computer.

Here are some tips for using slides and transparencies:

- Be sure you and the projector do not block participants' view. Align projector perpendicular to screen to avoid distortion.
- Dim lights directly over the screen.
- Point to the transparency itself rather than to the screen.
- Do not read what is on the screen. Comment on key points. Speak loudly to be heard above the hum of the machine.
- Remove transparency when going on to another topic or activity. Turn off the overhead or slide projector when not in use.
- Progressively reveal key points on a transparency by sliding down a cover sheet. For slides, the same effect can be achieved by using several slides or electronically when slides are on a computer.

Videotapes

Videotapes are used in college to gain attention; demonstrate skills, procedures, or interpersonal behaviors; present factual material and overviews; stimulate discussion of issues; introduce humor; present case study material for class exercises; and summarize lesson topics. Because video combines motion, color, narration, sound effects, and music, it is an especially effective medium for simulating real-life situations and for delivering attitudinal, motivational messages. Video is also useful in taping classroom interaction for playback and analysis. Videotapes add instant pizzazz to your lessons and are easy to use, transport, and store.

Two common formats are used: VHS or ½-inch tape and ¾-inch tape. Be sure to specify which you are using when you order equipment for playback! Besides the tape player, you need a monitor (TV). More than one, or an extra-large screen, will be needed for groups larger than 20.

Most university libraries have videotape collections you can use, and you may be able to borrow tapes from your workplace. You may even be able to use your university's production facilities to create your own teaching tapes. Contact your instructional media facility for advice on this.

Here are some tips for using videotapes:

- Select tapes that really fit your course objectives. Use "entertainment-value" tapes sparingly as attention getters only.
- Be thoroughly familiar with the tape before class. Check out equipment before class.
- Place monitor(s) for maximum viewing.
- Darken the room as necessary for visibility.
- Explain to the class the purpose of viewing the tape. Show how it fits into the overall instructional plan.
- Stress the points on which viewers should focus or questions they should seek to answer. You may even want to provide a worksheet to facilitate note taking and follow-up discussion. Structure the discussion following the tape. Use small group or whole-class interaction.

The use of these methods and strategies can produce professional lessons that include the adult learner in meaningful interactions. Consequently, genuine and lasting learning can take place, and you, as an adjunct instructor, can enjoy with the learner a mutually successful experience.

References

Daniels, W. R. (1986). *Group power I: A manager's guide to using task-force meetings.* San Diego: University Associates, Inc.

Davis, R. H., Fry, J. P., & Alexander, L. T. (1977). *The discussion method: Guides for the improvement of instruction in higher education.* East Lansing: Michigan State University, Instructional Media Center.

Additional Suggested Readings

American Society for Training and Development. (1985). *How to create a good learning environment* (InfoLine Publication Rep. No. 8506). Alexandria, VA: Author.

American Society for Training and Development. (1986). *Alternatives to lecture* (Info-Line Publication Rep. No. 8602). Alexandria, VA: Author.

American Society for Training and Development. (1986). *Creative effective workshops* (Info-Line Publication Rep. No. 8604). Alexandria, VA: Author.

American Society for Training and Development. (1987). *First-rate technical and skills training* (Info-Line Publication Rep. No. 8706). Alexandria, VA: Author.

American Society for Training and Development. (1987). *Top-notch training with partners: Team training, panel discussion, guest speaker* (Info-Line Publication Rep. No. 8705). Alexandria, VA: Author.

American Society for Training and Development. (1988). *Basic training for trainers* (Info-Line Publication Rep. No. 8808). Alexandria, VA: Author.

Bell, C. R., & Margolis, F. J. (1986). *Instructing for results.* San Diego: University Associates, Inc.

Brilhart, J. (1967). *Effective group discussion.* Dubuque, IA: William C. Brown.

Cranton, P. (1989). *Planning instruction for adult learners.* Toronto: Wall & Thompson.

Daniels, W. R. (1990). *Group power II: A manager's guide to conducting regular meetings.* San Diego: University Associates, Inc.

Decler, P. J., & Nathan, B. R. (1985). *Behavior modeling training.* New York: Praeger.

Department of Education, George Washington University. (1974). *Group methods and techniques.* Washington, DC: Author.

Doyle, M., & Straus, D. (1984). *How to make meetings work: The new interaction method.* New York: Berkley.

Gall, D., & Gall, J. P. (1976). The discussion method. In National Society for the Study of Education (Ed.), *The psychology of teaching methods* (pp. 166-216). Chicago: Author.

Hill, W. F. (1969). *Learning through discussion.* Beverly Hills, CA: Sage.

Maier, N. R. F. (1963). *Problem-solving discussions and conferences: Leadership methods and skills.* New York: McGraw-Hill.

McKeachie, W. (1965). *Teaching tips.* Ann Arbor, MI: George Wahr.

Olmstead, J. A. (1974). *Small group instruction: Theory and practice*. Alexandria, VA: Human Resources Research Organization.

Phillips, J. (1983). *Handbook of training evaluation and measurement methods*. Houston: Gulf.

Potter, D., & Andersen, M. P. (1963). *Discussion: A guide to effective practice*. Belmont, CA: Wadsworth.

Roseborough, M. E. (1953). Experimental studies of small groups. *Psychological Bulletin, 50*, 275-303.

Schmuck, R. A., & Schmuck, P. A. (1975). *Group process in the classroom*. Dubuque, IA: William C. Brown.

Sharan, S., & Sharan, Y. (1976). *Small-group teaching*. Englewood Cliffs, NJ: Educational Technology Publications.

Appendix 4.1
Checklist for Group Facilitation

■ Leader Responsibilities

_____ 1. **Arranges seating of participants** so that everyone can see and hear each other.

_____ 2. **States and confirms the agenda.** Obtains answers to
   A. What is the objective of this discussion?
   B. How much time should be spent on each topic?

_____ 3. **States and/or confirms "ground rules"** to be followed

   Typical Ground Rules for Group Discussion

   A. All points of view will be accepted and posted; criticism (evaluation) is ruled out until later.
   B. Interruptions will be "gatekept."
   C. Silence is okay; one needs time to think.
   D. Disagreement is okay as long as it's about ideas, not personalities.
   E. Evaluation of the content and the process comes last.

_____ 4. **Elicits ideas, opinions, feelings.** Uses recognition, silence, nonverbal coaxing, etc., to get participation "What do you think about the topic?"

_____ 5. **Posts and confirms key points generated.** Lists, publicly, brief summaries of what has been said

Quickly prints a summary statement of what has been said (in own words) and inquires, "Is this correct?"

_____ 6. **Elicits clarification or elaboration.** Asks for examples or illustrations

"Could you give us an example or illustration to help us understand?"

_____ 7. **Recognizes or encourages contributions.** Listens attentively to others' ideas. Reinforces them by adding own ideas or approves them verbally or nonverbally

Nod of head, smile, or "That's an interesting point."

_____ 8. **States or reflects feelings.** Describes own concerns or feelings about what is happening or restates what he or she thinks others are feeling and asks for confirmation

"It seems to me that we're confused. Is that true? Remember the topic we're discussing is . . ."

_____ 9. **Gatekeeps.** Asks someone to hold off introducing a new topic while another is being discussed; intervenes to prevent people from talking at the same time

"Hold it! Jane, please finish what you were saying. Then we'll get to you, Sam."

_____ 10. **Tests consensus.** Checks with others to see if they agree with points made or with conclusions stated or to see if everyone is ready to proceed to another topic, issue, or step in problem-solving sequence

"Are there any more ideas about this topic? Are we ready to evaluate or analyze what it means now?"

_____ 11. **Summarizes.** Pulls together related ideas; tries to draw conclusion

"Let's see, from what's been posted, it seems that we agree that . . ."

_____ 12. **Analyzes, evaluates.** Asks "Why?" about what has been posted; inquires about supporting assumptions, values, and facts

"Why do you think you felt this way about this topic?"

_____ 13. **Derives principles or generalizations.** Guides others into either discovering basic principles or transferring conclusions to new settings

"What basic principles seem to be at work here?" "How does this apply in your field?"

Participant Responsibilities (in Addition to Assisting With the Above)

_____ 14. **Gives information or opinions.** Offers facts or generalizations; makes suggestions honestly, forcefully, and spontaneously

"Here's what I see as the key point of . . ."

_____ 15. **Clarifies or elaborates.** Clears up confusion by restating (in his or her own words) what someone else has said or by asking for or giving examples or illustrations

"Let me see if I understand. Is this what you're trying to say?"

_____ 16. **Accepts others' ideas** or disagreements as ideas to be explored, not personal attacks. Looks for a positive side.

"You certainly see things differently. But that's interesting. Let's see . . ."

_____ 17. **Ignores aggressiveness,** attempts to impress, and competitive behavior, or points out their dysfunctional and counterproductive consequences

"When people dominate the discussion, I feel frustrated and soon 'tune out.' "

Appendix 4.2
Group Membership Behavior That Facilitates Discussion

▩ General

_____ Be open to and reflect on others' ideas and disagreements.

_____ Be honest and forceful in getting your ideas and disagreements out.

_____ Accept others' ideas or disagreements as ideas to be explored, not personal attacks. Look for a positive side.

_____ Speak out spontaneously; try to integrate or synthesize others' ideas.

_____ Ignore aggressiveness, attempts to impress, and competitive behavior; point out their dysfunctional and counterproductive consequences.

_____ Keep on the topic; be sure you know the goal of the discussion.

▩ Specific

_____ Restate (in your own words) what someone else has said to make sure you understand it.

_____ Give an example to clarify the meaning.

_____ Ask someone else in the group to give an example.

_____ Add to what someone else has said.

_____ State the ways in which your understanding or interpretation differs from that stated by another student.

_____ Ask for clarification on points you don't understand.

_____ Ask or state how new points contradict, substantiate, or amplify previously developed points.

_____ Summarize into compact statements points others have made.

_____ Ask for or give help in stating ideas more concisely.

_____ Listen carefully for and try to state puzzling aspects of the material that are giving the group trouble.

_____ Call the group's attention to and reinforce a comment that seems particularly helpful.

_____ Ask or state why and how new material can be useful to members.

_____ Test the usefulness of new material by describing a situation for which it should be useful.

_____ Give examples you know for which the new material helps to explain or helps you to apply it.

_____ State questions to help the group evaluate new material.

5

Connecting With Cooperative Learning

BARBARA J. MILLIS

This chapter on cooperative learning provides one of the most leading-edge ideas in the entire book. Barbara Millis points out that the "influx of diverse students precludes the practice of traditional delivery methods in which authority figures lecture to passive students." The premise of this chapter is that university teaching can no longer be just "adequate" but must be more creative and flexible. This message is of particular importance to adjunct faculty who may fall into the trap of teaching the way they were taught 10 years ago.

Millis carefully describes the theory, methods, and objectives of cooperative learning. This technique is predicated on active learning, cooperation, and respect for individual learning styles. It provides a unique classroom structure that can be used to balance more typical methods of learning, such as listening to lectures, reading predigested texts, memorizing, and taking multiple-choice tests.

On the surface, cooperative learning merely looks like "group work."
However, Millis outlines a definitive approach that requires detailed lesson
plans with carefully positioned transitions, checkpoints, and outcomes. As
she points out, "Too many students have been burned by haphazard group
assignments." In contrast, this chapter describes a series of disciplined
methods that ensures commitment, group monitoring, individual ac-
countability, equal contribution, and mutual coaching.

The beauty of cooperative learning is that it goes beyond teaching "just
content." An additional benefit is skill development in group process,
social interaction, problem solving, critical thinking, and writing and
presentation techniques. Through this chapter, adjuncts will discover the
behind-the-scenes work, creativity, and preparation that are required to
produce successful group assignments.

Boice (1992) painted a bleak picture of the academic landscape faced by new faculty members. Isolated and uncertain, they receive little support during their first few years in traditional academia. If these carefully selected, long-term faculty members receive so little, the fate of thousands of part-time, adjunct faculty members must be far worse. Adjuncts are now a permanent part of the academic workforce and teach substantial parts of college curriculum (Gappa, 1993). In fact, Masters (1992) noted that Department of Education statistics indicate that their ranks grew 18%, to 299,794, from 1983 to 1989. Too often, despite their numbers, part-time faculty—defined as teaching-oriented faculty in less-than-full-time non-tenure-track positions—are treated as second-class, marginal employees. Despite evidence that adjunct faculty members bring to institutions strong academic credentials often augmented by "real-world" experience, plus enthusiasm and energetic approaches to teaching (Gappa and Leslie, 1993), they often do not receive either the respect or the support their contributions deserve.

Because adjunct lecturers often face some of the toughest teaching challenges in academia, they must be unusually prepared to meet them. Adjuncts typically teach adult learners (learners who are both demanding and discerning) at unusual, extended hours (evenings when students and faculty have already put in a full workday, or weekends, when family, work, and recreational draws can siphon off energy or attendance) in unusual locations (locked doors or "No Parking" signs can be unpleasant realities).

Today's students require more creative and flexible approaches to teaching. They bring a different set of experiences and expectations. Some, for example—often adults successful in their professions—may view their instructors as equal partners, not as authority figures. As Giezkowski (1992) concluded, "Clearly, the range of roles that the teacher of adult students assumes is broader than that for traditional-aged college students" (p. 133). Furthermore, many of these adult learners will be from diverse backgrounds. The influx of diverse students precludes the practice of traditional delivery methods in which authority figures lecture to passive students.

To meet these teaching challenges, adjunct faculty members must muster all the known pedagogical ammunition. They cannot merely be adequate in the classroom: They must help their students—the nontraditional students as well as the traditional—to excel academically. Gaff (1992) emphasized that " 'business as usual' in any pedagogical program—listening to lectures, reading a predigested text, memorization, and multiple choice tests—will not allow students to learn what even the most fervently argued courses have to teach" (p. 35). Thus innovative teaching strategies must be introduced—proven ones predicated on active learning, cooperation, and respect for individual learning styles. Increasingly, both researchers and classroom instructors are recommending cooperative learning.

What Is Cooperative Learning?

Solidly grounded in theory, research, and practice, cooperative learning is a systematic, highly structured pedagogical approach that places students in small, often heterogenous groups to accomplish mutually rewarding tasks.

Underlying cooperative learning is a philosophical framework based on respect for students and a belief in their potential for academic success. Cooperative learning is not an elitist approach to education with a "weed 'em out, let the students fall where they may" mentality. Thus it is particularly appropriate for the nontraditional students that many adjunct faculty find in their classes.

To operationalize the egalitarian philosophy of cooperative learning, practitioners use specific tools called *structures*. Structures are essentially content-free procedures, such as a brainstorming technique called Roundtable, that can be used in virtually any discipline for a variety of purposes. When content is added to a structure—for example, when the Roundtable structure is used with small groups to ask composition students to generate possible topics for a classification paper or is used to challenge political science students to identify the ethical issues facing Congress—a specific classroom activity is created. When a series of activities are linked, they become a lesson or unit plan. Many cooperative learning practitioners plan class meetings with such care that they prepare ahead of time their own "script" with details such as transition cues and activity time estimates; often they post on the board a specific class agenda. Structuring class activities—which means being well prepared!—is a hallmark of cooperative learning, probably a welcome sign to those who fear group work will be considered a loose teaching philosophy practiced by lazy instructors intent on "winging it."

Far from being a loose teaching philosophy, cooperative learning, because of its structured and hence accountable approach, builds in components that lead to successful student learning and positive interactions. Two key components of cooperative learning that distinguish it from other, less structured forms of collaborative learning are positive interdependence (students have a vested interest in working together) and individual accountability (students cannot coast on the work of others; everyone must contribute).

Positive interdependence occurs when instructors set up a "win-win" situation. Students who help one another find that all group members benefit. Instructors can establish these win-win situations through careful planning. They can establish, for instance, mutual goals for students placed in permanent learning teams, such as reaching consensus on a problem's solution. They can offer mutual rewards, such as additional points for all team members based on a composite of the overall group's improvement after team members have coached one another for ongoing quizzes. They can encourage students to assume mutually dependent roles within a learning team, such as leader, spokesperson, or recorder, that are rotated frequently to ensure that everyone has an opportunity for growth and development. Perhaps most important, they can offer structured tasks that allow students to work together constructively—much as they do or will do in the workplace—on the meaningful "real-world" tasks that appeal in particular to adult learners.

Even though students may coach one another in learning teams, they—and the instructor—must always be mindful of the second key component of cooperative learning: individual accountability. Students cannot coast on the achievements of others; they must be responsible for their own learning. Hence most instructors assess student learning much as they always have, on the basis of individual quizzes and tests. If group projects are required (such projects are not necessarily a hallmark of cooperative learning), then instructors must determine—often through peer and self-assessment—the relative value of each student's contribution.

Appropriate grouping is also essential. As indicated earlier, students are placed in small groups. Most practitioners suggest four as the optimal number (Johnson, Johnson, & Smith, 1991, are an exception with three) because groups of this size will usually be inclusive (trios sometimes result in an odd-person-out dynamic); they can function meaningfully despite an occasional absence; they are small enough to allow equitable participation but large enough to contain the diverse talents useful for problem solving; and they lend themselves well to pair work. Most practitioners use instructor-selected groups to ensure heterogeneity, modeling workplace realities and making certain that each group will contain members of varying abilities and attributes to strengthen problem solving. Such groups, sometimes called *learning teams,* are usually permanent, remaining together throughout a semester, or semipermanent, re-forming at the midsemester point. Over time, such groups typically become both cohesive and supportive.

Two further attributes of cooperative learning—social skills and group processing or monitoring—contribute to the successful functioning of these groups. Social skills in a cooperative learning setting go beyond mere courtesy, although sometimes students can use some coaching in the basic social amenities. Skills include listening actively, paraphrasing accurately, questioning skillfully, and providing feedback constructively. Such skills should be modeled and reinforced by the instructor. As students work together in positive environments, they discover and provide both cognitive and motivational support. The team effort allows them to experience and value a variety of thinking patterns and problem-solving approaches. They can—within the comparative safety of the group—respond to different beliefs, ideas, and attitudes; in turn, they will have an audience encouraged to help their thinking grow and develop as they are asked, in constructive ways, to clarify, elaborate, or justify their own ideas.

Because these social skills are so critical to student learning, groups must be carefully monitored and encouraged to conduct their own processing activities to ensure that the environments do remain positive and that genuine learning is occurring. Group roles can contribute to the monitoring effort. Group leaders should be responsible for keeping the teams on task and for making certain that everyone has an opportunity to contribute equitably. They should allow no "put-downs." In addition, the instructor must be actively involved in the classroom activities, moving from group to group to be certain that they are indeed on task and that all members are encouraged to participate. Many benefits accrue from this mobility. Faculty members can determine and influence the degree of learning and pinpoint potential pitfalls that might lead to dysfunctional groups. By listening to student interactions, they can identify areas of confusion and benefit from hearing their lecture content or the textbook material "translated" by students for their classmates.

As should be evident, the instructor's role changes in a cooperative classroom. By becoming a "facilitator" or a "manager" in addition to a "dispenser of knowledge" (few instructors ever forgo lecturing, for good reason), instructors expand their areas of influence and dissolve what Finkel and Monk (1983) dubbed the "Atlas complex," a mind-set of instructor-student expectations that results in teachers bearing all responsibility for the success of a class. For example, if instructors observe inappropriate behavior as they are moving among the learning teams, rather than immediately intervening, they can instead take the leader aside and suggest that he or she address the problem. Monitoring can also be done more formally by the use of a classroom assessment techniques such as the "1-minute paper" (Angelo & Cross, 1993). Students can be asked to record on index cards their responses to such questions as "How did your group work today?" "What could help the group work more smoothly during the next class session?" "What stood in the way of your learning today?" and "What most contributed to your learning today?" It is useful to have students discuss their responses as a way of flushing out and resolving problems. Faculty members can also collect the cards for later review. Having students keep learning logs (journals) also gives instructors valuable insights into group processes, particularly if questions are focused on classroom dynamics and learning outcomes.

The Research Base for Cooperative Learning

The social dynamics and learning outcomes of cooperative learning have been thoroughly researched. Johnson et al. (1991) described the amount of research conducted over the past 90 years as "staggering" and concluded that "far more is known about the efficacy of cooperative learning than about lecturing, . . . the use of technology, or almost any other facet of education" (p. 28). In addition to finding a positive effect on student achievement, they found that cooperative learning significantly affects interpersonal relations:

> As relationships within the class or college become more positive, absenteeism decreases and students' commitment to learning, feelings of personal responsibility to complete the assigned work, willingness to take on difficult tasks, motivation and persistence in working on tasks, satisfaction and morale, willingness to endure pain and frustration to succeed, willingness to defend the college against external criticism or attack, willingness to listen to and be influenced by peers, commitment to peer's success and growth, and productivity and achievement can be expected to increase. (p. 44)

Faculty interested in an overview of the cooperative learning research base should consult this text in its entirety, particularly Chapter 3; Cooper et al. (1990); and the Cooperative Learning Special Interest Group (SIG) of the American Educational Research Association.

Perhaps the most compelling endorsement of cooperative learning has come from a highly credible source, Astin's (1993) comprehensive longitudinal study of the impact of college on undergraduate students. The final chapter makes a number of points significant for all faculty, including adjuncts. Astin concluded that because of the influence of the peer group and the influence of faculty, "How students approach general education (and how the faculty actually deliver the curriculum) is far more important than the formal curricular content and structure" (p. 425). He unequivocally endorsed cooperative learning as a valid and effective pedagogical approach:

> Under what we have come to call cooperative learning methods, where students work together in small groups, students basically teach each other, and our pedagogical resources are multiplied. Classroom research has consistently shown that cooperative learning approaches produce outcomes that are superior to those obtained through traditional competitive approaches, and it may well be that our findings concerning the power of the peer group offer a possible explanation: Cooperative learning may be more potent than traditional methods of pedagogy because it motivates students to become more active and more involved participants in the learning process. This greater involvement could come in at least two different ways. First, students may be motivated to expend more effort if they know their work is going to be scrutinized by peers; and second, students may learn course material in greater depth if they are involved in helping teach it to fellow students. (p. 427)

Given the solid research base on which cooperative learning rests and the testimonials of committed practitioners in all disciplines, adjunct faculty members can be confident that they are embracing a pedagogy that will pay enormous dividends, not just in student achievement, but also in affective ways. Students in well-conducted cooperative classrooms tend to have a more positive attitude toward their subject matter, their classmates, and their instructors.

Creating a Cooperative Classroom

A well-conducted cooperative classroom does not emerge merely because faculty encourage group work. On the contrary, too many students have been burned by haphazard group assignments neglecting the five key elements: positive interdependence, individual accountability, appropriate grouping, social skills, and group processing or monitoring. The worst-case scenarios probably occurred in the 1960s, when well-meaning, "with-it" instructors encouraged students to "get in a group and groove" without a structured focus, often while they were down the hall having a cup of coffee. Even now, however, probably the greatest disservice done to students—particularly adult commuter students with many other demands on their time—is to assign a group project with undifferentiated group grades for all members and expect the teams to "work it out," often out of class, under the rationalization that this is how things operate in the workplace.

As Cooper (1990) cautioned, "The three most important things in setting up a Cooperative Learning classroom are Structure, Structure and Structure" (p. 1). The instructor has an obligation to organize and orchestrate classroom activities. If these activities deviate from student expectations, a good starting point for clarification is the course syllabus. Faculty members should include clear explanations in the syllabus of the rationale for group work, its nature and purpose, and their expectations. They should also discuss all aspects of the educational process, including the evaluation system. Brookfield (1991) cautioned:

> Being clear about why you teach is crucial, but it is not enough in and of itself; you must also be able to communicate to your students the values, beliefs, and purposes comprising your rationale. You cannot assume that students will understand your rationale or be immediately convinced that your most deeply held convictions have value for them as well. (p. 22)

The syllabus, too, should be free of any classroom practices or course policies, such as grading on the curve, that pit students against one another competitively. The evaluation system, as indicated earlier, should be predicated on individual accountability. Everyone has an opportunity to excel—supported, but not carried by teammates—under an equitable, well-thought-out grading policy based on high but attainable standards.

Thus, when you are assigning students to permanent or semipermanent learning teams, an essential practice for genuine cooperative learning, it is useful to explain your basis for the groupings. In my junior-level children's literature class, for example, I collect data sheets from students and note on them during introductions ethnic or cultural distinctions so that I can carefully assign students on the basis of the following relevant criteria: gender (males are often in short supply), academic experience (I want an English major, if possible, in every group), age (I once deliberately formed a successful team with a grandmother auditing the course and an 18-year-old female first-year student), children (not a relevant concern in other courses, but important in children's literature because parents can share firsthand experiences with children and books), and ethnicity (because the course content deals with the value of multiculturalism, I am up front about wanting students to appreciate the viewpoints of a variety of classmates). Each discipline area will have important criteria that will ensure balance in the teams. Accounting professors, for example, may distribute students according to their intended emphasis.

Students need to be assured that the majority of their group work will be done in class. Part-time working adult students—but also an increasing number of working traditional-aged students—will be willing to "burn the midnight oil" on independent homework assignments but may be unable to coordinate schedules for team meetings outside of class. Setting up such teacher-directed expectations can create frustration for students unable to meet what they perceive as unfair demands on their time and can create frustration for teammates who perceive them as neglecting their necessary contributions.

After the up-front planning and group formation concerns are resolved, instructors need to know how to proceed on a daily basis. Here the "structure, structure, structure" admonition carries particular weight. All activities should be carefully tied to course objectives and their value emphasized. Adults, even more than traditional students, resist what they regard as frivolous activities.

One early activity, however, that may initially seem unimportant can pay enormous dividends down the road. Students, once they are in their learning teams and have become acquainted with each other and with the course expectations, can go through a relatively short but significant team-building exercise based on the behaviors they expect from teammates. The activity asks students to list their individual expectations of teammates' behavior, then to pair to consolidate their ideas, and finally to forge mutually agreed-on team expectations—expectations that can play a critical role in group processing or monitoring. If teams behave in nonproductive ways—a relatively rare occurrence in well-conducted classrooms—then the documentation established by the teams helps the leader and other teammates to resolve difficulties based on lapses from the team norms established early on. Students tend to place stricter demands on themselves than teachers would ever do: "We will attend all possible class meetings and notify team members of absences," "Absent members will be coached so that they are 'up to speed,' " "We will respect one another and listen attentively to all opinions," and so forth.

Another important classroom management technique is the quiet signal. Students placed in groups with structured tasks to complete with clearly defined roles and time limits will, almost without exception, wax enthusiastic. The instructor, however, must maintain control of the classroom dynamics, particularly because whole-class summaries and authority-driven lectures are important to all students, even those who embrace the team learning concept. Faculty members can sometimes make mistakes, for instance, if they fail to provide instructor-sanctioned closure for group activities, even if the closure only validates the conclusions of the team-generated results. It is important, therefore, that instructors have a quick and easy way to bring students back to attention.

With the adult learners/nontraditional students adjunct professors often teach, it is often best to work out an appropriate quiet signal with the class's consent. Most often, students will agree to accept a raised hand signal, one signifying that students should finish their sentence, turn to classmates and alert them to the signal, and then, raising their hand, turn their attention to the instructor. Within seconds, an instructor using this raised hand signal can regain the attention of a lecture hall. In smaller classes, instructors might want to substitute or augment the raised hand with an auditory signal such as a tinkling bell or even the shrill insistence of an electronic timer to signal the close of structured team activities. The timer has the added benefit of reinforcing a sense of on-task behavior.

Some Selected Cooperative Learning Structures

As has been emphasized earlier, a cooperative learning classroom is predicated on an underlying philosophy based on the potential of all students to succeed. It also operates under the assumption that such success is fostered by the student-to-student interactions that can take place in permanent or semipermanent student learning teams. The day-to-day classroom operations in a classroom, however, are carried out or "operationalized" by specific structures. Following is a brief descriptive list of some of the most common structures used in university and college classrooms; these structures work well with all students, but adjunct instructors will be particularly pleased with their efficacy with adult learners.

- *Think-Pair-Share.* In this activity, developed by Frank Lyman (1981), the instructor poses a question, preferably one demanding analysis, evaluation, or synthesis, and gives students about a minute to think through an appropriate response. This "wait-time" can be spent in writing also. Students then turn to their partners and share their responses. In the last stage, which may be omitted because much learning/processing has already occurred, student responses can be shared with a learning team, with a larger group, or with an entire class during a follow-up discussion. The caliber of discussion is enhanced by this quick technique, and all students have an opportunity to learn by both reflection and verbalization.

- *Concerns.* On the basis of a teacher-determined criterion such as their stands on a controversial issue, students divide themselves into four large groups. This structure results in homogeneous groups who, depending on the numbers involved, can participate in a group discussion if the overall groups are small or can be further divided for specific classroom activities into four-member teams or pairs.

- *Three-Step Interview.* Common as an icebreaker or a team-building exercise, this structure can also be used to share ideas such as hypotheses or reactions to a film or article. It can also be used to focus specific content. Students interview one another in pairs, alternating roles. They then share in a four-member learning team, composed of two pairs, the information or insights gleaned from the paired interview. Prior learning experiences can be highlighted in this exercise.

- *Numbered Heads Together.* Members of learning teams, usually composed of four individuals, count off: 1, 2, 3, and 4. The teacher poses a question, usually factual in nature but requiring some higher-order thinking skills. Students discuss the question, making certain that every group member knows the answer. The instructor calls a specific number, and a designated team member (1, 2, 3, or 4) responds as group spokesperson. Again, students benefit from the verbalization, and the peer coaching helps both the high and the low achievers. Class time is usually better spent because less time is wasted on inappropriate responses and because all students become actively involved with the material. Because no one knows which number the teacher will call, all team members have a vested interest in being able to articulate the appropriate response. Giving a team rather than a person answer helps usually reticent students to speak up with confidence.

■ *Roundtable.* In this brainstorming technique, adults in a learning team write in turn on a single pad of paper, saying their ideas aloud as they write. As the tablet circulates, more and more information is added until various aspects of a topic are explored. Within 3 minutes or less, teams can generate a wide range of ideas that can often be used in other class activities.

■ *Co-op Cards.* Useful for memorization and review, students coach each other using flashcards. Each student prepares a set of flashcards with a question on the front and the answer on the back. When a student answers a question correctly, the partner hands over the card. If the answer is incorrect, the partner gives a hint, then shows the answer and keeps the card. They continue going through the set until all questions have been answered correctly. The pair then reverse roles, using the second set of questions and answers prepared by the other partner until both students have mastered both sets of questions.

■ *Jigsaw.* The faculty member divides an assignment or topic into four parts, with one person from each "home" learning team volunteering to become an "expert" on one of the parts. Four expert teams with members from each home team then work together to master their fourth of the material and to discover the best way to help others learn it. All experts then reassemble in their home learning teams, where they teach the other group members. This strategy was originally described by Aronson (1978).

Once adjunct lecturers become accustomed to these structures, they will be able to mix and match or combine ideas creatively to invent class-room activities that encourage active learning and group affiliations.

Conclusion

In a review of the research literature on teaching and learning in the college classroom, McKeachie, Pintrich, Lin, and Smith (1986) concluded, "The best answer to the question, 'What is the most effective method of teaching,' is that it depends on the goal, the student, the content, and the teacher. But the next best answer is, 'Students teaching other students' " (p. 63). Hassard (1990) summarized some of the benefits of cooperative learning:

> Educational practitioners such as David and Roger Johnson, Robert Slavin, and Spencer Kagan reported that cooperative learning resulted in high academic achievement; provided a vehicle for students to learn from one another; gave educators an alternative to the individual, competitive model; and was successful in improving relationships in multiethnic classrooms. (p. viii)

Despite these benefits, faculty typically voice concerns about cooperative learning arising from three sources: (a) their own misgivings about implementation ("I will lose control," "It will take too much time away from content," "I don't handle groups well," "My classroom physically will not permit group work," "I don't have time for new preparations," "I don't know how to evaluate students fairly"), (b) their assumptions about student acceptance ("Students will perceive this as 'busy work,' " "Students expect me to lecture," "Some students won't want to participate"), and (c) their fears about censure by colleagues and/or administrators ("They will think I've given up demanding standards," "They will perceive my classroom as chaotic," "I will be accused of subverting department 'norms' ").

For new practitioners, all these concerns have validity, but many faculty, adjunct and otherwise, have successfully embraced cooperative learning techniques. Few ever return to "teaching as usual." To succeed, adjunct faculty should understand both the theory and the structures of cooperative learning; they should begin on a small scale, introducing new structures as they become comfortable with the old; and they should clearly explain to students (and perhaps to colleagues) the rationale and value of all activities.

"Teaching as usual" will no longer suffice in a global, connected world where new technologies demand lifelong learning and diverse societies require the ability to live and work harmoniously with many different people. As Ekroth (1990) noted, "Today's professors are challenged to teach a student population increasingly diverse in age, levels of academic preparation, styles of learning, and cultural background. Professors are now expected not only to cover material, but also to help students to think critically, write skillfully, and speak competently"

(p. 1). Adjunct faculty must strive to celebrate student diversity—minorities, older students, part-time learners, underprepared underachievers—and to find ways to both motivate and prepare their students for the complexity of the modern world.

References

Angelo, T. A., & Cross, K. P. (1993). *Classroom assessment techniques: A handbook for college teachers* (2nd ed.). San Francisco: Jossey-Bass.

Aronson, E. (1978). *The jigsaw classroom.* Beverly Hills, CA: Sage.

Astin, A. W. (1993). *What matters in college? Four critical years revisited.* San Francisco: Jossey-Bass.

Boice, R. (1992). *The new faculty member: Supporting and fostering professional development.* San Francisco: Jossey-Bass.

Brookfield, S. D. (1991). *The skillful teacher. On technique, trust, and responsiveness in the classroom.* San Francisco: Jossey-Bass.

Cooper, J. (1990, May). Cooperative learning and college teaching: Tips from the trenches. *Teaching Professor, 4*(5), 1-2.

Cooper, J., Prescott, S., Cook, L., Smith, L., Mueck, R., & Cuseo, J. (1990). *Cooperative learning and college instruction.* Long Beach: California State University Foundation.

Ekroth, L. (1990, Winter/Spring). Why professors don't change. *Teaching Excellence: Toward the Best in the Academy* [newsletter]. Stillwater, OK: Professional and Organizational Development Network in Higher Education.

Finkel, D. L., & Monk, G. S. (1983). Teachers and learning groups: Dissolution of the Atlas complex. In C. Bouton & R. Y. Garth (Eds.), *Learning in groups* (pp. 83-97). San Francisco: Jossey-Bass.

Gaff, J. G. (1992). Beyond politics: The educational issues inherent in multicultural education. *Change: The Magazine of Higher Learning, 24*(1), 31-35.

Gappa, J. M. (1993, March). *Integrating the invisible faculty: Strengthening academic programs with part-timers.* Presentation at the National Conference on Higher Education of the American Association for Higher Education, Washington, DC.

Gappa, J. M., & Leslie, D. W. (1993). *The invisible faculty: Improving the status of part-timers in higher education.* San Francisco: Jossey-Bass.

Giezkowski, W. (1992). The influx of older students can revitalize college teaching. *Chronicle of Higher Education, 38*(28), 133-143.

Hassard, J. (1990). *Science experiences: Cooperative learning and the teaching of science.* Menlo Park, CA: Addison-Wesley.

Johnson, D. W., Johnson, R. T., & Smith, K. A. (1991). *Cooperative learning: Increasing college faculty instructional productivity* (ASHE-ERIC Higher Education Rep. No. 4). Washington, DC: George Washington University, School of Education and Human Development.

Lyman, F. (1981). The responsive classroom discussion. In A. S. Anderson (Ed.), *Mainstreaming.* College Park: University of Maryland, College of Education.

Masters, B. A. (1992, October 21). Part-time profs: New campus class. *Washington Post,* pp. A1, A7.

McKeachie, W. J., Pintrich, P. R., Lin, Y., & Smith, D. A. (1986). *Teaching and learning in the college classroom: A review of the research literature.* Ann Arbor: University of Michigan.

Additional Suggested Readings

Bonwell, C. C., & Eison, J. A. (1991). *Active learning: Creating excitement in the classroom* (ASHE-ERIC Higher Education Rep. No. 1). Washington, DC: George Washington University, School of Education and Human Development.

Boyer, E. L. (1990). *Scholarship reconsidered: Priorities of the professorate.* Princeton, NJ: Carnegie Foundation for the Advancement of Teaching.

Cooper, I. L., & Mueck, R. (1989). Cooperative/collaborative learning: Research and practice (primarily) at the collegiate level. *Journal of Staff, Program, and Organization Development, 7*(3), 149-151.

Cottell, P., & Millis, B. (1992). Cooperative learning structures in the instruction of accounting. *Issues in Accounting Education, 8*(1), 44-59.

Cottell, P. G., & Millis, B. J. (1993). *Instructor's resource guide for financial accounting: Information for decisions.* Cincinnati: South-Western.

Davidson, N. (1990). The small-group discovery method in secondary and college-level mathematics. In N. Davidson (Ed.), *Cooperative learning in mathematics: A handbook for teachers* (pp. 335-361). Menlo Park, CA: Addison-Wesley.

Goodsell, A., Maher, M., & Tinto, V. (1992). *Collaborative learning: A sourcebook for higher education.* University Park, PA: National Center on Postsecondary Teaching and Learning.

Johnson, D. W., Johnson, R. T., Holubec, E. J., & Roy, P. (1984). *Circles of learning: Cooperation in the classroom.* Alexandria, VA: Association for Supervision and Curriculum Development.

Kagan, S. (1992). *Cooperative learning.* San Juan Capistrano, CA: Resources for Teachers.

Kohn, A. (1986). *No contest: The case against competition.* Boston: Houghton-Mifflin.

Michaelson, L. K. (1992). Team learning: A comprehensive approach for harnessing the power of small groups in higher education. In D. H. Wulff & J. D. Nyquist (Eds.), *To improve the academy: Resources for faculty, instructional, and organizational development, 11* (pp. 107-122). The Professional and Organizational Network in Higher Education, Stillwater, OK: New Forums.

Millis, B. J. (1990). Helping faculty build learning communities through cooperative groups. *To Improve the academy: Resources for faculty, instructional, and organizational development, 9* (pp. 43-58). Professional and Organizational Development Network in Higher Education, Stillwater, OK: New Forums.

Millis, B. J. (1991). Fulfilling the promise of the "Seven Principles" through cooperative small groups: An action agenda for the university classroom. *Journal on Excellence in College Teaching,* 139-144.

Natasi, B. K., & Clements, D. H. (1991). Research on cooperative learning: Implications for practice. *School Psychology Review, 20*(1), 110-131.

Sheridan, J., Byrne, A. C., & Quina, K. (1989). Collaborative learning: Notes from the field. *College Teaching, 37*(2), 49-53.

Slavin, R. E. (1990). Guest editorial: Here to stay-or gone tomorrow? *Educational Leadership, 47*(4), 3.

Slavin, R. E. (1990). Research on cooperative learning: Consensus and controversy. *Educational Leadership, 47*(4), 52-55.

Webb, N. M. (1989). Peer interaction and learning in small groups. *International Journal of Educational Research, 13*, 21-39.

Whipple, W. R. (1987, October). Collaborative learning: Recognizing it when we see it. *AAHE Bulletin, 40*(2), 3-7.

6

Active Learning Designs
Simple Techniques to
Make Your Teaching Dazzle

REBECCA BIRCH
CYNTHIA DENTON-ADE

Chapter 6 is a fun chapter that dramatically contrasts the effects of a "boring" class with the positive learning results of a lesson that "dazzles." Rebecca Birch and Cynthia Denton-Ade share a series of active learning designs that help students stay focused and energized. The strategies outlined in this chapter remind adjuncts that they must give students a reason and structure for learning.

The authors separate their learning designs into six categories: listening strategies, note-taking guides, learner-controlled strategies, controversy learning, review techniques, and summary techniques. The specifics of such interesting formats as raps, trial by jury, dyad review, and Jeopardy are discussed.

The chapter goes beyond the basics and suggests several activities that can add spice, enjoyment, and variety. Adjuncts are shown that success or failure of a class largely depends on the degree of planning, design, and innovation.

- It is 6:00 in the evening of a hot and muggy summer day. And it is the third week of a quarter-long course on project management. You are starting a lesson on scheduling techniques, and no one seems to be at all interested. You have three long hours to go.

- You are teaching a course on personnel policy. A large local company has contracted with your university to provide this course to everyone who is new to their human resources department, even employees who have had many years of experience in other companies. You do not want to insult these people, some of whom have more experience than you in this field. But according to the contract the university has with the company, and the contract you have with the university, certain topics *must* be covered. You wonder how to handle this delicate situation.

What do these situations have in common? The need to get students interested and actively involved in their own learning, in a classroom setting.

That is what active learning designs are for. They can help you add sizzle, get student input, assess learning needs and interests, and give you feedback. Active learning designs work with hard and soft skills, and with students at all levels of proficiency. They do not take much preparation, most require no extra materials or equipment, and best of all, they make teaching fun—for the instructors and the students.

Active learning designs are "templates" for activities that capture the learners' attention and keep it focused. They are content-free, so you can use them with any material.

This chapter contains descriptions of six different categories of active learning designs, and examples of specific designs in each category:

- Listening strategies
- Note-taking guides
- Learner-controlled strategies
- Controversy learning
- Review techniques
- Summary techniques

Listening Strategies

Here are some sobering data comparing the rate at which people can listen and the rate at which most people talk:

Speaking rate for normal conversation: 150-200 words per minute
Speaking rate in teaching presentations: 125-150 words per minute
Listening rate: 400-500 words per minute

This gives your students an "excess processing capacity" of about 300 words per minute, a capacity they will use to think about things unrelated to the course, such as dream vacations, sex, bills they need to pay, or groceries they need to pick up after class.

If you want people to stay alert and focused during a lecture, you need to give them both a reason and a structure for listening attentively. Listening assignments do both. Here are three specific listening assignments you might try.

What Fits?

This technique asks participants to listen to your presentation for ideas that fit with their experience and needs, ideas that do *not* fit with their experience and needs, and questions they have about the content of the lecture or its application. You can create materials on the spot by asking students to fold a piece of paper in thirds and write "What Fits?" "What Doesn't Fit?" and "Questions" in each third of the page. Or you could give them a handout like this:

During the lecture on Total Quality Management, please write notes on the following:

1. What fits for you? What ideas can you use?
2. What doesn't fit? What ideas do you disagree with or have trouble applying?
3. What questions do you have about the content of the lecture or its application?

You can add small group participation to this listening strategy by asking participants to meet and discuss the notes they have made; at the end of the discussion, take comments and questions.

Listening Teams

Whereas "What Fits?" is focused on students' personal reactions, "Listening Teams" is focused on the content of the presentation. Teams of participants are organized before a presentation starts; they receive an assignment that helps them listen actively and think critically about key points. Teams can be made up of

- Questioners, whose assignment is to ask at least two questions about the material at the end of the presentation
- Agreers, who listen for points they agree with
- Naysayers, who listen for points they disagree with
- Realists, who listen for specific ways to apply the key points to their work

At the end of the presentation, teams spend a few minutes discussing what they heard; then they report their questions, applications, and so forth and explain their reasoning.

Dyad Review

This is similar in concept to the other listening strategies, in that pairs of participants are given specific assignments for listening to the presentation; the difference is that the "teams" are pairs. This strategy can be especially useful in large groups and/or auditorium settings where getting together as a large team is logistically difficult.

Note-Taking Guides

Instructors often wonder what level of detail to give students in written text. If they give too much detail, the students may not take any notes because they think they have everything in their notes. If instructors give the students too little detail, the students may spend all their attention on note taking and possibly lose the sense of the lecture. Note-taking guides provide a happy medium.

Taking notes does help students to learn and remember. By opening up another channel for learning, the writing process reinforces what the instructor teaches. In addition to the kinesthetic learning path provided by the note taking, the notes themselves provide a visual reinforcement of key points.

A note-taking guide provides a structure for taking notes during a presentation. It could be an outline on the left-hand side of a page, with space for notes on the right-hand side. Another option—one that can keep students riveted to a trainer's every word—is a fill-in-the-blanks format.

For example, imagine that you are attending a course on managing organization change. Among your course materials you see a page like this:

Characteristics of Successful Change

- Senior management _____ the change effort.
- _____ is surfaced.
- Natural _____ is used as a catalyst.

Wouldn't you want to find out what goes in those blanks? So did our students, and they remained focused and were able to follow what might otherwise have been a "soft" discussion of organizational change.

A fill-in-the-blanks job aid can work the same magic. In a course on death investigations, an instructor used this job aid to support her lecture on identifying different types of bullet wounds:

How to Identify Bullet Wounds

If the Wound Looks . . .	And You See . . .	And There Is . . .	Then It Could Be . . .
Round	A reddish brown "_____"	Minimal bleeding	
Ragged, irregular	A wound larger than _____	Maximum _____ with protruding internal tissue	
Large, ragged	Stellate (_____-like) patterns	→	
Ragged, with torn skin and tissue radiating from the hole	Unburned or partially burned gunpowder below _____	A bruise pattern resembling the _____	

As the instructor lectured on characteristics of different wounds and what conclusions you might draw from those characteristics, the students filled in the blank lines and blank boxes of their job aids.

Learner-Controlled Strategies

On the continuum of active to passive learning designs, learner-controlled strategies are at the active extreme. In a learner-controlled lesson, the students have choices about the sequence of topics and the amount of time the instructor lectures on each one. In addition, students decide which of several different activities they would want to engage in to meet learning objectives. Allowing the learners to control their own learning generates intense interest in the learning activities.

For example, a professor is giving a lecture on computer security systems. The objective of the lesson is that students will be able to match security problems and risks to appropriate security methods. The professor reviews the objective and displays a set of topics for the lesson:

Objective: Be able to match security problems and risks with appropriate methods.

Topics:

- Passwords
- Voice prints
- Retina scans

The professor asks students to vote for the topic they are most interested in learning about. Then he sequences the topics in the order of greatest to least interest. Now his chalkboard looks like this, with the numbers indicating the order in which he will lecture:

Objective: Be able to match security problems and risks with appropriate methods.

Topics:

- Passwords (2)
- Voice prints (1)
- Retina scans (3)

Then the professor lectures on the first topic for a specific period of time—anywhere from 5 to 15 minutes. At the end of the time period, he asks if anyone wants more information to satisfy the objective. If enough students want more information, he continues; if few or no students want more information, he stops lecturing on that subtopic. Then he goes on to topic number two in the same way, until he has covered all of the topics.

Controversy Learning

In controversy learning, students learn two or more competing viewpoints of the same topic. It might be a topic that is controversial in the traditional sense of the word: for example, "Is there life after death?" Or it might be controversial in the sense that there are multiple theories or perspectives on the same issue: for example, "What motivates people?"

In the first instance, where opinion plays an important role, a controversy learning design helps students appreciate the range of viewpoints on a single topic. In the second instance, a controversy learning design helps students learn the viewpoints faster and remember them longer; it also helps students understand finer points of the competing theories that they might otherwise overlook.

Here are two ways of structuring controversy learning:

- *Trial by Jury.* This is a mock trial, complete with witnesses, prosecutors, defenders, friends of the court, and a jury. The instructor creates an "indictment" appropriate to the course material and organizes a jury and teams for the prosecution and the defense. Each side prepares for the trial, selecting evidence from class notes or reference material, coaching witnesses, and writing briefs. Then the students conduct the trial. A judge and/or jury—who could be students or the instructor—hands down a decision.

- *Structured Debate.* This design allows students to explore opposing sides of an issue. It is particularly useful when the objective of the learning is to increase students' understanding and empathy with other points of view. Two or more views of the same issue are displayed to the class. One team is assigned to each view. For example, if the issue is motivation, one team might be responsible for preparing and arguing in favor of "People are motivated by their desire for money." The teams select a captain who presents their argument. While one team is presenting, the other team(s) take notes. At the end of the first round of arguments, the teams prepare rebuttals. Teams can be assigned to argue in favor of the view they agree with or in favor of the one they oppose, or they can be assigned randomly. At the end of the debate, the instructor asks students to discuss what new insights they gained.

Review Techniques

Too often, a review is a rehash by the instructor. Students lose interest because they already know most of what the instructor reviews; by the time the instructor gets to material the student needs to review, the student has completely lost interest.

Games can rescue the review from terminal torpor. They also add excitement and challenge. Here are several ideas:

- *Team Quiz:* Students are organized into teams. Each team is assigned a portion of the material for which to develop quiz questions. Then teams take turns quizzing each other. You can add competition by giving points, bonus questions, and penalties for wrong answers. Make sure the quiz conditions mimic the exam or application conditions. For example, if you want students to use job aids and reference material on the exam, let them use these resources in the quiz.
- *It's Academic:* Much like the Team Quiz, except the instructor makes up the questions.
- *Jeopardy:* Like the TV game show, with a game board that separates questions into point values based on their difficulty.

Summary Techniques

Summaries typically produce the same soporific effect as reviews because the instructor tells the students what they have learned. How much more interesting—and reinforcing—it is to ask the students what they got from the class. Here are some ideas for active summaries:

- *Skits,* in which teams of students act out key points or techniques derived from the course.
- *Raps,* in which the instructor gives the first several verses and teams of students create raps to summarize some portion of the training. After the teams have prepared their raps, they present them to the class.
- *Sing-alongs,* much like raps, except that a song is used. Good ditties include "The Bear Went Over the Mountain," "Row Row Row Your Boat," and "Twinkle Twinkle Little Star"—in other words, tunes that are familiar and do not make huge demands on singing talent.

■ *Cheers, acronyms, or other mnemonic devices.* The instructor might select an acronym that characterizes the message of the course or lesson and ask teams of students to develop a phrase to go with it.

A small number of students might resist these techniques, thinking they are silly and inappropriate. Our experience is that less than 5% of adult students object to them; in fact, most people love the "requirement" to get silly. However, for those students who are uncomfortable singing, dancing, or rapping, you should allow lots of latitude in how they participate. The result—real learning that is fun!

7

Facilitating Classroom Learning

MARGARET SEARS
PENNY ITTNER

Chapter 7 is the capstone chapter for instructional methods and strategies. Sears and Ittner step back and analyze classroom strategies from the point of facilitation as opposed to content. How do you create a psychological learning environment? How do you use questions effectively? What should you say when a student gives a wrong answer? How do you deal with students who are too vocal or disruptive? How do you manage the diversity in today's classroom—age, gender, religious beliefs, or physical disabilities? Though the authors repeat several techniques that are mentioned in previous chapters, information is presented here in job aid format for quick reference and easy use.

The authors first give tips for creating rapport and setting up a classroom. Suggestions range from using tent cards, posting agendas, and displaying handouts to using humor, encouraging networking, and ac-

commodating special needs. "If/then" charts are provided to guide the use
of attending, observing, and active listening behaviors. More advanced
techniques are discussed for addressing problem situations, coaching, and
giving feedback.

As adjuncts soon discover, inappropriate style and process skills can
ruin even the most brilliantly designed lesson. The authors provide a series
of job aids that can help adjuncts think through, prepare, and practice the
facilitative side of classroom activities.

The purpose of this chapter is to summarize the role of the adjunct professor as a facilitator rather than his or her role as an expert or authority. As noted in previous chapters, your focus is primarily on the learning process. Your responsibility is to use tools and techniques to make learning easy or facile. Students are rich resources for their own and others' learning. Facilitating skills enable you to tap these resources.

This chapter provides you with a series of job aids that summarize facilitating behaviors. The topics are as follows:

- "Establishing an Environment for Learning" covers establishing a physical and psychological environment that facilitates learning.
- "Basic Facilitation Skills" covers the core skills of attending, observing, questioning, and active listening.
- "Facilitating Classroom Discussions" considers ways to provide for maximum involvement of students.
- "Handling Difficult Classroom Situations" covers strategies for dealing with problems you may encounter.
- "Facilitating Writing" offers ways to provide coaching in connection with writing assignments.
- "Facilitating Project Work" suggests approaches to make project work as close to students' real-life situations as possible.
- "Managing Diversity" covers valuing and managing diversity in the classroom.

This chapter is structured around key segments under each heading so as to be as user-friendly as possible. Where appropriate, checklists, decision charts, and tables are provided. A list of additional resources is included.

Establishing an Environment for Learning

You can facilitate learning by structuring the physical environment to minimize distractions and maximize interaction and by establishing rapport with your students. The following information provides help with setting up the classroom and building rapport:

1. Room Setup
   - ■ Arrange tables and chairs in configurations that facilitate discussion. A circle or U-shape is an effective arrangement.
   - ■ Have a place in the classroom for posting announcements by you or by students.
   - ■ Have course materials, learning aids, and supplies readily available. Ensure that all visual aids are in working order.
   - ■ Have a place for supplemental handouts. Use sticky-notes for signing up for additional handouts.
   - ■ Provide name tent cards.
   - ■ Post the agenda in a visible location.
   - ■ Play music before class and during breaks.
   - ■ Arrange for refreshments. Have students sign up to participate in bringing the refreshments.
2. Building Rapport
   - ■ Welcoming students
   - ■ Providing introductory activities
   - ■ Encouraging networking within the class
   - ■ Identifying and accommodating special needs and situations
   - ■ Closing the distance between you and the students by encouraging appropriate informality
   - ■ Using humor

Basic Facilitation Skills[1]

Adult learners bring prior experience to the classroom: work experience, educational experience, life experience. As a result, they are rich resources for learning. As an adjunct professor, your key role is to facilitate the educational process rather than to focus solely on course content.

Facilitation skills are skills that make learning easier. The core facilitation skills are attending, observing, questioning, and active listening.

Attending Skills

Attending means demonstrating that you are attentive to the students. This is accomplished by positioning your body to indicate full attention and mentally focusing to eliminate distractions. Adult learners learn best when they feel their time is being used efficiently. They also feel they deserve your attention and respect.

The following are important attending behaviors:

- *Facing the students.* For example, if you are recording ideas on the flip chart or white board, minimize time when your back is to students.
- *Maintaining eye contact.* For example, if class seating is in a wide arc, maintain eye contact with those on the edges of the arc.
- *Walking toward students.* For example, if a student makes a contribution, walk toward him or her.

Some barriers to attending are

- Distractions within the classroom
- Preoccupation with personal matters
- Formality in physical stance
- Stress
- Personal biases toward individual students

Observing Skills

Observing is taking in information about how students are responding to the learning. Awareness of student responses allows you to change course to maximize learning, if appropriate (see Figure 7.1).

Observation Cycle	Observe Behavior → Make Inferences About Feelings ← Choose to Act		
Examples	**Situation** A student yawns	**Inferences** Room temperature? Boredom? Low energy?	**Possible Actions** Do nothing Check it out Take a break Speed up Subgroup
	Students frown	Confusion? Disagreement?	Check it out Summarize Ask a question Test for agreement

Figure 7.1. The Observation Cycle

SOURCE: From *Train-the-Trainer: Practical Skills That Work,* by Penny L. Ittner and Alex F. Douds, published by HRD Press, Amherst, MA, 1988. Copyright 1988 by HRD Press. Reprinted with permission.

Questioning Skills

Questions are significant to the learning process. Asking the right questions at the right time, in the right way, contributes to the learning of all. Questions serve to

- Stimulate student involvement
- Check understanding
- Draw on resources in the group
- Add energy
- Broaden the discussion
- Focus discussion

The following list provides types of questions and examples:

- *Overhead:* Directed at the entire group to promote thinking. Example: "How will communication patterns change in the next decade?"

- *Leading:* Used to suggest an answer or prompt analysis. Example: "How might supervisors benefit from learning this?"
- *Clarifying:* Used to challenge old ideas, develop new thoughts, or check understanding. Example: "How would that work in today's environment?"
- *Redirected:* Returning a question posed by a student to the same student or to another in the class. Example: "That's a good question, Robert. What would you do in your organization, Barbara?"
- *Factual:* Used to obtain specific information, sometimes for the purpose of getting discussions started. Example: "How many of you work in matrixed organizations?"
- *Alternative:* Requires a decision between options; sometimes used to evaluate the options. Example: "Are the best managers strict, easy, or neither?"
- *Personal Experience:* Prompts sharing of past critical incidents, adding concreteness to the discussion and promoting ownership of the topic. Example: "What experiences have you had with TQM, and how has it affected the functioning of your organization?"

When framing questions:

- Be brief.
- Cover a single point.
- Relate the question directly to the topic.
- Use words that have meaning to the class.

Questions may be *open* or *closed.*

- *Open* questions cannot be answered by a "yes," a "no," or other one-word answers. They stimulate students' involvement by encouraging discussion. They generally begin with the words *what, when, where, which, how, who,* or *why:* for example, "Why are teams playing such an important role in industry today?"
- *Closed* questions can be answered by a "yes," a "no," or a one-word answer. They discourage discussion and may be seen as leading the class to an opinion. Closed questions generally begin with the words *is (are, aren't, was, wasn't), has (have, haven't), do (did, didn't), can (could, couldn't), will (would, wouldn't, won't),* or *shall (should, shouldn't).*

When directing questions, choose whether you want to direct your question to the class or to an individual. When you want to provide wider involvement, avoid putting individuals on the spot, or stimulate thinking, direct to the class. When you want to recognize a special resource, build on a previous contribution, or increase involvement from particular individuals, direct to an individual.

In general:

- Allow sufficient time for responses.
- Restate or reword the question if class members appear confused.
- If no one responds, select an individual for responding.
- Encourage the class to question one another.

The three kinds of answers students can give are right answers, partly right answers, and wrong answers. If the student gives a *right answer*, acknowledge and give positive reinforcement. For example, say, "Yes, that's on target" and nod approvingly. If the student gives a *partly right answer*, acknowledge and give reinforcement for the correct part. Develop the correct answer for the incorrect part. For example, say, "You're right about. . . . Let's explore your comment about. . . ." If the student gives a *wrong answer*, consider that you may not have asked the question clearly and rephrase the question. If you have been clear in your question, consider the self-esteem of the person and the effort made when correcting the response. For example, say, "That's not the answer I had in mind. I was thinking more about . . ." or "That doesn't apply here, but it could be applicable in some other circumstances. What do others think?"

Active Listening Skills

Active listening is more than just "hearing" your students. Rather, it includes behaviors that ensure that the message that has been communicated has been received and understood as intended. The purpose of active listening is to ensure understanding and demonstrate respect for the information and perspective of the student.

The core active listening skills are encouraging, paraphrasing, and reflecting feelings.

Encouraging behaviors are things you do to communicate that you care what the student is saying and you want him or her to continue talking. The behaviors include

- Nodding, smiling, saying "uh huh"
- Using a positive voice tone
- Asking open questions that elicit discussion

Paraphrasing involves rephrasing in your own words what someone is saying. The purpose of paraphrasing is to help the student feel listened to and to let you check your understanding of what the student said. For effective paraphrasing, your response should

- Be interchangeable, not adding to or subtracting from what was said
- Be brief
- Be original, in your own words
- Convey neither approval nor disapproval

Reflecting feelings goes beyond paraphrasing. When you reflect feelings, you express how the student feels in addition to paraphrasing the reason for the feeling ("You feel . . . because . . ."). The benefits of reflecting feelings are:

- It helps the student feel you understand the content and the feelings behind the content.
- It reduces defensiveness.
- It defuses emotional situations by helping the student calm down and devote energies to learning.

Facilitating Classroom Discussions

Classroom discussions stimulate and motivate students to learn. Students become involved in the learning process. The learning assumes relevance for them when they share their ideas and experiences.

If the class is large (over 20), you can

■ Select a random sample of 15 to 20 students for the discussion while the rest observe.
■ Break the class into small groups of five to seven students each and train students to be discussion leaders.

Make sure students can easily see you, each other, and the flip chart or white board. You can have students sit in a circle or a U-shape arrangement.

To prepare the students for the discussion:

■ State the goal or purpose of the discussion.
■ Clarify roles and responsibilities, including any requirements for before-class preparation.
■ Display the agenda, which includes the topics to be covered and the time allotted for each.
■ Help the students develop ground rules for the discussion: for example, "All points of view will be accepted and posted," "Evaluation will be deferred until later," "Silence is okay; thinking takes time," "Interruptions will be 'policed,' " and "Disagreement is okay; personal attacks are not."
■ Write the problem, issue, or topic on the flip chart or white board.
■ State that ideas are wanted. For example, say, "What ideas do you have on this topic?"
■ Use nonverbal means to elicit ideas: For example, indicate (coax) with your hand that ideas are wanted, cue with the marker that you are ready to write, and use attending skills (see "Attending Skills").

During the discussion:

■ Avoid dominating the discussion.
■ Accept, without evaluating, ideas and opinions.
■ Demonstrate willingness to explore ideas, even though you may not agree with them.
■ Accept that student participation and idea sharing are more important than getting through all the content planned for that class.
■ Let the group motivate and reward participation. Let them have control over the pace, and to some extent the content, of the discussion.

Table 7.1   Functions of the Instructor in Facilitating Discussion

Function	Description
Post and confirm information	Record all information quickly and succinctly on the flip chart or white board, abbreviating as you go. Confirm the accuracy of your recording as you proceed.
Gatekeep	Give a "green light" to the person who is speaking and a "red light" to others. Stop interruptions. Encourage more silent people to participate in the discussion.
Request examples or illustrations	Ask for elaboration on incomplete or vague ideas.
Encourage contributions	Verbally and nonverbally reinforce students for their participation.
Test consensus	Check that all have expressed their thoughts and that all "buy in" to important conclusions or decisions made.
Summarize and confirm	Provide understanding and closure to the discussion by restating what has happened and checking for accuracy.

Table 7.1 shows several functions of the instructor in facilitating discussion.

Handling Problem Situations in the Classroom[2]

Problem situations in the classroom are those in which learning is inhibited due to the behavior of one or more students. All adjuncts, even the most skilled and experienced ones, occasionally run into these problem situations.

Problem situations can revolve around the level and kind of participation of students. Some differences in levels of participation are a natural reflection of variations in students' personalities and their preferred ways of learning. A problem situation occurs, however, when students participate too much or too little or inappropriately.

If individual students are too vocal, other students may not be able to participate fully in the classroom activities. You may also run out of time before you complete all planned activities.

If individuals are too silent, their valuable input is lost from the group. Silent students pose another problem for you—you may have difficulty assessing whether they are learning.

If individuals participate in side conversations, this can be disconcerting to you and can also interrupt the group's process.

When learning becomes inhibited, you must take action. There are three key goals for handling problem situations that are negatively affecting learning:

1. *Eliminate or minimize the problem behavior.* You need to resolve the problem to the extent necessary for learning to resume unhindered.
2. *Maintain the self-esteem of the student.* You need to take care of the problem in a way that does not reduce the self-esteem of the student exhibiting the problem behavior.
3. *Avoid further disruption to learning.* You need to preserve a learning climate that is relaxed, comfortable, and conducive to learning.

When you are confronted with a problem situation, it is important to remain as emotionally neutral as possible so that you can identify the best strategies for handling the situation. Use a rational problem-solving approach:

1. Identify possible strategies—those you have seen other facilitators use as well as those you think will fit the situation.
2. Evaluate them against the three goals noted above, eliminating those that do not meet all three conditions.
3. Select a strategy to use in handling the problem situation.

The following are some specific problem situations and strategies for dealing with them:

1. Student is too vocal.
   - Interrupt and ask student to summarize briefly.
   - Say "thank you" and ask for input from others.

- Use procedures, e.g., round robin or brainstorming, that facilitate total group involvement.
2. Student is too silent.
   - Do some "warm-up" activities to increase comfort level.
   - Talk privately with the person.
   - Direct questions to the student when you know he or she has experience/ideas on the topic.
3. Students engage in side conversations.
   - Set ground rules at the beginning of the class.
   - Encourage the class to refocus on the topic at hand.
   - Talk privately with those involved.

Facilitating Writing

Your role as a facilitator extends to student writing. This includes *coaching* the student before the assignment is completed and *giving feedback* on the written assignment. The purpose of facilitating student writing is to

- Engage in dialogue with students about their strengths and areas for improvement
- Encourage students and help shape their writing behavior in alignment with course goals
- Improve writing skills
- Raise questions for revision
- Facilitate learning while maintaining a respectful posture with adult learners

You can coach students before they turn in a written assignment by

- Clarifying requirements for content and format
- Providing examples of other student papers
- Alerting students to potential problem areas, e.g., grammatical errors, lack of focus
- Providing coaching on appropriate topics and resources
- Encouraging peer review of draft materials

You can give students feedback on a written assignment by

- Making paragraph-by-paragraph comments on the paper
- Summarizing the strengths of the paper
- Outlining an approach for revision, if appropriate
- Allowing students to improve grades by revising written work
- In class, summarizing class strengths and areas for improvements

Facilitating Project Work

Projects provide opportunities for students to demonstrate learning through research and/or application. Adult learners need to translate classroom learning to real-life situations. Strategies for accomplishing this include

- Understanding individual students' contexts
- Using examples and exercises related to real-world situations
- Using applicability to students' experiences as a criterion for selecting textbooks
- Encouraging students to use their own real-world problems or situations as a basis for project work
- Holding students accountable for output quality and deadlines

To coach students in project work:

- Provide for project time in class.
- Meet with each student/project team to discuss status and areas of concern.
- Have students report on status of projects in class. Encourage other students to serve as coaches for problem areas.
- Provide opportunities for recognition/celebration of accomplishments.

Managing Diversity

You can facilitate learning by valuing and managing diversity in the classroom. Diversity is defined as differences within a group. Dimensions of diversity include age, education, gender, marital status, ethnicity, religious beliefs, race, geographical location, physical abilities, work experience, and sexual orientation. These dimensions provide individuals with unique perspectives on all aspects of their lives. Because of these differences, there will be different perspectives on tasks and different techniques for accomplishing tasks in the classroom.

In an educational setting, diversity management is important because it

- Provides richness to the learning environment
- Prevents discrimination in the classroom
- Serves as an important part of the relationship dimension (both adjunct-to-student and student-to-student)
- Serves as a model because the classroom is a microcosm of the world

The following are some effective ways to manage diversity:

1. Understand differences, and act in ways that support differences.
2. Create an environment where every student's potential can be maximized.
3. Avoid stereotyping. *Don't:*
   - Assign tasks based on stereotypes.
   - Use anecdotes and visual examples that reinforce stereotypes.
4. Use appropriate language. *Do:*
   - Use pronouns that include both genders.
   - Vary your examples to include different populations.
5. Use diversity criteria in
   - Selection of guest speakers
   - Providing students with leadership opportunities
   - Subgrouping students
6. Be aware of communication patterns you are encouraging in class. For example, if a few students are dominating, change the pattern.
7. Enhance community in the class by learning students' names and backgrounds and using team or class projects to stimulate group interaction.
8. Design exercises that promote equitable participation: for example, "Think-Pair-Share," in which first individuals think about a question or a problem, then pairs of students discuss the issue, and then pairs share ideas with the total class.

Summary

The role of the adjunct is to facilitate classroom learning. This is accomplished by

- Establishing a physical and psychological environment that facilitates learning
- Demonstrating that you are attentive to the students
- Observing how students are responding to the learning
- Asking questions that generate discussion
- Actively listening to ensure understanding and to demonstrate respect for students' perspectives
- Facilitating classroom discussions that provide maximum involvement of students
- Handling problem situations that inhibit learning
- Providing coaching in connection with writing assignments
- Making project work as close to students' real-life situations as possible
- Valuing and managing diversity in the classroom

Notes

1. Portions of this material drawn from the work, *Train-the-Trainer: Practical Skills That Work,* by Penny L. Ittner and Alex F. Douds, published by HRD Press, Amherst, MA, 1988. Used with permission.

2. Portions of this material drawn from the work, *Train-the-Trainer: Practical Skills That Work,* by Penny L. Ittner and Alex F. Douds, published by HRD Press, Amherst, MA, 1988. Used with permission.

Reference

Ittner, P. L., & Douds, A. F. (1988). *Train-the-trainer: Practical skills that work.* Amherst, MA: HRD.

Suggested Readings

Brookfield, S. D. (1990). *Understanding and facilitating adult learning.* San Francisco: Jossey-Bass.

Davis, R. H., Fry, J. P., & Alexander, L. T. (1977). *The discussion method: Guides for the improvement of instruction in higher education*. East Lansing: Michigan State University, Instructional Media Center.

Knowles, M. S. (1989). *The making of an adult educator*. San Francisco: Jossey-Bass.

Kolb, D. A. (1984). *Experiential learning: Experience as a source of learning and development*. Englewood Cliffs, NJ: Prentice Hall.

Schmuck, R. A., & Schmuck, P. A. (1988). *Group processes in the classroom*. Dubuque, IA: William C. Brown.

Schlossberg, N. K., Lynch, A. Q., & Chickering, A. W. (1989). *Improving higher education environments for adults*. San Francisco: Jossey-Bass.

White, E. M. (1985). *Teaching and assessing writing*. San Francisco: Jossey-Bass.

8

Evaluation of Students

LINDA M. RAUDENBUSH

Student evaluation—how, when, and why—is one of those topics that both new and seasoned adjuncts struggle with. There are many theories and approaches, and adjuncts must clearly assess two things: (a) What are my own beliefs concerning evaluation? and (b) what are the university's designated policies? Sometimes an adjunct will be in alignment with the university's process, and sometimes he or she will have to follow an approach that goes against his or her personal views.

In Chapter 8, Linda Raudenbush provides a set of questions to help adjuncts uncover both the written rules and the unspoken assumptions concerning evaluation. In discussing evaluation methods, the author provides an excellent description of the traditional norm-referenced approach versus the more student-centered criterion-referenced method. Of particular note are the tips for communicating the specific elements that make up a particular grade. As Raudenbush points out, "This careful attention to detail during the planning and communication phases will prevent the unfortunate scenario of students asking why they received a particular grade at the end of the semester."

This chapter continues by providing a road map for determining the best evaluation methods. Several exhibits and checklists are provided to aid the matching of methods with specific techniques: For example, a critique of a role play provides a qualitative measure, whereas a true/false test results in a quantitative score. Continuing to uphold an adult learning philosophy, the author covers a wide range of evaluation strategies, including learning contracts, simulations, journals, laboratory exercises, computer applications, group evaluations, and peer reviews.

One of the more enlightening aspects of this chapter is a discussion on giving students feedback. The reader discovers that giving feedback becomes easier when specific skills and knowledge are identified and communicated in the initial evaluation plan. Raudenbush also offers some helpful tips for handling student resistance during the feedback process. Again, the author suggests techniques that are more meaningful to the adult learner. These techniques look different from the traditional, unilateral methods.

Last, the author reminds the adjunct of administrative responsibilities that accompany every evaluation process: record keeping, deadlines, grade changes, cheating policies, and letters of recommendation.

Through this chapter, adjuncts gain an understanding of the importance, complexities, and benefits of an evaluation plan and strategy. Given recent trends toward competency-based curriculums and measurable outcomes, universities are requiring both adjuncts and full-time faculty to apply more rigorous evaluation strategies.

The evaluation of students is an increasingly important instructor responsibility, especially with the trends of competency-based curriculum, return on investment, and the view of education as a consumer product. The benefits of thorough and accurate evaluation are many and varied, including identifying a student's place in the learning hierarchy, determining teacher effectiveness as a facilitator of learning, controlling quality in the educational process, providing feedback for planning future learning experiences, managing classroom learning activities, opening communication about performance between instructor and student, and enhancing both the teaching and the learning processes.

The purpose of this chapter is to provide useful information about student evaluation in the areas of program philosophy, specific criteria, methodologies and techniques, feedback process, and administrative responsibilities. Specifically, this chapter deals with the mechanics of evaluation, particular approaches a university might use, and various evaluation tools that are appropriate for the adult learner.

Program Philosophy

In general, the instructor must identify the philosophy, policy, and procedures regarding the subject of evaluation held by the program, department, school, and university. You can start this process by asking questions, such as

- What are the written and unwritten guidelines?
- What is expected of me and of the students?
- Do most of the students work full time? What effect does this have on student expectations of academic workload and on types and grading of academic assignments?
- Are there standards of evaluation?
- What effect does attendance have on evaluation?
- Are midterm and final exams required?
- Are there standard tests that I or someone must administer?
- What do my program head, department chair, dean, and president think about evaluation?
- What is the impact of grades on the students? What are their expectations?
- What do my tenured colleagues do? What are their thoughts about giving A's and about using the bell curve?

In short, the new adjunct must scan the entire academic system to uncover written rules and unspoken assumptions concerning evaluation. For example, you might find written documentation that the university requires midterm grades to be given on all registered students by instructors or that some sort of final exam must be given during a specified period of time. Further, you might find that most of the university's graduate students work full time. Therefore it is customary to give assignments that are less theoretical and more applied in nature. This enables students to use real-life work examples and experiences. Thus, in a performance management course, it would be more appropriate to have students orally compare the types of annual evaluations used in their organizations with models discussed in class than to give a written test on performance evaluation methods and models.

The trend in evaluation is away from the norm-referenced methods of the past and toward a criterion-referenced (or *outcomes evaluation*) system. The latter is predicated on curriculum objectives and course goals; grades depend on each student's level of achievement. Changes in use of the two types of evaluation methods over time are presented in Figure 8.1, and definitions and examples are given in Table 8.1.

Therefore you may want to consider seriously using criterion-based evaluation. If you discover, during your environmental scan, that this method is little used in your system, you should discuss your planned usage with your program head and department chair.

Plan and Communicate Specific Criteria

The use of a criterion-based evaluation system requires several ingredients for success. They can be clustered under the two headings of planning and communicating.

First, you should address the tasks of planning for specific evaluation criteria:

1. Find out where your course fits into the school's curriculum. Identify the curriculum objectives, especially as they relate to your course. Ask the following questions:
   - What are students in this curriculum expected to know and be able to do when they finish?
   - What portion of the overall curriculum knowledge and skills do they learn in my course?
2. Identify the written and unwritten goals for your course.
   - What are the students in my course expected to know and be able to do when they finish?
   - How will I find out what my students know and can do?

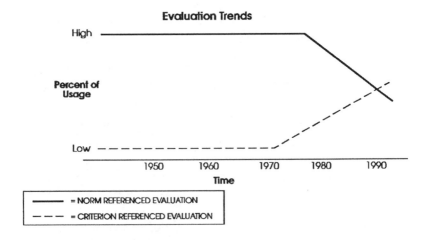

Figure 8.1. Evaluation Trends

3. Find out what else is being done at your university and others to evaluate students in your type of course.
   ■ What are other faculty who teach my course doing to evaluate students?
4. After a thoughtful analysis of all the above information, you are ready to develop specific course goals and objectives. Each goal must have observable standards of measurement that enable both you and the students to know when the goals have and have not been met. Be sure to include any special criteria in your course, such as
   ■ Quality
   ■ Energy
   ■ Motivation
   ■ Attendance
   ■ Participation
   ■ Creativity
5. Finally, you must document the evaluation plan for your course, along with its rationale, if needed. Do not skimp on details. Being explicit in the written plan will save you from lengthy explanations.

Now you are ready to communicate your plan, in the appropriate form, to students and other interested parties, such as the faculty who teach in your curriculum area, your program head, and your department chair. The most widely accepted location for your written evalua-

Table 8.1 Comparison of Evaluation Methods

Type	Norm-Referenced	Criterion-Referenced
Definition	Grade earned depends on other students' scores	Grade earned does not depend on other students' scores.
Basis of grades	Tests results distributed along a normal curve, using standard deviation	Individual student's completion of course objectives
Examples	Using a normal curve, approximately 70% will get a C, 10% a B, 10% a D, 5% an A, and 5% an F	Without the restriction of any curve, it is usual for at least 50% of a class to get an A, 30% a B, 15% a C, and 5% a D or F
Response to "Why did I get a C?"	"Using the normal curve, your score was X number of standard deviation units from the class mean."	"Let's look at each of the course goals, desired behaviors, maximum number of points allowed, and points earned by your work and behavior. All of this will explain the C."

tion plan is in your course syllabus. Other documentation requirements vary by university, so you need to identify the acceptable formats at your school.

You will want to communicate your evaluation plan carefully to your students at the beginning of each course. When you present your syllabus containing the evaluation details, take the time to explain the evaluation plan and how it works to your students. For example, start by explaining each course goal and the percentage that contributes to the total grade. The total of all goals should be 100%, as this marketing course example illustrates:

Goal 1	Facilitate a classroom discussion.	(25%)
Goal 2	Carry out a market analysis.	(25%)
Goal 3	Evaluate a marketing plan.	(25%)
Goal 4	Provide constructive feedback.	(25%)

Next, explain what the requirements are to achieve each goal. For example, using Goal 1:

3	Introduce discussion topic, guidelines, and goals.
1	Track time and stay within limit.
3	Post ideas and obtain confirmation.
3	Gatekeep information flow.
3	Solicit examples and elaboration.
3	Positively recognize each contribution.
3	Consensus-test each step in the discussion.
3	Summarize posted ideas.
3	Integrate into discussion goals.
25	points

This careful attention to detail during the planning and communicating phases will prevent the unfortunate scenario of students asking why they received a particular grade at the end of the semester. On the rare occasion when that happens, you can refer to your evaluation plan with its specific details, reminding the student that you covered all this at the beginning of the semester.

The tasks of planning for and communicating specific evaluation criteria are summarized in Table 8.2.

Considerations for Methodologies and Techniques

A wide variety of methods and techniques can be used with adult students. Some ideas have already been discussed in other parts of this handbook. It would be impossible to cover every option in one chapter, but the most useful will be outlined and discussed. Be creative. Remember, the goal is learning and learning transfer, not testing per se.

First, you should *choose an evaluation methodology: qualitative methods*, such as critique of a role play; *quantitative methods*, such as grading a true/false test; or a *mixture of both*, such as critique of a role play with specific behaviors that are acceptable and unacceptable. Using this example, you would identify and communicate in advance the points

Table 8.2 Planning and Communicating Specific Evaluation Criteria

Action	Questions to Ask
Investigate	1. Where does your course fit into the school's curriculum? 2. What are your course goals? 3. How does your school evaluate students?
Analyze	4. What are the implications for your course?
Develop	5. What are your specific, observable, and measurable course objectives?
Document	6. How will you write your course evaluation plan?
Communicate	7. How will you inform students and others about your evaluation plan?

given for acceptable behaviors and points lost for unacceptable behavior. The latter methodology is recommended because it increases the likelihood of obtaining a complete picture of the learning achieved by each student and because it adds variety to your classroom activities.

Next, you must *identify the specific evaluation techniques* that are best used to measure learning in your course. The course objectives in your evaluation plan will determine which of the qualitative and quantitative techniques are most suitable for the unique combination of you, your course, and your students. You can choose to evaluate student learning by *observing students' behaviors,* as in a role play; *reviewing students' oral and written products,* such as reports and presentations; or *using a mixture of both,* such as observation of students conducting a role play on conflict resolution and review of students' reaction papers describing how comfortable they felt using conflict resolution techniques in the role play. Again, it is recommended that you use a mix, for the reasons stated above. Regardless of the specific evaluation techniques used, you must always identify and communicate the evaluation criteria in advance. In the above example, you might determine that 90% of the grade will be based on your observation and critique of the conflict resolution role play, in which you award points for desirable behaviors and take off points for unacceptable behaviors, and that 10% of the grade might relate to the students' written expressions of individual comfort level with using conflict resolution techniques.

Now you must *determine what you will observe and review*. These simple and effective qualitative and quantitative evaluation techniques can be applied to an almost endless array of observable and measurable student activities, including but not limited to

- Questions/answers
- Small group problem solving
- Film/video discussion
- Field trip analysis
- Critique of articles
- Role playing
- Student panels
- Individual projects
- Research results
- Group projects
- Class discussion
- Completion of handouts
- Brainstorming
- Term papers
- Learning contracts
- Simulations
- Games
- Presentations
- Outside assignments
- Journals
- Computer work
- Laboratory exercises
- Quizzes/exams
- Essays

Again, it is recommended that you use a mix of student activities, for the reasons stated above.

Now let us examine more closely several student activities to see how they fit into a course. We will look first at the student activity of games. Suppose that the goals for a personal growth course are the following:

Goal 1	Increase awareness of one's own values.	(25%)
Goal 2	Increase awareness of values of others.	(25%)
Goal 3	Identify ways that values affect individual decision making.	(25%)
Goal 4	Identify ways that values affect group decision making.	(25%)

After the class has satisfactorily met the first three goals, you could conduct the student activity of a game with the purpose of clarifying the impact of values on group decision making. As the game was being conducted, you would observe student behaviors. After the game and the follow-up discussion, you might ask each student to write a brief paper on ways that values affect group decision making, based on the game and learning derived from playing it. This example uses the student activity of games to illustrate a mix of evaluation methodology and techniques.

Next, we will look at the student activity of presentations. Suppose that one goal for a public administration course is to give an executive presentation using varied media (20%). In advance, you would identify and communicate acceptable behaviors and related points—for example, as shown below:

3	Provide a one- to two-page executive summary (1 point for having the summary and 2 points maximum for the quality of the summary).
2	Give an introduction/overview to the presentation.
3	Provide attendees with a handout, including details, related studies, copies of slides, transparencies, etc.
3	Clarify critical points with examples and costs.
3	Integrate at least two different types of media into the briefing.
2	Provide an opportunity for audience questioning.
2	Handle questions expeditiously and accurately.
2	Summarize key points, decisions made, and action items.
20	points

As the briefing was being given, you would observe student behaviors, and determine the appropriate number of points to award, using the criteria. After the briefing and the follow-up discussion, you would ask each student to hand in the executive summary for your review. You would decide, on the basis of quality of content, how many points to give it. This example uses the student activity of presentations to illustrate a mix of evaluation methodology and techniques.

Now, you must *determine how to carry out the evaluations*. There are several options:

■ Instructor evaluates individuals or groups, as in the presentation example above.

■ Students evaluate individuals or groups (i.e., peer evaluation). This could be done with the presentation example if the points and acceptable behaviors were incorporated into a checklist (see Appendix 8.1) for use by students on fellow students.

■ Individuals or groups use self-administered evaluations (see Appendix 8.2).

■ You use a mixture of all of the above.

The mixture is again recommended because it provides the most diverse range of perspectives. In addition, observing and evaluating by students can develop their skills in these areas.

Thus far, we have discussed a variety of methods and techniques that can be used with adult students. When creating the unique combination for your situation, remember that the emphasis with evaluation should be learning and learning transfer, not testing.

Regardless of the specific options you choose to determine how each student has or has not met the course objectives, your methodologies and techniques should be in accordance with

1. *The many established principles of adult learning,* including, but not limited to, these three:
   ■ *Maintaining and increasing adults' self-esteem.* You can do this in many ways, such as enabling your adult learners to evaluate their own progress in meeting course objectives (e.g., by using a tool such as Appendix 8.1 to capture a student's self-evaluation, then using it as a discussion aid when you and the student review learning and grading

for that course goal) and using nonthreatening feedback processes, which will be discussed shortly.

■ *Using and building on adults' accumulated experiences.* When evaluating adults, you must be aware that accumulated experiences might both help and hinder new learning. Therefore, before evaluating, allow sufficient time and learning activities to enable learners to unfreeze fixed habits from previous experience. For example, in a communications course, you might have a series of group discussions and class debates that encourage students to verbalize views based on their past experiences about gender-stereotypic verbal and nonverbal behavior; because the students' ever-changing thoughts are being expressed, you can easily judge when they are ready to move on to new material, such as androgenous communication.

■ *Showing immediate application of new knowledge and skills to adult learners' lives.* Try to identify the adult learners' needs, problems, and applications within the context of your course. When evaluating their learning, you should use realistic situations that reflect possible applications for their newly gained knowledge and skills. For example, to complete the goal identified in Appendix 8.1, encourage students to choose topics on which they either have recently given a presentation or must soon give a presentation.

2. *Equitable treatment of the diversity needs of your students.* When considering evaluation methodologies, techniques, and options, you must maintain an awareness of student diversity in such areas as gender, age, race, ethnicity, religion, culture, sexual preference, and disability. Use the combination of evaluation methods and techniques that is most comfortable for all of your students. For example, some cultures value group accomplishments more than individual successes; in this case, you would consider using some group evaluation techniques.

3. *Competency-based evaluation.* You should be able to answer the following questions:

   ■ To what extent has each student acquired new knowledge and skills?

   ■ As a result, what can each student do differently?

   ■ What can the students do with the new learning?

Giving Students Feedback

Now that you have considered your evaluation methodologies and techniques, you must consider the process of giving feedback: letting students know the results of your evaluation procedures.

An instructor gives students feedback in several ways. It is recommended that you use a mix of written and verbal techniques to maximize the effectiveness of your evaluation methods and techniques. Regardless of the mix of techniques, giving students feedback requires at least two key considerations for success: (a) following a process and (b) using effective techniques.

The following feedback process is a useful model to master. If you are going to use any peer evaluation techniques, you should review appropriate feedback methods with the students also:

1. Plan and prepare for giving feedback.
   - Adopt the attitude of a coach/facilitator of learning, not a judge.
   - Have course and module goals and objectives available for easy reference.
   - Be ready to identify clearly accurate and acceptable knowledge and skills.
2. Ask the learner for a self-evaluation before you or others give feedback.
   - For significant feedback sessions, this should be done privately.
3. Make every effort to reduce student fear and anxiety.
   - Before your discussion, let the student know the date, time, and place for the feedback session.
   - At the start of a session, try to put the student at ease; give an overview of what will be covered and the benefits to the student.
4. Be candid, specific, direct, accurate, clear, and factual.
   - Criticize measurable knowledge and observable skills, not the individual. For example, it would be not appropriate to say, "You are so in love with your own voice that you did not provide the audience the opportunity for participating." A better way to give feedback about inadequate audience participation would be "Your presentation did not allow time for audience participation. In your next presentation, plan for at least 5 minutes of audience questioning. Keep your answers brief and to the point to encourage the maximum amount of audience participation."
5. Discuss how the student can improve knowledge and skills.
   - Involve the student in planning for improvement.
   - Set mutually acceptable, realistic goals for each student for a specified period of time that match the original course objectives.

- Include checkpoints when you will reevaluate student progress in meeting the objectives.
- Build on student strengths, rather than emphasizing shortcomings.

6. Ask for the student's reaction to receiving the feedback.
- Use effective listening techniques to get the full meaning of the student's attitudes, thoughts, and feelings.
- Be sure that the student understands the feedback and buys into the plan for improvement. Ask for concurrence and commitment.

7. Take the opportunity to enhance your relationship with the student.
- Help the student feel positive about objectives that have been accomplished and motivated to improve according to the agreed-on plan.
- End on a positive note by emphasizing the success of the feedback session.

Throughout the process, you want to focus on some techniques for making the feedback as effective as possible. They include but are not limited to the following:

- *Focus on specific knowledge and skills areas.* For example, for the public administration course example in Appendix 8.1, it is less effective to say, "That was a good briefing" than to say, "The example of the FCRS and its related costs was appropriate to your briefing because it illustrated the trend of providing incentives to respondents." This relates specifically to the fifth desired behavior.
- *Keep feedback impersonal.* Again using the example in Appendix 8.1, it is less effective to say, "Len, you're such a verbose speaker!," than to say, "Len, when handling questions, try to keep your responses short, approximately 2 to 3 minutes per question." This relates specifically to the seventh desired behavior.
- *Tie feedback to the course objectives.* After giving the student feedback similar to that illustrated in the above two examples, you could wrap it up with the statement "All of these points relate to your ability to give an effective presentation, using varied media. As you recall from our public administration syllabus, this is our first course goal, and you have achieved it according to the level we just discussed."
- *Make feedback well timed.* The shorter the interval between the evaluation and the receipt of feedback, the better.
- *Direct negative feedback at knowledge and behavior that the student can control.* For example, it is not effective to say, "Because you are a woman, your

voice is too quiet to be heard in the back of the room." It would be better to suggest the use of a microphone without any gender reference.

■ *Take the previous described adult learning and diversity principles into consideration* when giving feedback. Do what is comfortable for you and each student.

■ *Make sure that the recipient understands and accepts the feedback.* For example, you might want to ask the student to summarize the new behaviors that he or she will try in the future on the basis of this learning experience.

The last technique warrants a few more tips because overcoming student objections to feedback can be challenging. When you encounter student resistance, use the following process:

1. *Acknowledge the student's emotional reaction to receiving feedback.* A simple phrase such as "I can understand that you must feel that way" can help the student move closer to accepting feedback.
2. *Clarify the source and substance of the student's objection.* Try not to jump to conclusions or make assumptions about what you think the student is saying. Use effective listening and paraphrasing to clarify the real source and substance of the objection. You can say, "So in other words, what you mean is. . . ."
3. *Confirm your understanding of the concern* by rephrasing the objection in question form: e.g., "Are you really concerned about . . . ?"
4. Respond to the objection directly. Indicate any student misconceptions, give relevant information, and offer proof to substantiate your explanations.
5. If necessary, reiterate your response in a different form. Consider using analogies or examples to clarify the issues in a new light for the student.

Administrative Responsibilities

The first few sections of this chapter have focused primarily on instructor responsibilities regarding methods and strategies for student evaluation. However, evaluation also involves a list of administrative duties that require attention.

Perhaps the most mysterious and least enjoyable set of instructor responsibilities are those best described as *administrative*. The umbrella term is used here to include areas such as record keeping, university procedures and deadlines, course grades and grade changes, cheating, and letters of recommendation for students.

Record Keeping

There are several considerations with record keeping:

1. *What records to keep?* At the very least, the following data should be kept on all your students during any semester:
   - *Demographics:* Name, address, current day and evening telephone numbers, and, if used in university records, social security number. For an example of a form, refer to Appendix 8.3.
   - *Attendance:* You can use a sign-in sheet for each class session, thus creating an attendance list signed by each student. For an example of a form, refer to Appendix 8.4.
   - *Assignments:* Any student work, feedback given, and the grade earned.
   - *Other kinds of records:* notes about student participation, observation notes of individual student behaviors, and written descriptions of any difficulties with students.

2. *How should student records be kept?* There are basically two types of systems available. Records can be kept manually; long columnar accounting ledgers work well. Or records can be kept in an automated way, using either the university's computer or your own personal computer with spreadsheet software to meet your needs. Regardless of the system used, all student records must always be treated with strict confidentiality. The privacy of student data must be maintained at all times and shared only with the student and any university authorities with a need to know.

3. *How long should records be retained?* Records should always be kept during the semester while you are teaching the course and often during the subsequent semester because students may contact you for an explanation of their final grades. A few students might contact you quite some time after the end of the course for references for future study or assistance with career matters. Having records can assist you in recalling the

student's performance in your course. You should ask your university contacts if there is any unique school requirement for retention.

University Procedures and Deadlines

There are several considerations with procedures and deadlines. They all involve the university's registrar's office. So find out from your department secretary or other colleagues whom you should talk with in the registrar's office to get a full understanding of all requirements in the following areas.

Course Registration

You will need to discuss the following:

- How will you know if a student is properly registered for your course and section?
- How does a student add or drop your course? What are the time frames for doing so?
- What are your responsibilities and limits of authority?
- What should you do if a student thinks he or she is enrolled in your course but is not listed on your official roster?

Course Grading and Grade Changes

As with procedures and deadlines, the considerations regarding course grading and grade changes also involve your university registrar's office. So discuss each item with them:

1. What do the traditional grades of A, B, C, D, F, and P/F mean?
2. When are grades due? And in what format, paper or electronic?
3. How do you complete the grading process? Are there special forms? If so, where do you get them? Must you make copies for anyone, such as your program head or department chair?
4. How do you get the grades to the registrar's office? Often the instructor must personally carry them, between the hours of 9:00 a.m. and 4:00 p.m., Monday through Friday.

5. How are final grades communicated to the students? There might be a special area for posting grades. It is often not acceptable to tell students their grades orally.

6. Unusual grades: There are circumstances under which the traditional grades of A, B, C, D, F, and P/F are not appropriate. Following are several examples, with suggestions for handling them:

   ■ *Student asks to repeat your course.* Find out what the university policy and procedures are and how they should be communicated to the student. It might be possible, if the student plans to retake the course with you in the near future, for you to give a grade of Incomplete so that the student does not need to pay additional registration fees.

   ■ *Student asks for an Incomplete grade,* with the intention of completing the course in the future. Find out what the rules are. Usually, the student must have completed a majority of the course with a passing grade, and for reasons not under his or her control cannot complete the course.

   ■ *Student asks to withdraw from your course.* Giving a Withdrawal grade is usually only done by the registrar's office. Students must often submit a written request to withdraw.

   ■ *You need to change a grade after grades have been submitted.* In most schools it is not possible to change grades once they have been submitted. If the need should arise, due to an unusual situation, talk directly with the registrar.

Cheating and Plagiarism

Each school has its own rules about such matters. Your departmental secretary should be able to get you a copy of the policy and regulations. It is useful to note in your course syllabus that cheating, plagiarism, and dishonest behavior will not be tolerated.

Letters of Recommendation

It is likely that a few students will ask you for a recommendation some time after completing your course. Reasons vary, but postgraduate studies and career advancement are two favorites. If you have retained your student records, giving a recommendation, should you decide to do so, is easy. Otherwise, ask the student to draft a letter citing some of his or her accomplishments in your course.

Your best guideline for all administrative matters is "When in doubt, don't guess, find out."

Resources

If you choose to further your study of evaluation via a research and literature search, you will find a range of sources at the end of this chapter. Consider widening your investigation to include both graduate and undergraduate evaluation, as well as evaluation in specific professional fields, such as medical, dental, and legal services.

Evaluation is an important and complex instructional responsibility. Thus it is important for the instructor to cite specific evaluation criteria when creating and documenting a course evaluation plan. The plan must be congruent with the curriculum and the broader university environment and must contain a mixture of evaluation methods and techniques. The instructor must skillfully communicate the results of the evaluation to each student. Finally, the instructor must competently carry out administrative duties as directed by the university. When all aspects of the evaluation process are carefully managed, evaluation becomes the key for controlling quality in the educational process.

Suggested Readings

Astin, A. W. (1991). *Assessment for excellence.* New York: Macmillan.

Barnett, B. G. (1991, October). *Incorporating alternative assessment measures in an educational leadership preparation program.* Paper presented at the annual meeting of the University Council for Educational Administration, Baltimore.

Blake, V. M., & Dinham, S. M. (1988). *Teaching guidebook.* Tucson: University of Arizona, University Teaching Center.

Blumenstyk, G., & Magner, D. K. (1990). As assessment draws new converts, backers gather to ask "What works?" *Chronicle of Higher Education, 36*(43), A11.

Bouhuijs, P. A. J., Van der Vleuten, C. P., & Van Luyk, S. J. (1987). The OSCE as a part of a systematic skills training approach. *Medical Teacher, 9,* 183-191.

Burck, H. D., & Peterson, G. W. (1983). Doctoral comprehensive examination in one program. *Counselor Education and Supervision, 23,* 169-172.

Ceci, S., & Peters, D. (1984). Letters of reference. *American Psychologist, 39,* 29-31.

Cross, K. P. (1988). In search of zippers. *AAHE Bulletin, 40*(10), 3-7.

DaRosa, D. A. (1985). A comparison of objective and subjective measures of clinical competence. *Evaluation and Program Planning, 8,* 327-330.

Davis, K. J., Inamdar, S., & Stone, R. K. (1986). Inter-rater agreement and predictive validity of faculty ratings of pediatric residents. *Journal of Medical Education, 61,* 901-905.

Dinham, S. M. (1988, April). *Student assessment in architecture schools.* Paper presented at the annual meeting of the American Educational Research Association, New Orleans.

El-Khawas, E. (1987, August). *Campus trends, 1987* (Higher Education Panel Rep. No. 75). Washington, DC: American Council on Education, Division of Policy Analysis and Research.

Enteman, W. F., & Jackson, P. I. (1986, June). *Improving undergraduate education with value-added assessment.* Paper presented at the Conference on Value-Added Learning at Empire State College, Saratoga Springs, New York.

Erwin, T. D. (1991). *Assessing student learning and development.* San Francisco: Jossey-Bass.

Grace, E. G., & Cohen, L. A. (1991). A ten year follow-up of attitudes toward evaluation in behavioral aspects of clinical practice. *Journal of Dental Education, 55,* 166-168.

Harkin, P., & Sosnoske, J. (1992). The case for hyper-gradesheets. *College English, 54*(1), 22-30.

Hawkridge, D. (1983). Evaluation of the open university. *Higher Education in Europe, 18*(3), 39-45.

Henbest, R. J., & Fehrsen, G. S. (1985). Preliminary study at the Medical University of Southern Africa on student self-assessment as a means of evaluation. *Journal of Medical Education, 60,* 66-68.

Irby, D. M., & Milam, S. (1989). The legal context for evaluating and dismissing medical students and residents. *Academic Medicine, 64,* 639-643.

Knowles, M. (1984). *The adult learner: A neglected species.* Houston: Gulf.

McClain, C. J., Kreuger, D. W., & Taylor, T. (1986). Northeast Missouri State University's value-added assessment program. *International Journal of Institutional Management in Higher Education, 10,* 252-261.

McMillan, J. H. (1988, Summer). A synthesis with further recommendations. *New Directions for Teaching and Learning, 34,* 99-102.

Melvin, K. B. (1988). Rating class participation. *Teaching of Psychology, 15*(3), 137-139.

Mingle, J. R. (1986, July). *Assessment and the variety of its forms.* Report prepared for the Task Force on Planning and Quality Assessment of the South Carolina Commission on Higher Education.

Mudd, J. O. (1986, April). *Assessment for learning in law.* Paper presented at the annual meeting of the American Educational Research Association, San Francisco.

National Institute of Education. (1984, November). Trouble spots in higher education. In National Institute of Education, *Involvement in learning.* Washington, DC: Author.

Noel, G. L. (1987). A system for evaluating and counseling marginal students during clinical clerkships. *Journal of Medical Education, 62,* 353-355.

Norlander, K., Czajkowski, A., & Shaw, S. (1987, June). *The University of Connecticut program for learning disabled college students.* Hartford: University of Connecticut, School of Education, Special Education Center.

Nutter, N., Johnson, G. W., & Spangler, R. (1989, February). *Computers and professors.* Paper presented at the annual convention of the Association of Teacher Education, St. Louis.

O'Neill, J. P. (1986, October). *The political economy of assessment.* Paper presented at the National Forum of the College Board, New York.

Orphen, C. (1982). Student versus lecturer assessment of learning. *Higher Education, 11,* 567-572.

Pollio, H. R., & Humphreys, W. L. (1988, Summer). Grading students. *New Directions for Teaching and Learning, 34,* 85-97.

Shugars, D. A., May, K. N., & Vann, W. F. (1981). Comprehensive evaluation in a preclinical restorative dentistry technique course. *Journal of Dental Education, 45,* 801-803.

Stark, J. S., Shaw, K. M., & Lowther, M. A. (1989). *Student goals for college and courses* (ASHE-ERIC Higher Education Rep. No. 6). Washington, DC: George Washington University, School of Education and Human Development.

Stemmler, E. J. (1986). Promoting improved evaluation of students during clinical education. *Journal of Medical Education, 61*(part 2), 75-81.

Taylor, T. (1985). A value-added student assessment model: Northeast Missouri State University. *Assessment and Evaluation in Higher Education, 10*(3), 190-202.

Tonesk, X. (1986). MMC program to promote improved evaluation of students during clinical education. *Journal of Medical Education, 61*(part 2), 83-88.

Tonesk, X., & Buchanan, R. G. (1987). An AAMC pilot study by 10 medical schools of clinical evaluation of students. *Journal of Medical Education, 62,* 707-718.

Tori, C. D., & Cervantes, O. F. (1986, May). *The academic evaluation of minority graduate students in psychology.* Paper presented at the annual meeting of the Western Psychological Association, Seattle.

Turnbull, W. W. (1986, October). *Can "value-added" add value to education?* Paper presented at the National Forum of the College Board, New York.

Warren, J. (1987). What students say about assessment. *Liberal Education, 73*(3), 22-25.

Appendix 8.1
Sample Evaluation Checklist
Public Administration

▩ Evaluation Checklist for Goal 1

Goal 1: Give an effective executive presentation, using varied media. (20%)

> Given a group of participants (pretending to be executives), each student will do the following:

Maximum No. of Points	Desired Behaviors	Points Awarded/Explanation
3	Provide a one- to two-page executive summary (1 point for having the summary and 2 points maximum for quality of summary).	

Maximum No. of Points	Desired Behaviors	Points Awarded/Explanation
2	Give an introduction/overview to the presentation.	
3	Provide attendees with handout, including details, related studies, copies of slides, transparencies, etc.	
3	Clarify critical points with examples and costs.	
3	Integrate at least two different types of media.	
2	Provide opportunity for audience questioning.	
2	Handle questions expeditiously and accurately.	
2	Summarize key points, decisions made, and action items.	

20 points

Appendix 8.2
Sample Self-Administered Evaluation
Public Administration

■ **Self-Administered Evaluation**

Goal 2: As a group, work effectively and efficiently to prepare a quality presentation that uses varied media. (10%)

> Circle your response to indicate your evaluation of your group's effectiveness and efficiency in working together.

(1) To what extent did other team members pay attention to your ideas?

Very little	*Little*	*Some*	*Quite a bit*	*Very much*
1	2	3	4	5

(2) How frustrated did you become while creating the team product?

Very little	*Little*	*Some*	*Quite a bit*	*Very much*
1	2	3	4	5

(3) How responsible do you feel for the decisions that were made?

Very little	*Little*	*Some*	*Quite a bit*	*Very much*
1	2	3	4	5

(4) To what extent did you actively seek contributions from others?

Very little	Little	Some	Quite a bit	Very much
1	2	3	4	5

Write out your responses to the following, using the reverse side.

(5) What specific actions/statements were made that helped the group produce the product?

(6) What specific actions/statements were made that did not help the group produce the product?

(7) What would you recommend that your group do differently next time to be more effective and efficient?

Appendix 8.3
Sample Student Data Form

■■ **Student Data**

Date:

NAME: _____

ADDRESS: _____

CITY/STATE/ZIP:_____

PHONE: Home: (   ) _____ Work: (   ) _____

Other: (   )_____

FAX:_____

E-MAIL: _____

WORK EXPERIENCE: Include job and company

OTHER RELEVANT INFORMATION

Appendix 8.4
Sample Student Attendance Form

■ **Attendance List**

Session #: _____

Date: _____

Print Your Name	Sign Your Name	Social Security #

Evaluation of the Course and the Adjunct

EDWARD J. MARITS

We have all been there. It is the last session of the course, and the instructor distributes one of those notorious end-of-course evaluations that require you to rate the instructor and course on a scale of 1 to 5: Would you take another course from this instructor? Were the course goals, objectives, and topics outlined in the syllabus achieved? Were the reading materials relevant?

In this chapter, Edward Marits offers an enlightening look at course evaluation. He effectively explains that the "the primary purpose of evaluation of adjunct faculty is to provide a systematic feedback source that can be used to enhance the performance of an adjunct or a specific course." A good evaluation tool helps to determine two things: whether the course outcomes match the learning objectives and whether the areas of improvement are clearly defined.

Marits discusses the many issues associated with course/adjunct evaluation, including what to measure, how the evaluation will be used, whether the evaluation is valid and fair, and whether there is a process to deal with disagreements. It clearly behooves the adjunct to review the university's end-of-course evaluation tool at the time of hire. It is also wise to determine what follow-up actions are required as a result of the evaluation process. Will someone be observing my class? Will an administrator want to see my plans for revisions? Is it a meaningless process that I should ignore?

Marits explores a wide range of both formal and informal techniques, from the typical reaction questionnaire to more innovative end-of-class group interviews, peer visits, and self-analysis journals. The author also provides meaningful discussion on who does the evaluating (self, full-time faculty, administrator, students), how feedback is given (statistical analysis summary sheet, one-on-one discussion meetings), and how evaluation information is used (rehire, recognition, development opportunities, course changes).

By carefully reading this chapter, an adjunct can protect him- or herself from getting caught off guard by a university's evaluation process. But more important, an adjunct can create his or her own evaluation interventions so as to maximize his or her own teaching effectiveness and make midcourse corrections. By maintaining a proactive and continuous improvement attitude, an adjunct can ensure his or her own success and that of the course.

This chapter addresses two related types of evaluation of adjunct faculty professional performance—evaluation of the course and evaluation of the instructor. The purpose of evaluation is to produce continuous professional improvement of adjunct faculty. This discussion identifies various evaluation techniques and tools that can benefit the continued growth and professionalism of adjunct faculty, regardless of their experience or academic discipline.

This chapter is divided into two sections: first, an overview of the purposes and benefits of evaluation and common concerns about it, and second, a comprehensive look at the evaluation and assessment of adjunct faculty and the courses that they have developed and delivered.

What Is Evaluation?

What is systematic evaluation of college courses? What distinguishes casual assessments from more formal evaluation structures?

For the purpose of this book, evaluation is any formal or informal process of assessment conducted to generate information concerning the quality of learning for a college course. Conventionally formal evaluation of courses has two parts: evaluation of the instructor (performance) and evaluation of the course (syllabus, flow, objectives, difficulty, relevance, usefulness, etc.).

Evaluation of the instructor most frequently takes the form of student survey questionnaires of the instructor, generally done at the last class meeting, in which a student responds on a survey form using an intensity scale of satisfaction or agreement on questions or statements related to the instructor's role and performance. The intensity scale is then quantified, and a summarized readout is provided for feedback. For example, one questionnaire item might be "My instructor provides constructive feedback in writing to class members on presentations and projects," with response choices of *never* (1), *seldom* (2), *sometimes* (3), *frequently* (4), and *always* (5) and an average response of 4.24.

Evaluation of the course, also done at the end of the course by student surveys using an intensity scale, generally involves a wider range of variables. Often the survey includes questions about the course, the textbook, the class organization, the grading structure, communications, instructional style, and the classroom setting as well as the instructor. For example, one questionnaire item might be "This course was valuable and worthwhile," with response choices of *strongly disagree* (1), *disagree* (2), *sometimes agree* (3), *agree* (4), and *strongly agree* (5) and an average response of 3.5.

Alternative approaches to evaluation of the course and the instructor can be employed and will be addressed later. However, distinctions in structure, complexity, cost, and perception of objectivity can be made between formal and informal approaches to evaluation. Formal approaches incorporate systematized and standardized analysis procedures and are generally sponsored by the department, the college, or sometimes the student association. Informal approaches are usually sponsored by the adjunct faculty member him- or herself and are conducted as voluntarily solicited feedback during or at the end of a course. This difference is only relevant to the extent that the quantified survey evaluations are prudently used for comparison and are judged against some preset standard.

As mechanisms for feedback, both formal and informal systems work well. Because the purpose of evaluation is to improve the quality of learning, the choice of evaluation system should be based on what is most useful for translating feedback into improved quality.

Purposes of Evaluation

The overall goal of any assessment system is the improved quality of performance. The primary purpose of evaluation of adjunct faculty is to provide a systematic feedback source that can be used to enhance the performance of an adjunct or the quality of a specific course. Such enhancement manifests itself through the general reactions of students on completion of the course (their affective reactions); what students have learned, as demonstrated in their ability to perform within the classroom setting; what students take away from a course, as demonstrated in their ability to use their learning within their own professional context; and the ultimate effect of the learning experience on general performance and growth and development of student knowledge, skills, and attitudes (Kirkpatrick, 1959-1960).

An additional purpose is to compare learning objectives, course expectations, or curriculum goals with learning outcomes as measured by knowledge, skills, and/or attitudes. The results are the basis for determining areas of improvement and alternative approaches to syllabus, curriculum, delivery, or program outcomes.

Finally, evaluation serves to discriminate between classroom activities, instructor behaviors, and instructional strategies and styles that should be replicated because they worked well and those that should be modified or abandoned because they failed to support learning.

Benefits of Evaluation to the University

A number of benefits accrue to the university from support of both formal and informal evaluations and a systematic instructional assessment system. These include

- A comparative structure to identify areas in which resources can be applied for improvement
- A database of ideas, strategies, and techniques to be used as a resource for other faculty/courses/curricula
- An outline of possible problem areas that can be targeted by professional development activities
- A source for identification of mentoring opportunities
- A basis for specialized recognition of superior performance (merit pay, awards, salary raises)
- Data that help in understanding institutional feedback from students, faculty, or administrators

Benefits of Evaluation to Adjunct Faculty

What are some incentives for adjunct faculty to participate in assessments of their teaching? The general answer would be that evaluation can improve the quality of their courses' content and process so that in the future they and their students can have an enhanced learning experience. More specifically:

- Assessments that include feedback and discussion about performance can provide instructors with a model of professional performance.
- Assessments enable instructors to prioritize areas that need improvement so that action can be specifically directed.
- Assessments enable instructors to compare course goals with what is actually achieved and to revise their strategies accordingly.
- Assessments provide recognition for good performance.
- Assessments provide feedback from the "customer" (college student) to the institution, instructor, and department.

Common Concerns About Evaluation

Numerous issues are frequently raised in any discussion that involves judgment of performance. The intent here is to acknowledge the existence of these concerns and thus to give them credibility, without attempting to address each individually. The most important aspect of all concerns about evaluation is whether evaluation fulfills its purpose of improving the quality of learning.

In evaluation of faculty, the most notable concern is that an arbitrary or unreliable judgment made by students, other faculty, or administrators could cause the university to mandate some change of behavior, at best, or to refuse to renew the teaching contract, at worst. The following questions are those most frequently asked about evaluation:

- What will be evaluated (course, instructor, or both)?
- What will the evaluation be used for?
- Who will do the evaluation, and are they qualified to judge?
- Will the assessment be valid and reliable?
- What actions will come from the evaluation?
- What safeguards are built into the system to prevent arbitrary or unreasonable judgments?
- What are the criteria for judgment?
- When will evaluation happen?
- How do adjunct faculty make use of evaluation data?
- How will adjunct faculty receive evaluation information?
- What is expected of faculty when feedback is received?
- What weight is given to the adjunct faculty's perceptions?
- How can faculty and the administration support evaluation for the purpose of improved quality?
- Are conventions of data quality (validity and reliability) applicable and incorporated in the evaluation system?
- Is there a hierarchy of importance for evaluation elements?
- What constitutes recourse for disagreement?

Strategies for Evaluation

Everyone has a favorite method for gathering evaluation information, whether merely to modify and improve existing courses or to justify the continuation/rehiring of faculty members. But some types of evaluation provide more timely, relevant, and reliable information than others. The discussion of evaluation strategies below is based on theories that differentiate three fundamental kinds of learning—knowledge, skills, and attitudes—and on Kirkpatrick's (1959-1960) discussion of types of evaluation according to the sources and contexts of evaluation information; methods' complexity, value, and cost; and issues around the interpretation of assessment information.

The first strategy for instructional evaluation, and the one that is least complicated, least costly, quickest, most often used, and of most questionable reliability, is the simple reaction questionnaire. This strategy involves soliciting students' reactions (feelings or thoughts) to various elements of a course, such as

- The physical class environment
- The organization of the course content
- The course instructional processes
- The instructor
- The style of teaching
- The degree of difficulty of the course
- A perception of having attained the course outcomes
- A perception of self-assessed learning
- The instructional tools—textbook, handouts, audiovisuals, laboratory equipment

The reaction questionnaire can provide useful information for changing a course to improve learning. There are, however, many drawbacks to using such data:

- Reactions are based on a student's individual needs and expectations.
- Reactions may or may not have anything to do with what is being reacted to.

- Reactions are frequently based on the "most recent event" and do not necessarily represent the entire course.
- Reactions are subject both to spurious influence—some external issue not related to the course, the instructor, or the learning—and/or to events or factors that are misunderstood.
- The object of reaction is usually not the learning of the student.
- Reactions are, at best, biased perceptions of reality.
- There is a strong correlation between a person's learning style and his or her reactions to the learning context and instructional methodology (Kolb, 1984).

The use of a reaction strategy often assumes an expectation that a course should be entertaining and that the instructor should be a polished entertainer. For example, students may be asked to assess the extent to which an instructor was "stimulating." Whether learning outcomes are achieved is assumed to be related only to the degree of agreement with what has been done and discussed in the class. Worse yet, there is significant evidence that because learning is often an uncomfortable process in that it involves change, there exists an inverse relationship between the experiences that a student enjoys and those from which the most learning occurs.

Another critical issue in reaction evaluations is whether the student is qualified to give competent or knowledgeable responses in certain areas of the evaluation. For example, a student may not be qualified to assess the extent to which the instructor in a course was knowledgeable about the material.

Other strategies for evaluation involve the assessment of what has been learned. Those strategies are rooted in the notions that learning is measurable and that it is the terminal outcome of a college course. Such evaluation strategies change the focus of assessment from the aspects of the course (including the instructor) to the product of instruction— what is learned. The performance of the instructor is evaluated on the basis of the degree of learning demonstrated by the students, as measured by changes that occur within each student over the entire course.

The easiest way to assess the degree of learning is to use a student self-evaluation learning inventory. A series of questions is posed to students throughout a course to influence them to think about and record their individual learning. At the end of the course, their "learning logs" can be discussed; turned in for review by the instructor, academic program, or university; or used only by students for their own reflection or potential application.

Another technique for assessment of learning that requires a bit more sophistication and time to employ is the pre-post learning inventory. This is an inventory or performance test that measures, in a controlled setting (the classroom), students' knowledge, skills, or attitudes at the beginning of a course and again on completion of the course. For example, a course in professional ethics might start with an assessment instrument that measured the ability of a student to apply a series of ethical protocols to a given situation. Knowledge, skills, and attitudes might be reasonably assessed. At the completion of the course, the same situation would be presented again and a measurement taken of the changes in knowledge, skills, or attitudes that were demonstrated. Finally, when the changes of all students within a class were aggregated for the course, we could deduce a degree of effectiveness of instruction or performance of the course, instructor, and instructional context.

A third strategy for evaluation involves the assessment of knowledge, skills, or attitudes within an *applied* setting, or field situation. This requires students to demonstrate not only that they have learned knowledge, skills, or attitudes but that they can select and apply knowledge and skills that are appropriate for the "real" situation. Because this evaluation strategy must be employed after some time has been allocated for the learning to "germinate" and because it occurs outside the setting of the university, it generally has the disadvantages of being expensive, time consuming, and difficult to design and implement. Therefore it is not typically used to test for instructional quality or to generate specific information that might suggest changes to a course.

Finally, the strategy that is most difficult, time consuming, and sophisticated in design and application is the assessment of the impact of learning on the individual or the organizations with which the student will engage. Although this strategy would probably provide the best information on the true impact of the course, it is clearly prohibitive, because of time, complexity, and cost, for the evaluation of a single course.

What, then, should adjunct instructors use to evaluate or assess a course when they are seeking information that will help them to improve future offerings? Below are a few questions to begin the evaluation process:

- What am I/are others going to use this information for?
- What are the requirements of the institution, department, program, or special interest groups (e.g., the graduate student association, full-time faculty)?
- What kind of information will be most useful to me for feedback?
- Can the needs of the university and my needs be made compatible?
- What techniques have already been developed, and which of these can I use?
- What costs and benefits will be generated by the technique that is selected?
- What techniques have been useful to me in the past?

Evaluation Techniques

Below are some specific instructional evaluation techniques that are commonly used by universities. Examples are given, and sample instruments are provided in Appendices 9.1, 9.2, and 9.3 at the end of this chapter. You will note that some of the techniques suggested for course evaluation are similar to those suggested for student evaluation in Chapter 8. With slight modification or careful construction, similar methods can be used. Where specialized resources are available, they are identified.

End-of-Course Survey Questionnaire (Closed-Ended Questions)

An example of a closed-ended question is "I consider this course to be a valuable part of my education," with the choice of answers as *strongly agree, agree, neutral, disagree,* and *strongly disagree.* For other examples, see Appendix 9.1.

End-of-Course Survey Questionnaire (Open-Ended Questions)

An example of an open-ended question is "Please provide your personal comments about the following for both the course and the instructor: strong points, weak points, and suggested improvements." For a sample form, see Appendix 9.2.

Midcourse Evaluation

A midcourse evaluation is designed to provide *formative evaluation* so that the instructor can improve while the course is still going on. The students might be asked, for example, whether the instructor "provides clear instructions for projects and exercises," "reviews the agenda at the beginning of each semester," and "uses a variety of media and teaching methods," with the choice of answers being *almost never, seldom, sometimes, frequently,* and *almost always.* For a sample form, see Appendix 9.3.

End-of-Course Group Interview

This technique involves the use of focus group interviews to generate feedback related to a course or instructor. Any reference material on interview technique can act as a resource for the design of focus group interviews. The interviews can be conducted by an outside instructor, proctor, or facilitator; the adjunct who conducted the course; or selected students, who facilitate and record interview information for feedback to the instructor. The focus group technique is particularly applicable to collecting and analyzing evaluative interview information.

Peer Visits

This technique involves the selection of a competent peer by either the adjunct or the institutional faculty to make periodic announced visits to observe the instructional process and provide individual feedback concerning what might be changed to enhance or improve the instructional process. Areas of possible peer evaluation of a class session and feedback to adjunct faculty are listed in *A Handbook for Faculty Development* (Berquist & Phillips, 1981):

- Logical organization
- Pacing
- Student participation
- Closure
- Level of challenge
- Creativity
- Individualization
- Enthusiasm/inspiration

Appendix 9.3, already cited as a sample form for midcourse evaluation, is also a form that could be used by a visiting peer.

Self-Report/Self-Analysis/Self-Checks

This technique, developed by Millis (1989), uses a formal checklist that permits the instructor to perform an assessment periodically to determine where improvement in instruction might occur. There are many variations, from an informal reflective assessment technique in which you think about what went well and what went poorly and ask yourself, "What changes can I make for the next course/class?" to formal learning logs, as described above, that you collect and monitor.

The 1-Minute Paper

This technique, also called the Half-Sheet Response, is a quick and simple way to collect written feedback on student reactions. It consists of a few short questions, offered to students at the end of a class (including individual sessions), that the students then answer in writing on a sheet of paper or index card. A resource for further information about this technique and other reaction techniques is *Classroom Assessment Techniques* (Cross & Angelo, 1988).

Needs Assessments

Needs assessment involves setting an early and accurate context for a course that helps improve the learning by identifying the needs of all learners; establishing clear objectives and expectations about content, style, and student competence entry levels; and recognizing the differences in needs, expectations, backgrounds or experience, interest, preknowledge or skills, and learning styles. This technique is most useful if conducted before development of the curriculum and might employ contact with potential students before the first class session.

A variation of the needs assessment evaluation technique is the *needs reassessment* during the course, sometimes called the *midcourse correction technique*. This can be done at the midpoint and even at course completion to create a "course database" on needs that must be met in the future.

Another variation of the needs assessment technique is sometimes called the *mini-needs assessment*. This technique involves a frequent and informal evaluation of where a group of students are in their learning and what can be done at the moment to enhance the process. A variation of the mini-needs assessment is the "How-Goes-It?"—a simple one-question solicitation of what is working and what is not.

Resources to support needs assessment include any general instructional evaluation source, but particularly *Figuring Things Out: A Trainer's Guide to Needs and Task Analysis* (Zemke & Kramlinger, 1982).

Outcome Assessments

Outcome assessment is a comparative assessment of stated or desired outcomes for a course and achieved outcomes, as measured by various tools such as examination, discussion, and performance simulation. A simple and focused outcome assessment is a quick, easy, and effective way to provide information about whether and to what degree course objectives have been met. Procedure can vary according to preference or focus, but there are four general steps in any outcome assessment:

1. Set the objectives for the course.
2. Determine how to measure the outcomes (with what measurement tools).
3. Measure the output either periodically or at the end.
4. Systematically compare the outcomes to the objectives.

For example, in a graduate course in macroeconomics, one objective is that course participants will be able to apply a specific economic theory to current economic conditions in a specified geopolitical setting. The outcome assessment would require students to apply economic theory to the designated geopolitical setting through a classroom case demonstration.

A resource for outcome assessments is *The Evaluator's Handbook* (Humen, Morris, & Fitzgibbons, 1987).

Informal Evaluation

This is more an approach than a technique. Informal evaluation involves somewhat arbitrary observation or interviewing concerning what is useful, clear, or helpful and what should be changed to improve on utility, clarity, or helpfulness. Generally, informal evaluation is done unobtrusively and occasionally even subconsciously. In fact, each of us in our daily lives is conducting informal evaluations on an almost continual basis.

Who, What, and When?

Who Evaluates?

Evaluation of adjunct faculty needs to be done by one or more of the following:

- The adjunct instructor
- Full-time/permanent faculty
- Student association members

- Peers/other adjunct faculty
- Independent evaluator
- Administrative staff
- Students

All evaluators must understand the basic assessment issues and techniques for collecting valid and reliable data about instructional elements. They must be clear about the purpose and intended use of the evaluation information and how it will help to improve the existing course. In addition, they must be committed to the assessment for improvement and have the available time to conduct a quality evaluation.

Beyond these qualifications, two characteristics determine the choice of who evaluates. First is the use or purpose of the evaluation. Student association questionnaires are used to publish "statistics" about a course or faculty member. Permanent/full-time faculty evaluations are sometimes used to qualify an adjunct for continuation or for a full-time position. Second is the means of giving feedback to the instructor. In informal situations, adjunct faculty conduct their own assessments. A formal feedback situation may use a full-time professor. In the case of surveys, who conducts the evaluation is based on sponsorship.

Who Receives the Evaluation?

Another important factor to consider in adjunct evaluation is who receives the evaluation. Who, besides the instructor, has access to the information, who will review it, and what are the levels of official and unofficial review? Is a formal record of the information retained? What if you, the adjunct, do not agree with the evaluation?

What Is Evaluated?

Far more important than who evaluates is the question of what is evaluated and how extensive the evaluation is. Conventional evaluation theory suggests that specific and measurable criteria be identified so that the assessment can be focused and can differentiate factors for specificity. Table 9.1 lists the many elements of a course that can be evaluated.

When Does Evaluation Take Place?

One final parameter of evaluation for adjunct faculty is when the evaluation should be done. The answer depends primarily on the purpose of the evaluation, what is to be evaluated, who will do the evaluation, how extensive the evaluation will be, and what methods of evaluation will be used. Evaluation usually occurs either *summatively*, at the end of a course, or *formatively*, sometime during a course so that changes can be made to improve the course as it is being conducted. The important issue of timing involves generating assessment information that is representative of the entire course of instruction and does not reflect a single event or point in time (e.g., the last class period).

In addition, one special consideration regarding timing of evaluations is important when the evaluation is done by the students who are being evaluated by the adjunct faculty member on their performance. Students rarely receive formal training or instruction in the evaluation process. Therefore they may perceive the task of evaluating their instructors as threatening and difficult. Occasionally they may see the evaluation as a means of "getting back" at an instructor who has not met individual needs or is otherwise perceived unfavorably. Therefore confidentiality or anonymity is often assured to control for the potential threat to a student who might provide less than complimentary feedback. The procedure that is generally followed when anonymity or confidentiality is desired is to use written feedback instruments in which the evaluators do not identify themselves. These instruments are turned in to a person designated to collect them for the sponsoring faculty member, department, or institution. They are analyzed and returned after the instructor has reported final grades so as to preclude the perception of retribution for less-than-favorable comments. When a system of oral feedback by students is used, timing of assessment may need to take this issue into consideration.

Table 9.1   Course Instructional Elements That Can Be Evaluated

Psychological environment	Level of trust
	Degree of displayed respect
	Demonstrated willingness to help
	Safety of experimentation/risk
Physical environment	Classroom climate
	Classroom equipment
	Class location
	Scheduled time
	Availability and adequacy of support resources
Instructor	Background and experience in teaching
	Background and experience with discipline
	Credible and recognized expertise
	Willingness to support learning
	Commitment to learner
	Predominant teaching style
	Fairness and equity
Organization of course/outcomes/ methods/resources	Planned objectives
	Expected outcomes
	Instructional methodologies
	Organization/flow/timing of curriculum/lesson plans
	Availability of intellectual resources and extra help
	Difficulty of course
	Usefulness of assignments and requirements
	Usefulness of materials (texts, etc.)
	General interest of subject matter
Student	Needs (short-term/long-term)
	Learning style
	Background/experience
	Concerns
	Capacity for work and availability of time
Learning/knowledge/behavioral skills/attitudes	Content knowledge (models, theories, conventions, procedures)
	Skills in demonstrating learned material
	Skills in learning
	Skills in generalization to nonclassroom applications
	Belief systems
	Values
	Feelings/reactions as they affect learning

Communicating Evaluation to Adjunct Faculty

The usefulness of any evaluation depends on whether the information can be clearly communicated and understood by the person evaluated so that improvements in course content or process can be made. The responsibility for the generation of reliable and clear assessment information lies with the sponsor of the evaluation. If the department has a course evaluation system, the department chair needs to ensure that the information is processed and fed back in a timely manner.

Consideration should be given to when and how feedback is provided to adjuncts. Feedback of evaluation information is most meaningful and useful when

- Information is specific about course content and process.
- The purpose of the evaluation is clearly stated and understood.
- Level of quality (validity and reliability) of the data is explicated through discussion of the possible limitations and biases of the evaluation method.
- Who provides feedback, his or her stake in the feedback, and how, where, and when feedback is given are carefully considered.
- It is recognized that the most useful feedback is that solicited by the faculty member.
- Evaluations include assessment and discussion about change strategies or improvement.
- Evaluations identify both strong points and improvement opportunities.
- Evaluations are nonjudgmental.

Use of Evaluation Data

Once you, as an adjunct, receive the feedback of evaluation information, you can put it to the best use by (a) critically reflecting on each component of the information to be sure that you understand what is being said and can analyze it with any significant contextual data that might make it more meaningful and (b) soliciting, through reflection or discussion with a colleague, some actions that can be taken (tested) in the future to improve the quality of your course.

University departmental chairs, administrative managers, academic deans, and program directors can use assessment information in a variety of ways. The most important mandates concerning the use of evaluation information are (a) to be explicit and public about the purpose and intended use for the evaluation both before and after the evaluation has taken place and (b) to ensure that assessment information is used in an ethical and professional manner. The use of evaluations for judgment of awards, special recognition, or selection demands the highest possible degree of objectivity and systematization and the minimization of bias and political motives. Information from evaluations, like other performance data, needs to be kept confidential.

"Ad Hoc" Evaluation

Occasionally a student will make a public complaint about an instructor, course, or program. When a real or perceived threshold, agreement, or standard is violated to such an extent that quick or immediate action is warranted, an "ad hoc" evaluation is necessary. The most important consideration in conducting such an evaluation is the recognition of its importance to the complainant. Whether the charge ultimately proves to be valid or malicious, a clear need exists to assess whether the specific breach has occurred, the extent to which it has occurred, and what action should be taken and by whom. The most common charges that are made concern

- Unprofessional conduct by an instructor
- Violation of a formal agreement or covenant
- Arbitrary or prejudicial judgment or action in grading
- Consistent substandard performance

Another form of "ad hoc" evaluation is the unsolicited testimonial, in which a student, faculty colleague, or administrator recognizes an act of superior performance that is so extraordinary that specific and usually formal recognition is warranted. Though less systematic and objective than formal evaluations, the testimonial should be considered not only as praise but as feedback that may enable the instructor to repeat a superior instructional performance in future courses.

The Evaluation Process

The evaluation process and assessment system do not have to be complicated, expensive or technically perfect. The basic process consists of the steps outlined below:

1. Decide why evaluation is needed (needs assessment).
2. Decide how evaluation is to be used (usage assessment).
3. Decide who will evaluate, analyze, record, and provide feedback.
4. Decide who has a stake in evaluation (stakeholder identification).
5. Decide how assessment is to be conducted (process assessment).
6. Design evaluation tools to meet purpose (instrumentation).
7. Conduct evaluation—collect information.
8. Analyze information.
9. Draw conclusions and provide a report to stakeholders (outcome assessment).
10. Decide any action that needs to occur as an outcome of the evaluation.

A comment about adult learners is warranted. Adults have evaluation interests and concerns that are different from those of younger students because (a) their learning styles are different; (b) other life activities compete with learning for their time and energy; (c) they have more experience with evaluative processes; and (d) they evaluate on the basis of their "context" or worldview, which is shaped by their age and experiences. Therefore evaluation systems that are used for assessment of adjunct faculty should incorporate a recognition of the special characteristics of the adult learner population.

Appendix 9.4 is a short checklist that you can use in developing or participating in a quality assessment process for your teaching.

References

Berquist, W., & Phillips, S. (1981). *A handbook for faculty development* (Vol. 3). Washington, DC: Council of Independent Colleges.

Cross, K. P., & Angelo, T. A. (1988). *Classroom assessment techniques: A handbook for faculty* (Task. Rep. No. 88-A-004.0). Ann Arbor: University of Michigan.

Humen, J., Morris, L., & Fitzgibbons, C. (1987). *The evaluator's handbook.* Beverly Hills, CA: Sage.

Kirkpatrick, D. (1959-1960). Techniques for evaluating training programs: Reaction, learning, behavior and results. *Journal of the American Society for Training and Development.* November 1959, December 1959, January 1960 and February 1960.

Kolb, D. (1984). *Experiential learning: Experience as the source of learning and development.* Englewood Cliffs, NJ: Prentice Hall.

Lewin, K. (1951). *Field theory in social sciences.* New York: Harper & Row.

Millis, B. (1989). Peer visit packet: The University of Maryland University College Peer Visit Program. *Journal of Staff, Program and Organization Development, 7*(1).

Zemke, R., & Kramlinger, T. (1982). *Figuring things out: A trainer's guide to needs and task analysis.* Reading, MA: Addison-Wesley.

Additional Suggested Readings

Acheson, K. (1981). *Classroom observation techniques* (Idea Paper No. 4). Manhattan: Kansas State University, Center for Faculty Evaluation and Development.

Centra, J. (1979). *Determining faculty effectiveness.* San Francisco: Jossey-Bass.

Evertson, C., & Holley, F. (1981). Classroom observation. In J. Millman (Ed.), *Handbook of teacher evaluation* (pp.). Beverly Hills, CA: Sage.

Greive D. (Ed.). (1989). *Teaching in college: A resource for college teachers.* Cleveland: INFO-TEC.

Greive, D. (1990). *A handbook for adjunct/part-time faculty and teachers of adults.* Cleveland: INFO-TEC.

Pace, C. (Ed.). (1973). *Evaluation learning and teaching.* San Francisco: Jossey-Bass.

Seldin, P. (1984). *Changing practices in faculty evaluation: A critical assessment and recommendations for improvement.* San Francisco: Jossey-Bass.

Whitman, N., & Weiss, E. (1982). *Faculty evaluation: The use of explicit criteria for promotion, retention and tenure* (AAHE Research Rep. No. 2). Washington, DC: American Association of Higher Education.

Appendix 9.1
Sample End-of-Course Survey Questions (Closed-Ended)

Responses can be made along some kind of rating scale
(1 = *very poor, strongly disagree,* or *never;* 5 = *excellent, strongly agree,* or *always*)
or can be short answer.

▓ Overall

What is your overall evaluation of the course?

What is your overall evaluation of the professor?

Would you take another course from this instructor?

How would you rate this course as an educational experience?

Do you think you learned from this course?

If you were dissatisfied with this course, did you ever discuss it with the instructor during the semester?

Would you recommend this course to other students?

Were the course goals, objectives, and topics outlined in the syllabus achieved?

Was the course syllabus completed?

▆ Assignments

Were tests, papers, reports, and projects assigned in time for adequate preparation?

Were assignments too heavy?

Were assignments sufficiently challenging?

Compared to other courses you have taken at this university, the workload was _____.

Were the reading materials/homework assignments effective and relevant?

Please indicate the number of exams required in the course: _____

Please indicate the number of papers required in the course: _____

Were textbooks valuable? _____

Were handouts valuable? _____

▆ Grading

Were the tests/exams and papers/assignments graded fairly?

Were exams, papers, and/or evaluations discussed?

Was the instructor fair in grading and treatment of students?

Were the instructor's comments constructive?

What grade do you expect to get in this course? _____

On the basis of course objectives, class participation, test grades, and assignments, what grade do you think you deserve? _____

▆ Teaching

Did the instructor seem prepared for class?

Was the instructor clear in his/her presentation?

Did the instructor make the objectives, grading policies, and classroom procedures clear?

How would you rate the effectiveness of teaching used by the instructor?

In your experience, was the professor accessible out of class? _____

Was the instructor on time for class?

▧ Other

Were the classroom facilities satisfactory?
How many times were you absent from class?
Were there too many students in the class?

Appendix 9.2
End-of-Course Survey Questionnaire (Open-Ended Questions)

▒ Instructions

Use this sheet to record personal comments about strong points, weak points, and your suggested improvements for both the course and the instructor. These narrative comments are made available to the instructor only after the final grades for the course have been submitted. Individual instructors may, at their sole discretion, share these comments with colleagues and administrators.

AUTHOR'S NOTE: Taken from the American University Student Narrative Comment Form, Washington, DC. Reprinted with permission of the American University.

Course Number	Instructor	Semester
Strong Points		
Weak Points		
Suggested Improvements		

Evaluation of courses and instructors by students is the standard policy of The American University. Information provided by students is part of the documentation used in faculty personnel and annual merit-pay review. In addition, the information, particularly the narrative comments, may also be used for faculty development—the strengthening of both teaching and courses. The statistical information from tabulation of the machine-scanned questionnaires will be available—after final grades for the course have been submitted—to the instructor, the teaching unit administrator, the department rank and tenure committee and/or merit pay committee, other university officials and committees, and the university community.

Appendix 9.3

Behavior Observation Scale (BOS) for School of Business Administration Professors

▰ Introduction

This Behavior Observation Scale (BOS) has been developed for professor development. For example, it specifies what is expected of them and provides feedback about areas where they are doing well and areas where improvement is needed. It is designed to provide *formative* evaluation, so the professor can improve while you are still in the course, as opposed to *summative* evaluation, which is administered by the University at the end of the semester. For this reason, you should be receiving this instrument during the middle of the semester. To ensure frank, honest feedback, you are asked to complete this form anonymously:

AUTHOR'S NOTE: The Behavior Observation Scale, Marymount University, Arlington, VA, is reprinted with the permission of its developer, Dr. John Fry.

PROFESSOR: _____ COURSE NO: _____

COURSE NAME: _____ DATE: _____

LOCATION: _____

* * * DO NOT SIGN YOUR NAME * * *

■ Instructions

Please consider the above named professor's behavior *only* during the class you are currently taking. Circle the number that indicates the frequency with which you believe this professor has demonstrated this behavior.

"1"	for	"Almost Never"	0 to 64% of the time
"2"	for	"Seldom"	65 to 74% of the time
"3"	for	"Sometimes"	75 to 84% of the time
"4"	for	"Frequently"	85 to 94% of the time
"5"	for	"Almost Always"	95 to 100% of the time
"N/A"	for	"N/A"	Not applicable or unable to evaluate

An example statement is shown below. If the professor posts an agenda about 50 percent of the time at the beginning of your classes with him/her, then you should circle a "1." If the professor always posts an agenda, then you should circle "5."

■ Example

	Almost Never	Seldom	Sometimes	Frequently	Almost Always	N/A
Posts an agenda at the beginning of the class.	1	2	3	4	5	N/A

	Almost Never	Seldom	Sometimes	Frequently	Almost Always	N/A

■ Preparation

		Almost Never	Seldom	Sometimes	Frequently	Almost Always	N/A
1.	Designs class sessions so that skills and knowledge can be transferred from the classroom to the workplace.	1	2	3	4	5	N/A
2.	Arranges classroom to minimize distractions and maximize class member interaction.	1	2	3	4	5	N/A
3.	Has course materials, learning aids, and supplies readily available.	1	2	3	4	5	N/A
4.	Posts agenda and other relevant information in a clearly visible location.	1	2	3	4	5	N/A
5.	Assigns readings and activities in advance as homework.	1	2	3	4	5	N/A
6.	Comments:						

■ Presentation

		Almost Never	Seldom	Sometimes	Frequently	Almost Always	N/A
7.	States learning objectives (rationale) at the start of each session.	1	2	3	4	5	N/A
8.	Reviews the agenda at the beginning of each session.	1	2	3	4	5	N/A
9.	Relates the reading assignment to the class session.	1	2	3	4	5	N/A

	Almost Never	Seldom	Sometimes	Frequently	Almost Always	N/A

▬ Presentation (continued)

	Almost Never	Seldom	Sometimes	Frequently	Almost Always	N/A
10. Relates the content of the session to the expressed needs of class members and to their work environments.	1	2	3	4	5	N/A
11. Maintains the interest of the class by showing where key content points fit into the session outline.	1	2	3	4	5	N/A
12. Uses examples from own or class members' past experience to illustrate learning points.	1	2	3	4	5	N/A
13. Uses a variety of media and teaching methods over the course of the semester.	1	2	3	4	5	N/A
14. Provides for student involvement in practicing the ideas/concepts/principles presented.	1	2	3	4	5	N/A
15. Maintains interest (e.g., eye contact, speaking clearly).	1	2	3	4	5	N/A
16. Encourages class members to ask questions and is responsive to them.	1	2	3	4	5	N/A
17. Provides rationale for course activities, exercises, and examples.	1	2	3	4	5	N/A
18. Summarizes each session to emphasize key learning points.	1	2	3	4	5	N/A
19. Comments:						

		Almost Never	Seldom	Sometimes	Frequently	Almost Always	N/A

■ Communication

		Almost Never	Seldom	Sometimes	Frequently	Almost Always	N/A
20.	Provides *constructive* feedback, in writing, to class members on presentations and projects.	1	2	3	4	5	N/A
21.	Encourages class members to give feedback on course content or process during each class session.	1	2	3	4	5	N/A
22.	Provides clear instructions for projects and exercises.	1	2	3	4	5	N/A
23.	Is approachable; makes it easy to ask for help.	1	2	3	4	5	N/A
24.	Provides convenient times for consultation with class members, whether on campus or at their workplace.	1	2	3	4	5	N/A
25.	Follows the syllabus and class agendas unless modified by mutual agreement.	1	2	3	4	5	N/A
26.	Uses time effectively: starts on time, ends on time.	1	2	3	4	5	N/A
27.	Follows through on commitments made to me.	1	2	3	4	5	N/A
28.	Comments:						

	Almost Never	Seldom	Sometimes	Frequently	Almost Always	N/A

■ Grading/Assessment

		Almost Never	Seldom	Sometimes	Frequently	Almost Always	N/A
29.	Sets challenging course requirements, but not so difficult as to cause frustration.	1	2	3	4	5	N/A
30.	Grades all course requirements against the criteria described in the syllabus.	1	2	3	4	5	N/A
31.	Provides grades and feedback on presentations and projects promptly.	1	2	3	4	5	N/A
32.	Provides opportunity to discuss grades and explains reasons when requested.	1	2	3	4	5	N/A
33.	Comments:						

■ Course Introduction

34.	Introductions were conducted in a manner that put class members at ease, facilitated networking, and determined their learning objectives.	Yes	No	Other: _____ _____
35.	A syllabus was provided that described the course purpose, objectives, teaching method, requirements, grading criteria, schedule (with date, subjects and assignments for each session), required texts, and suggested readings.	Yes	No	Other: _____ _____
36.	An overview was presented that provided a course "road map, "with a clear path and skill/knowledge destination.	Yes	No	Other: _____ _____

37. What do you like *most* about this course thus far? _____

_____

38. What do you like *least* about this course thus far? _____

_____

39. What *recommendations* would you make for improvement? _____

_____

Thank you for your assistance in providing feedback that will help in the development of the Business School professors at Marymount University.

(Revised: 9/29/94)

Appendix 9.4

Checklist for Developing or Participating in a Quality Assessment Process

_____ Recognize the value and need for an evaluation system.

_____ Determine need and use for evaluation information.

_____ Determine existing evaluation procedures for department, course, student associations, and other stakeholders.

_____ Discuss evaluation publicly with colleagues, department chair, and students.

_____ Advocate for the value of and need for a feedback system to improve quality.

_____ Determine and seek specific (criterion-referenced) information that will be useful to you.

_____ Solicit feedback that is based on specific criteria, and listen carefully.

_____ Solicit feedback that is not based on specific criteria but that might be useful, and listen carefully.

_____ Consider the feedback provided, and propose change as necessary.

_____ Accept what is useful and ignore what is not, but avoid explanation.

_____ **Act!**

10

Professional Development of Adjunct Faculty

EDWARD J. MARITS

The very act of becoming an adjunct professor suggests a belief in applying one's skills in a variety of ways and situations. Consequently, professional development is something that most adjuncts would believe in. But as Edward Marits points out in this chapter—and as Bianco-Mathis and Cooper mention in the first chapter—how much or how little professional development is offered an adjunct depends on the university. Some univer- sities provide an entire professional development infrastructure, complete with workshops, career development programs, and recognition systems. Within other universities, adjuncts may need to beg for copies of their evaluation forms and seek reimbursement for textbooks that they have to read on their own.

It clearly benefits a university to provide professional development options. It ensures continual improvement in the quality of the instruc- tional product. It also provides a system for weeding out poor adjuncts or developing borderline instructors. Marits discusses a variety of professional development methods but specifically addresses criterion-referenced development and mentoring programs. Both of these systems involve targeted improvement areas and systematic plans. A good professional development infrastructure can target development activity in line with an adjunct's specific needs and in support of the university's overall philosophy and direction.

As emphasized in the last chapter on course/adjunct evaluation, it is wise for an adjunct to be proactive in his or her own professional development. This should not be hard to do because many adjuncts seek college teaching as a development strategy within their "overall" life development.

This chapter defines professional development of adjunct faculty, discusses its benefits to both faculty and the university, lists common concerns about the establishment of a professional development program, and describes a variety of professional development activities.

What Is Professional Development?

The professional development of adjunct faculty involves all formal or informal activities that ultimately help faculty to improve instructional quality. Professional development as discussed here is limited to activities that are directly related to either the academic discipline (content) of courses or the instructional process, although some scholars have offered broader definitions that include personal health and growth and career management. Millis (1989) suggested that professional development programs should have both a remedial focus (i.e., working to improve instructional shortcomings) and a developmental focus (i.e., working to increase or expand both instructional and intradisciplinary competence).

Professional Development Activities

Some professional development activities might include

- *A peer visit* or *peer feedback program* (possibly tied to evaluation) in which an interested colleague periodically visits the classroom for feedback to and discussion with the instructor. Within the evaluation context, peer visits involve observation and assessment of teaching methods and applications of content so that the instructor can continue to develop in teaching and scholarship.

- A more comprehensive *coaching program* (variously called *peer development, mentoring, companion,* or *colleague development program*) in which colleagues are invited to participate, as resource persons or mentors, in adjuncts' instructional planning, syllabus preparation, classroom activities, and evaluation and to help develop both adjuncts' instructional technologies and their particular scholarly discipline

- *A manual or other handouts* that provide sample syllabi, suggest teaching methods, or outline educational philosophy

- *A recognition system* that acknowledges and rewards excellence in instruction for the purpose of emulation

- *Internal instructional workshops* using faculty or other expert resources from within the university, where interested faculty can develop specific instructional skills, methods, or testing instruments

- *External education/workshops,* in which interested faculty can develop enhanced skills within their scholarly discipline or instructional practice

- *Training in new instructional technology*

- *An evaluation system,* in which assessment information is given to the adjunct, permanent faculty, and program coordinators, directors, and administrators

- *A communications network* with which faculty can access information concerning specific instructional problems or cases or can offer their thoughts about a new instructional product

- *A media system* to share information within and between faculty, which might include newsletters, professional journals, teleconferencing, and video presentations

- *Participation in faculty meetings* and retreats and other developmental activities of full-time faculty

- *Participation in university, college, or departmental committees, task forces, and research initiatives*

- *A formal program of grants* for extraordinary performance

- *An orientation program* to help adjunct faculty acclimate to the new learning environment

- *A career development program* that encourages adjunct faculty to develop a career plan and to map out goals and interests (e.g., courses desired)

■ A *documentation system* that enables adjunct faculty to develop a portfolio of their teaching experiences and efforts for future appointment or use by colleagues

■ A *"visiting scholar" program* in which adjunct faculty are invited to visiting scholars' talks on discipline-related innovations, ideas, or theories

■ A *professional presentation forum,* in which adjunct faculty are encouraged and supported to develop and present at professional associations and conferences as faculty representatives of the university

One specialized professional development program deserves separate discussion: criterion-referenced development. In criterion-referenced development programs, assessment tools are used on a regular basis to determine preference or need for additional training and development in either instructional technique or disciplinary knowledge. This information is made the basis for the development or modification of a university-, college-, or department-supported individual action plan that outlines activities, times, and support requirements for its execution.

The most important advantages of a criterion-referenced development system are that it is focused specifically on the needs of the individual adjunct faculty member and permits the evolution of a formal plan for addressing those needs. Many of the professional development activities listed above might be specifically targeted to individual faculty developmental criteria.

Common Concerns About Professional Development

The establishment of a system of professional development for adjunct faculty raises many questions. The following are some of the most common concerns:

■ Who is responsible for the development of adjunct faculty?

■ What resources are available for adjunct faculty development?

■ Will resources used for adjunct development be taken from professional development opportunities for full-time and tenured faculty?

■ Why should the institution support professional development?

Other questions are:

- When evaluation reveals an unacceptably low level of instructional competence, is it cost-effective to attempt remediation by professional development, or would it be better just to hire an alternative adjunct?
- The hiring of adjunct faculty presumes their technical instructional competence, so if adjunct faculty are performing below standard, is it not to their benefit to get their own "help"?
- What professional development strategies can be created that are not "cost-intensive?"
- Is time in professional development for adjunct faculty part of contracted time to be reimbursed with augmented salary?
- What if adjunct faculty do not avail themselves of professional development opportunities?
- What creative and new professional development strategies can be devised to provide individualized growth and development?
- How can we link professional development activities to performance within the classroom?

Benefits of Professional Development to the University

Although there is some disagreement concerning who should be responsible for adjunct faculty development, it is generally accepted that some formal and continuing plan for providing growth and development opportunities contributes to continuous improvement in the quality of the instructional product. Specifically, a professional development system for adjunct faculty offers several benefits to the institution that sponsors it:

- An efficient system for distributing developmental resources
- An organized plan for assessing faculty growth and development
- A "blueprint" for individual adjunct faculty development
- Better integration of adjunct faculty into the institution and conformance of their work to institutional philosophy and goals
- A selling point for attracting new adjunct faculty

Benefits of Professional Development to the Adjunct

For you, the adjunct, there are three primary benefits to participating in professional development programs:

■ You set an example for your students of continued openness to learning and show them that learning is a lifelong process.

■ You gain the opportunity to explore new areas in which you can enhance your skills and are exposed to new technology in your discipline or in the area of instructional methods.

■ You are intrinsically compensated for work that sometimes goes unrecognized.

Resources for Professional Development

Professional development should be voluntary because it generally requires additional work that is not formally compensated by the university, school, college, or program. No prejudice can be attached to voluntary nonparticipation by adjuncts.

Nevertheless, adjunct faculty have a vested interest in promoting their own continued growth, and if they recognize this interest, they must be proactive advocates for professional development for themselves and their colleagues. Where a formal professional development plan exists, it is only as sound as the combined commitment of both adjunct faculty members and the institution to support it. Where institutional support for such a plan does not exist, professional development becomes the sole interest of the adjunct.

Adjunct faculty are encouraged to contact specific departments and university development offices to offer and learn about opportunities for collaboration in individual growth and development. Some universities actually have an Office of Faculty Development. Also, there are annual award/recognition programs sponsored by the American Association of University Professors (AAUP) and the American Association of University Women (AAUW).

For adjunct faculty members, the essential issue is that teaching a course is not only about showing up one night a week for a semester and providing some instruction. Rather, it involves the commitment and confidence to create, seek, and participate in activities that will enhance the learning experience for both themselves and their students.

Reference

Millis, B. (1989). *Peer visit packet*. University of Maryland, University College.

Additional Suggested Readings

Berquist, W., & Phillips, S. (1975). *Handbook for faculty development* (Vol. 1). Washington, DC: Council for the Advancement of Small Colleges.

Berquist, W., & Phillips, S. (1981). *Handbook for faculty development* (Vol. 3). Washington, DC: Council of Independent Colleges.

Carroll, J., & Goldberg, S. (1985). The teaching consultant: A pragmatic approach to faculty and instructional development. In *Issues in Higher Education. Proceedings of Academic Chairpersons: Leadership and Management, 17*. Manhattan: Kansas State University, Center for Faculty Evaluation and Development.

Case, C. (1976). *Professional staff development: A community college model*. Pittsburgh, CA: Community College.

Centra, J. (1979). *Determining faculty effectiveness*. San Francisco: Jossey-Bass.

Clark, S., & Lewis, D. (Eds.). (1985). *Faculty vitality and institutional productivity: Critical perspectives for higher education*. New York: Teachers College.

Eble, K., & McKeachie, W. (1985). *Improving undergraduate education through faculty development*. San Francisco: Jossey-Bass.

Millis, B. (1992, October). Faculty development: An imperative in the 1990s. *MAHE Journal, 15*, 9-21.

Weimer, M. (1988). *Higher education: Faculty evaluation, faculty development*. Seminar at the University of Maryland, University College Center for Adult Education.

11

Putting It All Together

CYNTHIA ROMAN

The techniques mentioned in the preceding chapters sound perfectly logical and doable. An adjunct may dutifully develop good objectives, design a dynamic course, practice facilitation skills in front of the mirror, and visit the classroom for a dry run. But when that first night arrives and those students are staring expectantly, "putting it all together" may still seem intimidating.

In this chapter, Cynthia Roman has created four scenarios that dramatize the typical mistakes that new (and even experienced) adjuncts make. Following each vignette is an analysis that emphasizes one of the points made in the previous chapters. Reviewing these stories from time to time should be mandatory for all instructors.

Some final tips: Relax. Trust the process. Be authentic. Laugh.

Case 1: Susan Sanchez's Syllabus

Problem

Susan Sanchez's first semester of teaching at the university was not going as well as she had hoped. She worked as director of corporate communications for a large software company and was delighted when she was offered the opportunity to teach the graduate-level course "Communication Skills for Managers." She worked hard at planning the course lectures to make sure the curriculum included those topics she knew were critical for effective managers. However, almost from the first night of class, she was continually confronted with questions indicating that students were unsure about what was expected of them. The quality of the assignments she received from her students was so poor that Susan began to question not only the intelligence of her students but her own abilities as a teacher. In addition, students were arriving late to class and in some cases missing entire sessions. It was not unusual for Susan to get phone calls from students at work and late at night asking her for clarification of grade requirements and course material.

In desperation, Susan called Dr. Luce, the college faculty member who coordinated management courses, to ask for advice. Dr. Luce suggested that Susan meet with him and bring along a copy of the course syllabus. Following is a copy of Susan's course syllabus.

SYLLABUS

NORTHERN UNIVERSITY

Course:
MGT 403: Communications Skills For Managers

Instructor:
Ms. Susan Sanchez
ph: work: 213-794-5226
     home: 213-815-2339

Textbooks:
Bovee, C. L., & Thill, J. V. (1992). *Business Communication Today* (3rd ed.). St. Louis: McGraw-Hill.
Arredondo, L. (1991). *How to Present Like a Pro.* St. Louis: McGraw-Hill.

Attendance:
Acknowledging that the varied schedules of students might require missing a session during the course, the instructor will construct a learning contract to ensure that the class material has been covered sufficiently.

■ Philosophy and Overview of Course

The successful business operations of virtually any organization rest on its ability to establish and maintain effective communication channels among its members. On the basis of this premise, information is interpreted and decisions are made and disseminated through the appropriate channels, and problems are solved. For such a fundamental model to be effective, managers at all levels should be skilled in oral and written communications.

Managers should know how to communicate relevant information to different groups and should consistently develop, test, and actively seek feedback on communication skills. This process enables them to identify possible barriers within the organization that may inhibit effective teamwork and delay meeting organizational objectives and goals.

COMMUNICATION SKILLS FOR MANAGERS will give a close-up look at communication techniques that can lead to sound organizational decision making.

▇ Course Objectives

- ▇ Students will have a comprehensive understanding of how managers effectively use oral and written communications.
- ▇ Students will know how reports and proposals are used in a business setting.
- ▇ Students will know the characteristics of good speech delivery.
- ▇ Students will be able to identify the qualities of a good business report or proposal and be able to prepare all the necessary parts of a formal report.
- ▇ Students will be able to prepare for and speak in problem-solving discussions.
- ▇ Students will be able to write effectively.

▇ Class Sessions

Date	Session	Assignments/Exercises
Aug. 14	1	1. Principles of Speaking/Presenting Like a Pro
Aug. 21	2	1. Impromptu oral presentations. Use information provided in *How to Present Like a Pro.*
Aug. 28	3	1. Identify five topics related to written communication skills that you would like to improve from *Business Communication Today*. Turn in to me: List topic, chapter, and pages, and give brief explanation of why you want/need to improve in this area. 2. Bring two samples of written office communications that you authored: one that you judge to have a communication style that is very good (effective) and one with a style that is very bad (ineffective). Bring several copies to class. 3. Group project: proposal preparation

Date	Session	Assignments/Exercises
Sept. 4	4	1. Chapters 19 & 20—*Business Communication Today* 2. Final oral presentation 3. Group presentation

▀ Grading

1. Participation in class	20%
2. Oral presentations	45%
▪ Individual	30%
▪ Group	15%
3. Written submissions	35%

Discussion

During their meeting, Susan Sanchez and Dr. Luce discussed how the course syllabus might be contributing to the problems with her class. In addition, they talked about ways Susan might help her students focus on the specific learning outcomes she desired.

Questions

1. What are the weaknesses of the syllabus? How might these weaknesses be contributing to the problems in Susan Sanchez's class?

Susan's syllabus could be improved in several critical areas to help overcome student confusion and anxiety. First, the learning objectives are too vague and general. They do not support the goals of the course by specifying what the learner will actually do to achieve the goals of the course. It is apparent that Susan requires her students to give both impromptu and formal speeches during the class. Yet the learning objectives do not state this. It is not enough to state that students will know the characteristics of a good speech. They must actually deliver one. A learning objective that states that students will give an 8- to 10-minute oral presentation is a good example of a terminal learning objective. Susan's specific lesson plans could be guided by a series of enabling learning objectives that students must achieve before they will be able to deliver the final oral presentation. The following enabling objectives could have been written into the course calendar to correspond to specific session topics:

- Students will define the purpose of, analyze the audience of, and plan a speech or presentation.
- Students will develop the following components of a speech or presentation: introduction, body, close, question-and-answer period, and visual aids.

The second area of weakness in Susan's syllabus relates to the course calendar and grading criteria. Susan's course calendar includes a column labeled "Assignments/Exercises." Here Susan includes some session topics, class assignments, and specific reading requirements. To improve clarity, Susan should have addressed each session's learning objectives in this column and described assignments separately for each date. For each session, students need to know what they should read, what they should bring to class, and what assignments are due on that date.

Students typically are quite interested in what they are expected to do "to get an A." Let's look at each item on the "Grading" list. The syllabus states that participation in class counts for 20% of the final grade. Yet nowhere does she describe what *participation* means. Does it mean attendance? Or does it mean contributing to the learning environment? Or both? It would be easy for students to be confused regarding how their participation is measured, especially because Susan states that they can construct a learning contract in lieu of attending class. The individual and group presentations should be explained fully, including guidelines, procedures and measures for evaluation. The "written submissions" requirement needs to be explained. For example, do the individual and group presentations require supporting reports, and are they graded separately? Are the assignments listed under Session 3 graded? If so, how?

Finally, Susan needs to be clear about course contingencies and her own constraints. A section in her syllabus labeled "Other Issues" could address late work, makeups, extra credit, canceled classes, and so forth. Susan is not expected to be available at all hours to her students. Her syllabus should indicate when she is available to receive calls and when she holds office hours, if required by her school. With the advent of e-mail, many instructors can now offer their students an opportunity for dialogue while also better managing their time.

2. What can Susan do now to improve her class's learning outcomes?

Susan can do several things to clarify her expectations and help her students achieve the course goals. First, she can lead a discussion of student concerns. By being responsive to her students' questions, Susan will open the door to better communication, and her students' anxieties will be alleviated. Susan can also develop a syllabus supplement, explaining each assignment and how it will be evaluated. At the beginning of each class session, she can write the learning objectives and agenda on the board, including the next week's assignment. This will help her students to focus on what they are learning and not always be wondering how what they are learning relates to how they are being evaluated.

Finally, and perhaps most important, Susan needs to regard herself as being in a mutual learning relationship with her students. Adult learners have much experience to offer to the learning environment. Susan could include methods other than lecture in her class sessions to capture student interest and motivation. By designing her lesson plans around her learning objectives and not around topics, she can think about the best way to help adult learners achieve the objectives and apply them to their professional and personal lives.

Case 2: Terry Thompkins' Teaching

Problem

Terry Thompkins walked into the classroom prepared to teach this session as he teaches all his sessions. Terry teaches "Introduction to

Systems Engineering" to practicing engineers at a navy research and development laboratory. He was hired as an adjunct instructor to teach this class because the course was held on site and the full-time graduate engineering faculty did not want to commute from the university's main campus 4 hours away. Terry has a Ph.D. in engineering and works as a project manager for a telecommunications company. He enjoys teaching graduate courses because it allows him to keep up with the rapidly changing engineering technologies.

In this fifth session of the course, Terry took the first 15 minutes to write notes from his planned lecture on the board. As he filled up the board with flowcharts, mathematical equations, and complex algorithms, he overheard students behind him whispering about how they had not finished the homework for this session. Terry sighed and thought to himself, "Students just don't take their education as seriously these days as when I was in school."

He turned to his class, said, "Good evening," and began his lecture. The topic for tonight was fiber optics, and Terry knew that this is an important area for these engineers. The navy is adapting fiber optics technology to many of its weapons and communications systems, and Terry was sure that some of his students were working in related project areas. He lectured from his notes, occasionally referring the students to textbook material. After about an hour of lecture, Terry paused and stated, "Given the rapidly changing nature of fiber optics technology, it appears that the navy would be advised to contract out all research and development. The private sector is better equipped to incorporate advances in a more cost-efficient, timely manner." Terry was unprepared for the firestorm that followed. Everyone started talking at once, and the volume of the discussion started to rise.

As Terry struggled to regain control, one student raised his hand. Grateful for some semblance of organized discussion, Terry called on him. The student began a long, rambling story of his various negative experiences with contractors and how contractors would cause the downfall of the navy's proud tradition. As other students began fidgeting, Terry interrupted the student and said, "Your comments don't have any relevance to our discussion of fiber optics research." As the student slid down further into his seat, Terry was relieved that he could continue with his lecture. He had a lot of material to cover.

After another 45 minutes of lecture, Terry asked if anyone had any questions. One student asked a question that was clearly covered in the assigned textbook reading. Terry replied, "If you'd read the homework assignment, you wouldn't have asked that question." Another student made a comment that indicated to Terry that he had given a great deal of thought to what he had read. Terry said, "Yes, I agree." When another student offered a comment that merely restated what she had read, Terry responded with "You need to be more clear with your comments."

At this point, it was apparent to Terry that most of the class had not done their assigned reading. Terry moved away from the podium and stood closer to his students with his hands on his hips. He said, "It's obvious that most of you haven't done the reading. Why?" After what seemed like an eternity of silence, Terry added, "I know you all lead busy lives, but if you want to get through this program, you are going to have to make your schoolwork a priority." As he turned to walk back to the podium, a student stated, "We'd be more motivated if you could show us how all this theory relates to our jobs."

This was all Terry needed. He had suspected all along that these students were not really interested in graduate-level education. They really wanted job training, and they wanted academic credit for it! Terry launched into a lengthy lecture on his views of the difference between training and education, concluding with the admonition "My job is to give you the latest engineering information that research has generated. If you want job training, I suggest that you talk to your supervisor and sign up for some of the continuing education courses available." There was quiet in the room until two students slammed their books shut, got up, and walked out. Terry gave out the reading assignment for next week and reminded students that the midterm was scheduled for the seventh session. He left his classroom feeling that maybe this would be the last engineering class he would teach.

Discussion

1. *How could Terry have improved his teaching methods in the following areas: (a) instructional methods, (b) classroom discussion, and (c) presentation aids?*

Terry relied much too heavily on lecture as an instructional method. Although graduate engineering students are probably accustomed to lecture, there are many ways that Terry could "gently stretch" his students to become more actively engaged in their learning. Let us first discuss how Terry could improve his use of the lecture method and then what supplemental methods he could use.

A lecture is an appropriate method when a large amount of information must be covered quickly, but Terry missed important opportunities to help his students go beyond information acquisition to higher levels of learning, such as integration, analysis, and critical thinking. Instead of repeating textbook material in a lecture, Terry could begin his lesson by asking for reactions to the reading assignment, eliciting areas where students need explanation or reinforcement. A variation of this approach is the "pop quiz" to evaluate student understanding of reading assignments. This approach not only focuses the session but gives Terry important information about his students' learning needs, interests, and experiences. Terry's lecture could then be oriented around more recent research, giving information not available in the textbook. He should include examples from his own experience as well as from the literature. An adult version of "show and tell" in the form of demonstrations and illustrations helps adult learners apply concepts to the real world. One engineering professor used a fishing pole to illustrate certain motion dynamics. Another brought in a telephone to illustrate electrical engineering principles. Just as important, Terry should invite students to provide examples from their own work experience with the topic.

Terry could make his lectures more participative by facilitating orderly brainstorming on a topic raised in the readings. He could record ideas on overhead transparencies or flip chart paper, making copies for everyone in the class. His hour-long lectures are too long to maintain attention and interest. Every 15 to 20 minutes he should shift the energy to his students, having them engage in problems, case studies, or debates. Hands-on application exercises using computers or engineering resources will enable students to apply and practice what they hear in a lecture.

One of the most effective instructional methods with students with technical backgrounds is the applied project. This can be done by individuals or groups to give students practice on course objectives.

Instead of the traditional midterm or final exam, students choose a project of most interest and application to their work settings. Applied projects usually result in a paper and/or a concrete product or design. When students are allowed flexibility in choosing areas of work interest, they are more motivated to accomplish course objectives.

Terry's contentious statement regarding the contracting out of fiber optics technology could have been the start of a valuable class discussion. Instead, his authoritative, "nonacceptance" language shut down the opportunity for his students to learn to think analytically about the issues. If Terry had organized his use of the lecture method better, he could have used the class discussion to shift the emphasis away from teaching and toward learning. Discussion does take time, but the benefits of learning to think critically and solve problems are sizable.

As the fiber optics discussion "took off," Terry could have posted all the ideas on the board. Instead of cutting off discussion, he could have used "gatekeeping" skills to allow all students to contribute and build on ideas. Terry could have tested consensus until all ideas were posted, integrated similar ideas, and summarized the whole discussion. This approach turns a free-for-all discussion into a learning opportunity to achieve course objectives.

Terry needs to be sensitive to his students' behavior to deal with problems related to the learning environment. His aggressive words and body language probably contributed to the "eternity of silence" he experienced when he asked why the students had not done their reading assignment. The students may have been afraid to reveal their true feelings for fear of the consequences (poor grades, criticism, etc.). In fact, when the one brave student did express his views, all the students were indeed punished by being subjected to Terry's diatribe on the differences between training and education. This unfortunate sequence of events could have been avoided if Terry had tolerated the silence and probed into the meaning behind the comment regarding student motivation. A nonevaluative stance and good listening skills would have eventually reduced the tension until the students were ready to engage in problem solving.

Terry's only presentation aid was the chalkboard. Although this is certainly the presentation aid used most in the education setting, Terry used it inappropriately by filling it up with material already presented in the textbook and in his lecture. All presentation aids, including the chalkboard, should support the message, not take its place. Terry should have prepared a package of handouts, including an outline of his lecture material, copies of slides or transparencies and preboarded flip chart material, and any other exercise materials. He could have used the chalkboard to post output from spontaneous discussions and to illustrate diagrams or calculations. Not only did Terry lose time when he spent 15 minutes at the beginning of class copying lecture material on the board; he also lost the opportunity to include his students in learning interaction. By taking the time to prepare his presentation aids in advance, he will be able to concentrate during class on how his students are learning.

Case 3: Ed Esterbrook's Evaluation

Problem

Ed Esterbrook just received a call from Dr. Sanford, the head of the Administrative Sciences Department at Southern University. The results of the student evaluations from Ed's course, "Introduction to Computers," had been compiled, and Dr. Sanford wanted to discuss them with him. It was December 15, 1 week after the last session of the class. The last thing Ed wanted to think about 1 week before the holidays was evaluation. But he agreed to meet with Dr. Sanford the next day.

Dr. Sanford began the meeting with Ed by asking him how he thought the course had gone. Ed replied that he assumed everything went well because no one had complained. Dr. Sanford began to discuss how important it was to keep the students happy because of the growing competition from other area colleges and universities. He cited one horror story after another of students who had complained about unfair grading and uncaring instructors. As he went on, Ed began to get worried. What did his student evaluations look like?

Finally, Dr. Sanford produced a copy of the compiled results of the student evaluations, as shown below.

ADMINISTRATIVE SCIENCES PROGRAM

Student Evaluation—Fall 1994
Professor Esterbrook
ADSC 221. Introduction to Computers

Your evaluation of this course and the instructor will be helpful for future planning. A student volunteer will collect all completed forms and seal them in an envelope. The instructor will see only summary results for the entire class, not your individual responses. Please circle your answer to each question. Also to further protect anonymity, please do not put your name on this evaluation.

Course Methods

1 = *strongly disagree*, 2 = *disagree*, 3 = *neutral*, 4 = *agree*, 5 = *strongly agree*

	Average
1. The course goals and objectives were made clear.	2.5
2. The exams and papers/other assignments were graded fairly.	2.0
3. Evaluate each instructional method that was actually used in the course.	

1 = *very poor*, 2 = *poor*, 3 = *adequate*, 4 = *good*, 5 = *excellent*

	Average
a. Class discussions	3.5
b. Laboratory/practice	4.0
c. Lecture	1.5
d. Research paper	3.0
e. Project(s)	2.0

▰ Course Materials

4. Evaluate each text/reading material listed below. Circle one number in each row.

1 = *very poor*, 2 = *poor*, 3 = *adequate*, 4 = *good*, 5 = *excellent*

	Average
a. McLeod, *Management Information Systems*	2.0

▰ The Instructor's . . .

1 = *very poor*, 2 = *poor*, 3 = *adequate*, 4 = *good*, 5 = *excellent*

	Average
1. knowledge of this field was:	4.0
2. preparation and organization for this class was:	3.0
3. communication with students was:	2.0
4. interaction and response to student learning needs was:	2.5
5. overall effectiveness was:	2.0

▰ Total Course Evaluation

1 = *strongly disagree*, 2 = *disagree*, 3 = *neutral*, 4 = *agree*, 5 = *strongly agree*

	Average
1. I would take another course taught by this instructor.	2.5
2. Overall, this course was a valuable learning experience.	3.0
3. The course was enjoyable. 2.5	

1 = *heavy*, 2 = *above average*, 3 = *average*, 4 = *below average*, 5 = *light*

	Average
4. Compared to other ADSC courses, the workload was:	1.5

▰ Additional Comments

- ▇ Professor played favorites.
- ▇ Instructor never made his expectations clear.
- ▇ Instructor was too dry and boring.
- ▇ I never knew what it took to get an "A," and I never got one!
- ▇ This course was too difficult for our level.
- ▇ The instructor didn't seem to realize that we have some experience—he talked down to us.

As Ed looked at his "scores," he started feeling angry. Was this going to be the way this university evaluated him—by letting the students "get even" with him? Well, maybe he should go teach at some other university where academics was more important than whining students.

Dr. Sanford broke the silence by saying, "These scores aren't too good, Ed. I am probably partly to blame—I should have told you that I had received a few student complaints during the semester. But I dismissed the complaints because this is the first semester you have taught for us. Perhaps I should set up regular meetings with you adjuncts. But we do have a problem, you know; some of these students might decide that they would be happier at a different university. We need to figure out a way to make sure you don't get evaluations like this next semester. What do you think you'll do about this?"

Discussion

1. What can you say about the purpose of evaluation at this university, and what should it be?

It appears that the purpose of evaluation of adjunct faculty at this university is to keep students happy. The overall goal of any assessment of instruction should be the improved quality of performance (instruction). Quality of instruction is manifested by the extent to which students learn what they were taught and are able to apply it within their own professional context and by the effect of their learning on their growth and development. In addition, evaluation enables the instructor to compare learning objectives with learning outcomes. As a benchmark, evaluation assists in determining areas of improvement and alternative approaches to syllabus, curriculum, or delivery.

2. How should Ed use the evaluation information he received?

Instead of becoming defensive, Ed should take the opportunity of this meeting to clarify the purpose of evaluation at this university. He could ask Dr. Sanford some of the following questions:

- What is the purpose of evaluation in this department?
- What other evaluation methods are used besides student evaluations?
- What will this evaluation be used for?
- What is expected of faculty when feedback is received?
- What weight is given to the adjunct faculty's perceptions?
- What kind of university support can an adjunct faculty member expect for the purpose of improved quality?
- Are some elements for evaluation more important than others?

Next, Ed should reflect on each component of the student evaluation to determine where improvement efforts should be applied. In the meeting with Dr. Sanford, he should describe exactly what he did in each area assessed. For example, what were his course goals and objectives, and how did he communicate them? What papers and exams were assigned, and how did Ed determine criteria for evaluation? How were these evaluation criteria communicated to the students? The focus of this part of the discussion should be on Ed's actual behaviors, verbal, nonverbal, and written communications, methods used, and time frames. In addition, Ed should analyze any contextual data that might make the data more meaningful. Were there any unusual circumstances or instances of communication with the class or individual students that might help explain the data?

After reflecting on each aspect of his class experience, Ed should determine which areas are the most critical for improvement. How the university views the purpose of evaluation will help Ed to determine which areas to focus on. In discussion with Dr. Sanford, Ed should create a plan for instructional and/or course improvement. In addition, Ed would benefit by talking with other faculty, both full-time and adjunct.

Finally, Ed should discuss with Dr. Sanford how to assess the effectiveness of his improvement plan. At the very least, he should plan regular meetings with Dr. Sanford throughout the next semester to discuss his progress.

3. Should Ed develop some additional strategies for evaluation for next semester? If so, what kinds should he use and for what purpose?

The most popular and least costly strategy for instructional evaluation is the student reaction questionnaire. However, it has limits with regard to providing data for instructional improvement. Whether students "like" something is not necessarily correlated with learning outcomes. As most adjunct instructors know, students react to many issues not related to the quality of the course. Ed should explore with Dr. Sanford the advisability of methods that emphasize assessment of learning in addition to student reactions. Pre-post learning inventories and learning logs are good examples of ways to gather data throughout the course regarding learning. Because Ed's course is technical and skill based, he might use the outcome assessment method, also called *criterion-based evaluation,* to determine whether and to what degree course objectives have been met.

It is important for Ed to get ongoing feedback from his students instead of waiting until the end of the course. He might consider the "1-minute paper" and the "midcourse correction" techniques so that he can modify his instructional approach during the semester. One example of such a midcourse evaluation is included in Chapter 9's Appendix 9.3. At the end of the course, he might conduct a focus group interview to get informal, verbal feedback regarding course effectiveness.

Finally, Ed should discuss with Dr. Sanford how to assess and improve other aspects of the course not included in the student evaluations. These elements include

- Logical organization
- Pacing
- Student participation

■ Closure
■ Level of challenge
■ Creativity
■ Individualization
■ Enthusiasm/inspiration

These elements of instructional quality could be assessed by the adjunct instructor him- or herself, other faculty, students, or independent evaluators. Rather than merely assessing whether an instructor is liked, they assess his or her effectiveness as a facilitator of learning.

Case 4: Sarah Evert's Evaluation of Students

Problem

Sarah Evert was called the middle of August to teach a new university course, "Training Methods: Behavior Modeling," starting September 1. The adjunct instructor who had been hired to teach the course was unable to teach due to illness, and the university's department head was in a panic. Could Sarah teach the course, and could she throw together a syllabus in a week? Sarah had never taught a college course before, but she was experienced in designing and delivering behavior-modeling-based training courses. She reluctantly said "yes" and asked if she could see an example of a syllabus. As it turned out, the syllabus was not very helpful. It listed course goals, session topics, and grading criteria. Because of the time constraints, Sarah wrote her syllabus in a similar fashion. Her grading criteria were listed as follows:

Needs Assessment	20%	A	= 95-100
Facilitation	20%	A–	= 90-95
Group Presentation	40%	B+	= 87-89
Evaluation	10%	B	= 83-86
Exams	10%	B–	= 80-82
TOTAL:	100%		

Her syllabus also listed five course goals and a narrative description of each assignment. She spent a great deal of time on the first night of class describing the course.

Sarah did a masterful job of teaching her class that fall, or so she thought. She was pleased at the effort her students put into their group presentations. In fact, she would have liked to give all A's, but she was mindful of the memo from the dean advising faculty members to give more B's. So she gave B's to approximately 60% of her students, A's to 30%, and C's to 10%.

All of Sarah's self-confidence disappeared when students received their final grade reports. She received irate telephone calls, one after another, from students demanding to know why they had gotten B's or worse when Sarah had told them their presentations had been good. Sarah struggled to explain her evaluation methods, but there was nothing in her syllabus to defend what had essentially become a subjective response to the required bell curve grading system.

In addition to the irate telephone calls, several students demanded to meet with Sarah personally. Sarah planned carefully for these meetings, going over each student's work to justify how the A performers' work was superior. It was a difficult job. When Sarah meet with Hadim, she not only had to explain why he had gotten a C but was confronted with some unanticipated problems. Sarah had given Hadim's group a B on their video-based presentation, but she had given Hadim a C for his final grade. Hadim discovered through the grapevine that his group members had received B's for their final grade. Sarah tried to explain that it did not seem that Hadim had participated equally in the group effort because he had not taken part in the group's class presentation. Hadim responded that because English was not his first language, he could not handle the video script or the role-play practice sessions that made up the presentation. He had contributed in other ways, such as setting up group meetings, typing workbooks, and copying materials. Sarah could not bring herself to say that these tasks were not university-level learning activities. She also did not have the heart to tell him that his group members had complained that he was not pulling his weight in the group. When Sarah pointed out that he had received a C for the facilitation portion of the class, Hadim replied that she was discriminating against him because of his language barrier. Sarah hastily ended the meeting and said she would "get back to him."

Discussion

1. How did Sarah's evaluation methods contribute to the problems she experienced? How could Sarah use a criterion-referenced system to avoid these problems in the future?

Sarah's evaluation plan was based on the traditional norm-referenced methods in which the grade earned depends on other students' scores. The trend in evaluation is away from the norm-referenced methods of the past for some of the reasons Sarah experienced. The criterion-referenced evaluation method bases grades on the individual student's completion of course objectives.

Under the criterion-referenced method, goals and objectives have observable standards of measurement that enable both the instructor and student to know when the objective has and has not been met. With such a system in place, Sarah could have included specific criteria for participation in the group presentation and avoided the misunderstanding she had with Hadim. Sarah needs to include a variety of evaluation methods in her plan to meet the diverse learning needs of her adult students and to add variety to the classroom activities. Some of these methods might include role-play practice sessions, quizzes and tests, and written papers. She also should use a mixture of evaluation techniques to measure learning, such as observation of behavior and review of written papers. Under each learning objective, Sarah needs to identify and communicate acceptable behaviors and related point allocation. An improved example of Sarah's required group presentation is shown below:

Objective 3: Design/develop an interpersonal skill training module.

Given identified performance discrepancies, students will complete all design requirements contained in Worksheet II. This worksheet is to be reviewed with the instructor to ensure that feedback is obtained on the design before it's too late to change it.

4   Outline behaviors/key principles for the scenario for your video model, and review it with the instructor before you produce your video model.

4   Outline skill practice problem situation data.

2   Outline instructor notes.

2   Hand in Worksheet II by date designated.

12   TOTAL

Objective 4: Present an interpersonal skill training module.

Given a simulated group of trainees, student teams will prepare a behavior-modeling-based training module, demonstrating all the competencies noted on the Instructor Competency Worksheet. These competencies are organized under the following headings:

3   Advance preparation

3   Introduction/overview

3   Presentation of the video model

2   Skill practice coaching

2   Appropriate management of feedback to trainee

3   Overall facilitation

16   TOTAL

Sarah could also use a mixture of methods for who should carry out the evaluation and how. Peer and self-evaluations could be combined with the more traditional instructor evaluation to provide more diverse perspectives and maintain the self-esteem of adult learners. An example of how to incorporate peer evaluation in the evaluation plan follows:

Objective 5: Provide constructive feedback.

Given the need to provide feedback to other students, each student will

3   Give descriptive (rather than evaluative) and specific (rather than general) feedback.

3   Provide consequences or rationale for all feedback.

3   Suggest alternative positive behaviors where improvement could be made.

5   Provide feedback via "Behavior Observation Scales" to the
        instructor and team members. Note: Feedback on team
        members will be used to assess degree of individual
        contribution to the team's overall performance.

14   TOTAL

---

2. *How could Sarah improve her feedback sessions with her students?*

Having a comprehensive and well-communicated criterion-referenced evaluation plan will go a long way toward helping Sarah conduct
successful feedback meetings with students. However, Sarah should
also ask the learner for a self-evaluation before giving individual feedback. During the meeting itself, Sarah needs to put the student at ease
by creating a comfortable, private setting. Sarah should focus her feedback around measurable knowledge and observable skills, not the
individual. For example, Sarah could point out which facilitation skills
Hadim did not demonstrate well and ask him for ideas on how he could
improve. If Sarah had met with Hadim immediately following his
facilitation experience, she could have set mutually acceptable goals for
improvement so that Hadim could have a chance to meet the original
course objectives. If Hadim continues to reject her feedback, Sarah
should respond directly to the objection and restate her feedback in
different ways, offering additional supporting examples. Throughout
the interview, Sarah needs to demonstrate good listening skills and
respect for the student's diversity-based perspective.

Index

Academic conduct, fostering honest, 9
Acronyms, 141
Active learners, 16
Active learning designs:
  as content-free templates, 133
  benefits of, 133
  controversy learning, 132, 133, 139
  learner-controlled strategies, 132, 133,
   137-138
  listening strategies, 132, 133, 134-135
  note-taking guides, 132, 133, 135-137
  review techniques, 132, 133, 140
  summary techniques, 132, 133, 140-141
Active listening:
  in communication, 23
  purpose of, 148
  See also Active listening skills
Active listening skills, 145, 148-149
  encouraging behaviors, 148, 149
  paraphrasing, 148, 149
  reflecting feelings, 148, 149
Adjunct instructors:
  dealing with student evaluations of,
   238
  evaluation method mistakes made by,
   244-248

  key role of, 144, 156
  making part of academic community,
   3
  perks for, 8, 12
  professional development of, 220-226
  support available for, 7-8, 12
  syllabus mistakes made by, 228-233
  teaching method mistakes made by,
   233-238
  See also Learning facilitators
Adjunct positions:
  filling, 2
  interviewing for, 3
  possible candidates for, 3
Adult interaction skills, 14
Adult learners, characteristics of, 16,
  116-117, 144
Adult learning principles, 14
Adult learning styles, 15
  ascertaining, 18
Adult learning theory, 13, 56
Affective learning, 33
  levels, 33
Agendas, posting, 142
Alexander, L. T., 84
Alternative questions, 147

American Association of University
    Professors (AAUP), 225
American Association of University
    Women (AAUW), 225
Americans With Disabilities Act, 5
Andragogy, definition of, 15
Angelo, T. A., 120
Application exercise:
    definition of, 59
    strength of as instructional method, 59
Arden, E., ix
Aronson, E., 127
Assessment process, quality:
    checklist for
        developing/participating in, 219
Astin, A. W., 121
"Atlas complex," 120
Attending:
    barriers to, 145
    behaviors, 145
Attending skills, 145

Behavior Observation Scale (BOS), 212-218
Bloom, B. S., 32
Bloom's taxonomy of educational
    objectives. See Educational
    objectives, Bloom's taxonomy of
Boice, R., 116
Brookfield, S., 14
Brookfield, S. D., 123
Buzz session, 56
    advantages of, 97
    as participative teaching technique,
        96-97
    characteristics of, 96
    disadvantages of, 97

Caffarella, R., 14
Case study, 56
    definition of, 59
    in lectures, 65
    strength of as instructional method, 59
Chalkboards:
    as presentation aids, 101, 102, 237-238
    See also White boards/slickboards
Cheers, 141
Clarifying questions, 147
Class meetings, scheduling, 4

Classroom presentations/exercises,
    continuous quality improvement
    guidelines for, 17
Closed questions, 147
Cognitive learning, 33
    levels, 33
Communication, 22-24
    active listening in, 23
    importance of listening in, 23
    listening responses increasing, 23-24
    listening responses inhibiting, 23
    tips for effective, 24
Concerns:
    as cooperative learning structure, 126
Constructive criticism, 9
Contact person, university:
    as valuable resource, 4-5
"Continuous education" schools:
    within universities, 2
Contract, importance of
    adjunct-university, 4, 13
Cook, L., 121
Co-op Cards:
    as cooperative learning structure, 127
Cooper, J., 121, 123
Cooperative learning:
    appropriate grouping in, 119, 122, 123
    benefits of, 116, 128
    description of, 117-121
    effects of on interpersonal relations,
        121
    faculty concerns about, 128
    key components of, 118
    learning teams in, 119, 123, 125
    philosophical framework of, 117
    research base for, 121-122
    structuring class activities in, 118
    tenets of, 115
    versus traditional pedagogy, 122
    See also Cooperative learning
        classroom; Cooperative learning
        structures; Group
        processing/monitoring in
        cooperative learning; Individual
        accountability in cooperative
        learning; Positive interdependence
        in cooperative learning; Social
        skills in cooperative learning

Cooperative learning classroom:
  creating, 122-125
  importance of structure in, 123
Cooperative Learning Special Interest
  Group (SIG), American
  Educational Research Association,
  121
Cooperative learning structures, 117-118
  Concerns, 126
  Co-op Cards, 127
  Jigsaw, 127
  Numbered Heads Together, 126-127
  Roundtable, 118, 127
  Think-Pair-Share, 126, 156
  Three-Step Interview, 126
Course content, 9
Course materials, 9
Cross, K. P., 120
Cuseo, J., 121

Daniels, W. R., 81
Davis, R. H., 84
Deming, W. Edward, 15
Demonstration, 56, 57
  advantages of, 94-95
  as participative teaching technique,
    94-95
  characteristics of, 94
  definition of, 59
  disadvantages of, 95
  in lectures, 65
  strength of as instructional method, 59
Detail learners, 16
Discussion, 56, 57, 67-89
  basic group process and, 82-83
  conditions for facilitating student,
    67-69
  definition of, 59, 67
  facilitating classroom, 149-151
  group membership behavior
    facilitating, 113-114
  initiating positive group dynamics
    and, 83
  initiation of, 69-70
  instructor's functions in facilitating,
    151, 237
  requirements for initiating effective,
    81-82

strength of as instructional method, 59
  using in large classes, 89
  when to use, 67
  See also Discussion leadership skills;
    Discussion topics/strategies
Discussion leadership skills:
  encouraging/recognizing
    contributions, 71, 73-74, 151
  feeding back expression of emotion
    and confirming, 77, 79-80
  for emotion-laden situations, 76-81
  for information-laden situations, 70-76
  gatekeeping, 71, 72-73, 151, 237
  hearing out, 77, 78
  inviting expressions of emotion, 77,
    78-79
  making inquiries/probing, 77, 237
  posting and confirming, 71-72, 151,
    237
  requesting examples and checking
    with others, 71, 73, 151
  summarizing, 71, 75-76, 151, 237
  testing consensus, 71, 74-75, 151, 237
  tolerating silence, 76-77, 237
  turning loaded questions into
    problems to solve, 77, 80-81
Discussion topics/strategies:
  issue, 83, 86-87
  problem-solving, 83, 87-89
  shared-experience, 83, 84-86
Diversity, definition of, 155
Diversity, managing, 155-156
  effective methods of, 155-156, 248
  importance of, 155
Douds, A. F., 146, 156
Dramatization, 56
  advantages of, 95-96
  as participative teaching technique,
    95-96
  characteristics of, 95
  disadvantages of, 96
  See also Role play
Dyad review, 132, 135

Educational objectives, Bloom's taxonomy
  of, 29, 32-34
  affective learning levels in, 33
  analysis, 29

application, 29
cognitive learning levels in, 33
comprehension, 29
evaluation, 29
knowledge, 29
synthesis, 29
Ekroth, L., 128
Engelhart, M. D., 32
Enrollment roster, 6, 12
final, 6, 12
Ethics:
adjunct as school representative, 8
avoiding inappropriate classroom
friendships, 10
avoiding sexual harassment, 10
classroom, 8-10
comments in recommendation letters,
9
comments on student work, 9
ensuring students' freedom to learn, 8
fostering honest academic conduct, 9
protecting students' freedom of
speech, 8
protecting students' right to due
process, 9
protecting students' right to privacy, 8
selecting course content, 9
selecting course materials, 9
testing, 9
Evaluation:
"ad hoc," 204
benefits of to university, 190
concerns about, 191
definition of, 188-189
formal, 188-189
informal, 189
purposes of, 189
questions to begin process of, 195
See also Evaluation, adjunct faculty;
Evaluation, course; Evaluation,
criterion-based; Evaluation,
student; Evaluation process;
Evaluation strategies; Evaluation
techniques
Evaluation, adjunct faculty, 187, 188
benefits of to adjunct faculty, 190
communicating results of to adjunct
faculty, 203
concerns about, 191

evaluation criteria and, 200-201
evaluation timing and, 201
evaluators of, 199-200
form of, 188
purposes of, 186, 189, 241-242
recipient of evaluation and, 200
using information from, 242
Evaluation, course, 187, 188
elements to be evaluated in, 202
forms of, 188
purpose of, 186
Evaluation, criterion-based, 161-164, 243
Evaluation, student:
benefits of, 159
cheating/plagiarism and, 175
choosing methodology of, 164
competency-based, 169
determining options for carrying out
evaluations, 168
determining what to observe and
review and, 165
giving feedback and, 169-172
grading/grade changes and, 174-175
identifying specific evaluation
techniques and, 165
letters of recommendation and, 175
maintaining awareness of equitable
treatment of students' diverse
needs and, 169
maintaining/increasing adults'
self-esteem and, 168-169
program philosophy of, 160-161
record keeping and, 173-174
sample checklist for, 179-180
sample self-administered, 181-182
showing immediate application of
new knowledge/skills to adult
learners' lives, 169
trends, 162
university procedures and deadlines
and, 174-175
using/building on adults'
accumulated experiences and, 169
See also Evaluation, criterion-based;
Evaluation methods
Evaluation data, use of, 203-204
Evaluation methods, norm-referenced
versus criterion-referenced, 163,
246. See also Evaluation, student

Evaluation process, steps in, 205
Evaluation strategies:
    applied setting assessment, 194
    assessment of impact of learning on
        individual/organization, 194
    pre-post learning inventory, 194, 243
    reaction questionnaire, 192-193, 243
    self-evaluation learning inventory,
        193-194
Evaluation techniques, 195-199, 246
    end-of-course group interview, 196
    end-of-course survey questionnaire
        (closed-ended questions), 195
    end-of-course survey questionnaire
        (open-ended questions), 196
    informal evaluation, 199
    midcourse evaluation, 196, 243
    mini-needs assessment, 198
    needs assessments, 198
    needs reassessment, 198
    1-minute paper, 120-121, 197, 243
    outcome assessments, 198-199
    peer visits, 196-197
    sample end-of-course survey
        questionnaire (closed-ended
        questions), 207-209
    sample end-of-course survey
        questionnaire (open-ended
        questions), 210-211
    self-report/self-analysis/self-checks,
        197

Facilitation skills, definition of, 145. See also
    Active listening skills; Attending
    skills; Observing skills; Questioning
    skills
Factual questions, 147
Faculty syllabus checklist:
    academic integrity statement, 41
    attendance policy, 41
    course information, 40
    grading information, 41
    instructor information, 40
    late work policies, 41
    makeup exam policies, 41
    procedures for special
        accommodations, 41
    schedule information, 40-41

    unique class procedures/structures,
        41
    university-specific exam policy
        statement, 41
Feedback:
    role play example of giving and
        receiving, 27
    tips for giving, 26, 248
    tips for observing, 26-27
    tips for receiving, 26
Field experiences/trips, 57, 56
    advantages of, 99
    as participative teaching technique,
        98-99
    characteristics of, 98
    disadvantages of, 99
Finkel, D. L., 120
Flip charts:
    advantages of, 104
    as presentation aids, 56, 101, 102, 236,
        238
    suggested uses for, 104
    tips for preparing, 104
    tips for using, 104-105
Friendships, instructor-student, 9-10
Fry, J. P., 84
Furst, E. J., 32

Gaff, J. G., 117
Games, 140
    definition of, 60
    strength of as instructional method, 60
Gappa, J. M., 116
George Mason University, syllabus
    recommendations from, 37
George Washington University
    Continuing Education Program,
    dependence on adjunct instructors
    in, 2
Giezkowski, W., 117
Goal analysis, 29, 31-32
    process, 32
Goals, definition of, 31
Goals and objectives, setting, 28, 31-35
Grading system, 6, 12
Group facilitation, checklist for, 110-112

Group processing/monitoring in
  cooperative learning, 119, 120-121,
  122

Handout materials:
  as presentation aids, 101, 102, 238
  displaying, 142
  suggestions for use of, 103-104
  to summarize, 103
  to supplement class content, 103
  to support in-class activities, 103
  to support lectures, 103
Hassard, J., 128
Hill, W. H., 32
Humor, using, 142

Individual accountability in cooperative
  learning, 118, 119, 122
Instructional media, 7, 12
  electronic slides, 57
  overhead transparencies, 57
  print handouts, 57
  types of, 57
  videotapes, 57
  See also Presentation aids
Instructional methods:
  definition of, 57
  examples of, 56, 57, 59
  lecture-heavy, 236
  participative, 236
  strengths of various, 59
  See also specific instructional methods;
    Instructional method selection
Instructional method selection, 57-66, 236
  examples of, 58-62
Instructional objectives, developing, 28
Isaac, S., 32
It's Academic, 140
Ittner, P. L., 146, 156

Jeopardy, 132, 140
Jigsaw:
  as cooperative learning structure, 127
Johnson, David, 119, 121, 128
Johnson, Roger, 119, 121, 128

Kagan, Spencer, 128
Kazanas, H. C., 32

Kemp, J. E., 31, 38
Knowles, M. S., 15, 20
Knowles, Malcolm, 14
Krathwohl, D. R., 32

Laboratory exercise:
  definition of, 60
  strength of as instructional method, 60
Leading questions, 147
Learners, types of, 16
Learning:
  as learner-controlled internal process,
    22
  facilitating, 156
  See also Adult learning principles;
    Adult learning styles; Adult
    learning theory; Affective
    learning; Cognitive learning;
    Cooperative learning; Learning
    categories; Psychomotor learning
Learning categories:
  affective, 33
  cognitive, 33
  psychomotor, 33
Learning environment, establishing, 144
Learning experience, factors contributing
  to:
  physical, 15
  psychological, 15
Learning facilitators, 13-14, 143
  as "champions of change," 14
  as good communicators, 23
  basic competencies of, 15-24
  communication and feedback, 22-24
  managing diversity, 155
  modeling behaviors, 19
  motivation enhancement, 20-22
  project work and, 154-155
  relationship building, 19-20
  student writing and, 153-154
  understanding adult learning styles,
    15-18
  valuing diversity, 155-156
Lecture, 56, 57, 90
  advantages of, 63
  definition of, 59, 62
  disadvantages of, 63
  preparation tips for, 64

strength of as instructional method, 59
things to avoid in, 64
when to use, 63
See also Lecture, interactive
Lecture, interactive:
    debates, 66
    energy shifts, 65, 236
    feedback, 66
    making, 65-66, 236
    modeling, 65
    participative, 65, 89-101
    practice, 66
    problem-solving, 65
    role playing, 66
    use of drama, 66
    use of music, 66
    use of slides, 66
Left brain dominant (analytic) learners,
    16-18
    demonstration and, 18
    lectures and, 18
    programmed instruction and, 18
    readings and, 18
    teaching approaches for, 18
Leslie, D. W., 116
Lesson planning, 28, 29
Lesson plans, developing, 28, 35-36
Library, importance of, 7, 12
Lin, Y., 127
Listening teams, 135
Lyman, F., 126

Mager, R., 31
Main idea learners, 16
Martens, G. G., 36
Masia, B. B., 32
Masters, B. A., 116
McKeachie, W. J., 127
Merriam, S., 14
Michael, W. B., 32
Millis, B., 221
Millis, B. J., 36, 37, 38
Mnemonic devices, 141
Monk, G. S., 120
Motivation, learner:
    blocks associated with, 21
    competency and, 22
    definition of, 20

payoffs of, 21-22
Mueck, R., 121

National Center for Research to Improve
    Postsecondary Teaching and
    Learning (NCRIPTAL), 39
Networking, encouraging, 142
Nonthreatening environment, creating, 21
Numbered Heads Together:
    as cooperative learning structure,
    126-127

Objectives:
    definition of, 31
    terminal, 35
    writing enabling, 34-35
Observing, definition of, 145
Observing skills, 145
    observation cycle and, 146
Open questions, 147
Overhead questions, 146

Panel discussions, 56
    advantages of, 98
    as participative teaching technique,
    97-98
    characteristics of, 97-98
    disadvantages of, 98
Participative teaching techniques:
    and fewer demands on instructor, 91
    and flexibility in teaching
        methodology and timing, 92
    benefits of, 90-91
    definition/description of, 89-90
    group size and, 93
    importance of preparedness and,
        92-93
    practical applications of, 91
    sensitivity to interpersonal and group
        dynamics and, 94
    tips for, 92-94
    to create motivating learning
        environment, 90
    to demonstrate interest in students, 91
    *See also specific participative teaching
        techniques*
Passive learners, 16
Personal experience questions, 147

Picture making:
    advantages of, 100
    as participative teaching technique,
        99-100
    characteristics of, 99-100
    disadvantages of, 100
Pintrich, P. R., 127
Positive interdependence in cooperative
        learning, 118, 122
    win-win situations in, 118
Prescott, S., 121
Presentation aids:
    commonly used, 101
    general guidelines for, 101-102
    reasons for using, 101
    types of, 56, 101, 102-107
    See also specific presentation aids;
        Instructional media
Problem classroom situations:
    handling, 152-153
    key goals for handling, 152
    specific, 153
Professional development:
    activities, 222-223
    benefits of to adjunct instructor, 225
    benefits of to university, 224
    concerns about, 223-224
    criterion-referenced, 223
    definition of, 221
    of adjunct faculty, 220-226
    resources for, 225-226
Project:
    definition of, 60
    strength of as instructional method,
        60, 236-237
Project work, facilitating, 154-155
    coaching and, 154-155
    strategies for, 154
Psychomotor learning, 33

Questions:
    directing, 147-148
    framing, 147
    purpose of, 146
    significance of, 146
    types of, 146-147
    See also specific types of questions;
        Questioning skills

Questioning skills, 145, 146-148. See also
        Questions

Raps, 132, 140
Reading/workbook assignment, 57
    definition of, 59
    strength of as instructional method, 59
Recommendation letters, 9
Redirected questions, 147
Registration procedures, 6, 174
Relationship building, 19-20
    establishing ground rules in, 19
    providing service in, 19
    sensitivity to group process in, 19
    student-centered teaching in, 20
Right-brain dominant (global) learners,
        14, 16
    case study and, 18
    games and, 18
    group discussion and, 18
    panels and, 18
    simulation/role play and, 18
    teaching approaches for, 18
Rogers, Carl R., 14, 20, 22
Role play:
    definition of, 59
    in lectures, 66
    strength of as instructional method, 59
Rothwell, W. J., 32
Roundtable:
    as cooperative learning structure, 118,
        127
Ryan, M. P., 36

School of Inservice Education, George
        Mason University
    dependence on adjunct instructors in,
        2
Sexual harassment policies, 10
Schermerhorn, J. R., Jr., 22
Simulation, 56
    advantages of, 100-101
    as participative teaching technique,
        100-101
    characteristics of, 100
    disadvantages of, 101
Sing-alongs, 140
Skits, 140
Slavin, Robert, 128

Slickboards. *See* White
    boards/slickboards
Slides:
    as presentation aids, 101, 102, 238
    disadvantages of, 105
    suggested uses of, 105
    tips for preparing, 106
    tips for using, 106
Smith, D. A., 127
Smith, K. A., 119, 121
Smith, L., 121
Social skills in cooperative learning,
    119-120, 122
    listening actively, 119
    paraphrasing accurately, 119
    providing feedback constructively, 119
    questioning skillfully, 119
Special needs, accommodating, 142-143
Standards of academic freedom, 8
Structured debate, 139
Student attendance form, sample, 185
Student-centered teaching, 13
    assumptions of, 20
Student data form, sample, 183-184
Students' freedom of speech, protecting, 8
Students' freedom to learn, ensuring, 8
Students' right to due process,
    protecting, 9
Students' right to privacy, protecting, 8
Syllabi, designing, 28, 36-38
    class calendar, 37-38
    grading information, 38
    testing information, 38
    See also Faculty syllabus checklist
Syllabus:
    as informal contract between
        instructor and students, 29, 36
    as roadmap to navigate course, 29, 36
    course calendar problems in, 232
    course contingency problems in, 233
    elements of good, 29, 37
    grading criteria problems in, 232
    problems with, 228-233
    sample, 42-52
    vague learning objectives in, 231-232
    See also Faculty syllabus checklist

Teacher evaluations, 6-7, 12. *See also*
    Evaluation, adjunct faculty

Teaching preparations:
    adjunct-university contract, 4, 11
    check classroom size/configuration,
        5-6, 11
    class coordination, 4-5, 11
    class location, 5-6, 11
    class meeting scheduling, 4, 11
    familiarize self with grading system,
        6, 12
    familiarize self with registration
        procedures, 6, 12
    meet with university contact person,
        4-5, 11
    student administration, 6-7, 12
    visit classroom, 5, 11
Teaching styles, learning style and, 14
Team Quiz, 140
Tent cards, using, 142
Testing, 9
Test/quiz:
    definition of, 59
    strength of as instructional method, 59
Textbooks, 7, 12
Think-Pair-Share:
    as cooperative learning structure, 126,
        156
Three-Step Interview:
    as cooperative learning structure, 126
Transparencies, overhead:
    advantages of, 105
    as presentation aids, 56, 101, 102, 236,
        238
    creating, 105-106
    tips for preparing, 106
    tips for using, 106
Trial by jury, 132, 139

U.S. Department of Education, 116
University of Maryland University
        College:
    dependence on adjunct instructors in,
        2
    syllabus checklist, 37
    Syllabus Construction Handbook, 38

Videotapes:
    advantages of, 107
    as presentation aids, 56, 101, 102
    formats used, 107

  suggested uses for, 106-107
  tips for using, 107

What fits? technique, 134-135
White boards/slickboards:
  as presentation aids, 56, 101, 102
  disadvantage of, 105

  suggested uses for, 105
  tips for effective use of, 105
Wilson, D., 16
Writing, facilitating, 153-154
  coaching, 153, 154
  giving feedback, 153, 154
  purpose of, 153

About the Editors

Virginia Bianco-Mathis is Associate Professor of Human Resources at Marymount University, where she teaches organizational development and human resource development. She is an independent consultant for major companies and government agencies in the areas of organizational diagnosis, team building, strategic change, and executive development. Previously, she held the positions of Vice President of Human Resources at The Artery Organization, Manager of Training and Development at Martin Marietta, and Training Specialist at C&P Telephone. She received her master's from Johns Hopkins University and her doctorate from George Washington University. Some of her other published titles include *A Multidisciplinary Approach to Implementing Total Quality; Change in Organizations: Best Practices; The Role of Human Resource Development During Strategic Organizational Change; The Internal Consultant and the Eternal Struggle;* and *Consultant Dilemmas.*

Neal Chalofsky is the Director (and a Professor) of the Human Resource Development Graduate Program at the George Washington University, Washington, D.C., and President of Chalofsky Associates, a human resources development consulting firm. Formerly, he was a Professor and Director of Human Resource Development Graduate

Studies at Virginia Tech. He was also an internal human resource development practitioner, manager, and researcher for several federal and corporate organizations for 10 years.

He has consulted with such organizations as Mobil Research & Development Corporation, the U.S. Department of Commerce, Computer Sciences Corporation, the U.S. Chamber of Commerce, the Smithsonian Institution, Ernst & Young, Inc., the World Bank, and the National Alliance of Business. He has been a member of the national board of directors and chair of several national committees of the American Society for Training and Development, as well as past president of the Washington, D.C., chapter. He is currently on the review panel of the *Human Resources Development Quarterly*. He has been a speaker at numerous national and international conferences. He is coauthor of *Effective Human Resource Development* and *Up the HRD Ladder* as well as numerous chapters of edited works and journal articles. He is currently writing a book on learning in organizations.

About the Contributors

Rebecca Birch, President of Birch & Company in Churchton, Maryland, is an organization consultant with 25 years' experience training adults in a classroom setting. She conducts dozens of seminars each year, primarily in management and executive development, and training of trainers and consultants. She works with major corporations and federal agencies. She is on the faculty of the Executive Potential Program of the U.S. Department of Agriculture Graduate School, and she has been an adjunct faculty member with the Johns Hopkins Center for Management and Professional Development.

Dede Bonner is the founder of New Century Management, Inc., a management consulting and training company in Leesburg, Virginia, whose clients include *Fortune* 500 corporations and over 30 federal agencies. She has been an adjunct instructor in Marymount University's graduate programs in human resources for 5 years. She teaches classes in adult learning principles, organizational development, and career strategies. She is completing her doctoral work in George Washington University's Executive Leadership Program and is researching how downsized employees approach learning. She has taught hundreds of university classes and corporate workshops using participative and interactive methods of teaching.

Lorri Cooper received a master's degree from Vanderbilt University, concentrating on training and consulting in the human development counseling program. While in the Washington, D.C., area, she pursued a career in human resources management, first as Benefits and Compensation Manager at a large bank and then at Miller & Smith Companies, where she established the Human Resources Department and managed the entire human resources function. Currently she resides in Charlottesville, Virginia, where she is working on a dissertation in educational leadership. She is also associated with the Dean's Office of the Darden Graduate Business School and is an adjunct faculty member of Marymount University.

Cynthia Denton-Ade is an instructional designer with more than 18 years' experience. As head of CDA Performance Systems in Burke, Virginia, she develops technical and job skills training for clients such as Manor HealthCare, MCI, the Department of Defense, the Department of Energy, and the U.S. Postal Service. She consults with organizations on how to refocus their training from knowledge-based lectures to performance-based learning. She conducts many workshops each year in instructor training, problem solving, and communications. She is sought after as a speaker for professional conferences and meetings. She is a contributor to the *1996 McGraw-Hill Team and OD Sourcebook* and the *1996 McGraw-Hill Training and Performance Sourcebook*. She holds a master's degree in human development from the University of Illinois.

John Fry is Associate Dean and Director of Human Resource Development Graduate Programs at Marymount University. He has had over 22 years' experience in training design consulting and training management positions. He holds a Ph.D. in engineering psychology and an M.A. in industrial psychology from Michigan State University. Previously, he held positions as Program Development Specialist at American Hospital Supply Corporation and Associate Professor and Consultant on College Instruction at Michigan State University. He has managed several research projects that pioneered the use of behavior modeling methodology and has published extensively in the areas of adult learning, classroom techniques, and instructional methods.

Penny Ittner is President of Ittner Associates, Inc., which provides training and organization development consulting to national and international public and private sector clients. She also serves as an adjunct faculty member at Marymount University in Arlington, Virginia, where she teaches graduate courses in the School of Business. She holds a B.S. degree in business administration and an M.S. degree in human resource management from Johns Hopkins University in Baltimore, Maryland. Her publications include three nationally published training courses, *Train-The-Trainer; Managing High-Impact Presentations;* and *Managing Your Stress,* coauthored with Alex F. Douds.

Edward J. Marits is Manager for Quality Improvement at Vitro Corporation, an engineering systems development company headquartered in Rockville, Maryland, where he manages projects to measure, evaluate, and change organizational performance. In addition, he is an independent business consultant in the areas of organization development and program evaluation. Previously, he spent 20 years as an officer in the U.S. Navy, flying carrier-based aircraft. A perfect example of a "model adjunct," he has taught for over 20 years as an undergraduate and graduate adjunct professor at nine universities in the areas of research methods, statistics, and applied behavioral science. Currently, he is appointed as an Adjunct Professor in Management at the George Washington University. He holds an undergraduate degree in psychology, a master's in human resource management and organization development, and a doctorate in human resource development and program evaluation.

Karen Medsker is a Professor in the School of Business Administration at Marymount University, where she specializes in training design, development, and evaluation. She earned her Ph.D. in instructional systems from Florida State University, worked as an instructional technologist at AT&T Bell Laboratories, and served as Director of Instructional Development at Indiana University-Purdue University at Indianapolis. She consults regularly with businesses and government agencies on training and performance improvement issues. She has written several articles and book chapters on training-related topics and coauthored *The Conditions of Learning: Training Applications* with Robert M. Gagne (1996).

Barbara J. Millis, who has a Ph.D. in English literature from Florida State University, is Associate Director for Faculty Development at the U.S. Air Force Academy. Previously, she served as Assistant Dean of Faculty Development at the University of Maryland University College. She frequently offers workshops at professional conferences and institutions of higher education and publishes articles such as "Introducing Faculty to Cooperative Groups," "Fulfilling the Promise of the 'Seven Principles' through Cooperative Learning," "Conducting Effective Classroom Observations," "Putting the Teaching Portfolio in Context," "Enhancing Teaching Through Peer Classroom Observations," "Shaping the Reflective Portfolio: A Philosophical Look at the Mentoring Role," and "Faculty Development: Why We Can't Wait."

Kathy M. Naylor is currently a Human Resources Manager for Sprint International, Reston, Virginia, where she directs all aspects of human resources for 800 employees on- and offshore in five business units. Previously she was Process Improvement Manager for Sprint International in Reston, Virginia, where she served as a Project Leader and Internal Consultant to Executive Management in cultural change and business reengineering. Prior to this assignment, she held high-level positions in both the public and private sectors, including the Executive Office of the President at the White House in the areas of Total Quality Management implementation, human resources management and development, labor relations, strategic planning, and presidential personnel. She has been a guest speaker at numerous domestic and international conferences, where she has spoken on Total Quality Management implementation, leadership, and transformation, and has published four pieces on related topics. She is also a Mediator within the D.C. Superior Courts and a member of the graduate-level adjunct faculty at George Washington University's Division of Management Continuing Education. She has an M.S. in human resources development from American University, Washington, D.C., and a B.S. in business administration from Robert Morris College in Pittsburgh, Pennsylvania.

Linda M. Raudenbush received her B.A. in mathematics from St. Joseph College in Emmitsburg, Maryland; her M.S. in Applied Behavioral Science from Johns Hopkins University in Baltimore, Maryland; and her Ed.D. in Human Resource Development from George Washington University in Washington, D.C. She has held adjunct faculty positions with National-Louis University in McLean, Virginia; Strayer College in Washington, D.C.; and University of Maryland in Baltimore County, where she still teaches management courses. She has worked as a training manager with C&P Telephone Company, ITT, The Wyatt Company, and and the U.S. Department of Agriculture's National Agricultural Statistics Service, where she currently coordinates human resource development and organizational development programs.

Cynthia Roman is President of Roman and Associates, a consulting firm specializing in human resource and organization development. With over 17 years of experience in the public and private sectors, she conducts action research projects, consults in organizational change, and delivers large-scale training projects. Previously, she held the positions of Assistant Extension Director for the University of Virginia, Marketing Director for Virginia United Methodist Homes, and Senior Human Resource Development Specialist for Dynamic Systems, Inc. She received her doctoral degree in human resource development from Virginia Tech, and her graduate research involved the study of teaching and learning strategies in off-campus graduate education. She is an adjunct faculty member of George Washington University, Marymount University, and National Louis-University, where she teaches courses in planned change, behavior modeling, diversity, consulting skills, team building, and problem solving.

Margaret Sears is Director of Organization Development at Bell Atlantic and has worked in the training and consulting field for over 15 years. She currently provides consulting services for Bell Atlantic, with particular interest in large-system change and team-based organizations. She received a B.A. degree and an M.A. degree in English from the University of Maryland, where she was a member of Phi Beta Kappa. Her doctorate is in human resource development. She has taught at the University of Maryland and George Mason University. She has served as an adjunct faculty member for graduate programs at Marymount University and Johns Hopkins University, and she currently has a special appointment to the graduate faculty of the University of Maryland.

Theodore E. Stone is the Director of Learning Technologies and Media Center for the School of Nursing, University of Maryland at Baltimore. His main work is to seek out and implement new technologies that can improve the quality of how students learn. A large part of this work involves computer-aided instruction and distance learning technologies. He is also an Assistant Professor in the Department of Education, Administration, Health Policy and Informatics in the University of Maryland School of Nursing, where he teaches courses on instructional strategies and computer-aided instruction. He earned his Ph.D. from the University of Maryland in 1991 in curriculum and instruction.